The Burma–Thailand Railway dominates the experience of Australian prisoners of war of the Japanese.

Between November 1942 and October 1943 a force of about 60 000 prisoners of the Imperial Japanese army, together with an even greater number of locally conscripted labourers, was mobilised to construct a railway from Kanchanaburi in Thailand to Thanbuyzayat in Burma. Many died in the construction process, including 12 000 POWs (2800 of them Australian). They died from overwork, beatings, exhaustion, malnutrition and disease. Survivors have carried the physical and psychological scars ever since.

The crimes committed to build the railway need to be understood. In this book some of the Australian survivors and Japanese and Australian historians offer a real understanding of what happened on the railway and why.

The book combines the reminiscences of Australian prisoners Tom Morris, Tom Uren, Hugh Clarke and Sir Edward (Weary) Dunlop, with the tortured memories of a Korean guard. Australian and Japanese historians provide valuable insights as they describe the attempts to bring the perpetrators to justice and the ways in which individuals and nations have remembered the horrific destruction of lives on the railway.

The Burma–Thailand Railway: memory and history

edited by
Gavan McCormack and Hank Nelson

ALLEN & UNWIN

Front cover: Murray Griffin, *Changi trailer party carrying logs*, 1942, gouache with watercolour over pencil, 25 × 36.8 cm. Australian War Memorial (26488)
Back cover: Murray Griffin, *Working party returning to Changi camp*, 1944, brush and brown ink and wash over pencil, 51.2 × 34.4 cm. Australian War Memorial (25108).
Cover design: Peter Schofield

First published in hardback in 1993 by
Allen & Unwin Pty Ltd
9 Atchison Street, St Leonards, NSW 2065 Australia
This edition published in 1993 by
Allen & Unwin Pty Ltd

National Library of Australia
Cataloguing-in-Publication entry:

The Burma–Thailand railway.

Bibliography.
Includes index.
ISBN 1 86373 577 1.

1. Burma–Siam Railroad. 2. Prisoners of war—Australia
3. Prisoners of war—Asia, Southeastern. 4. World War,
1939–1945—Prisoners and prisons, Japanese.
I. McCormack, Gavan. II. Nelson, Hank, 1937– .

940.54725209593

Set in 10/12 Times by DOCUPRO
Printed by McPherson's Printing Group, Maryborough, Vic.

10 9 8 7 6 5 4 3 2 1

Contents

Tables

Figures

Map

Illustrations

Note on the artist

The illustrations used on the front and back covers and on pp. 31 and 76 were painted by Vaughan Murray Griffin who was born in Melbourne in 1903 and trained at the National Gallery School. Appointed as an official war artist in 1941, he flew to Singapore to spend time with the 8th Division. He painted the troops preparing for war in the east of Malaya, but after the Japanese attack he was trapped with the troops on Singapore and joined the march to Changi. By accident Australia had an official war artist with the prisoners of war. Early in captivity Murray Griffin had oil paints and canvas, but later his paints were exhausted and some of his sketches were made on waiters' day sheets from a British officers' mess.

The heavily-built Australian diggers of early 1942 deteriorated into monochrome skeletal forms. As a prisoner, Griffin did not leave Changi except on trailer parties around Singapore, but he recorded the return of the men from the Burma–Thailand Railway, and those gaunt, haunted figures are among the most eloquent statements on the Australian prisoner-of-war experience.

Murray Griffin documented something of the breadth of prisoner of war behaviour in Changi as well as the relationships between prisoners and Asians—as guards and victims.

Contributors

David W. Barrett, ex-POW. Served in 2/9 Field Ambulance Unit; 'L' (medical) Force on railway. Later on War Graves Commission. Organised Queensland ex-POW Association's appeal for reparations. Produced *Nippon Very Sorry—Many Men Must Die* (Boolarong Publications, Brisbane, 1990). Studied marketing and advertising and was state manager for a publishing house.

Hugh V. Clarke, ex-POW. Enlisted in 2/10 Field Regiment; captured in Singapore; worked on Thai end of railway; was later shipped to Japan and experienced the bombing of Nagasaki. Books include *Last Stop Nagasaki, Twilight Liberation, A Life for Every Sleeper* and the novel, *The Tub*. Was director of Information and Publicity in the Department of External Territories and Aboriginal Affairs before his retirement.

Sir Edward (Weary) Dunlop, ex-POW. Educated Benalla High School and Melbourne University; represented Australia at rugby union; distinguished surgeon. Enlisted in Royal Australian Army Medical Corps; served in Middle East; captured in Java; Commander of POW troops on Thai end of railway. Later served as team leader, Australian Surgical Team in South Vietnam 1969. *War Diaries* published in 1986.

R.H. (Dick) Gilman, ex-POW. Served in 2/10 Field Regiment; was sent to Burma with 'A' Force. After completion of the railway construction he joined a maintenance team and was in Burma to end of the war. After the war, joined the diplomatic service, completed BA degree at Australian National University, and was sent back to Burma for his first overseas posting.

Gavan McCormack. Professor of Japanese history in the Division of Pacific and Asian History, Research School of Pacific Studies, Australian National University. Author of various studies on modern Japanese history.

J.G. (Tom) Morris, ex-POW. Enlisted under age and served as a corporal in headquarters, 22nd Infantry Brigade; captured in Singapore and worked on the railway, finishing the war at a railway camp in Thailand. Trained as a school teacher on return from the war; retired as headmaster from a major Canberra primary school. Has written a privately distributed autobiography and supplemented his memories with research in the Australian War Memorial.

Yoshinori Murai. Professor at Sophia University, Tokyo. Specialist on the 'social economy' of South-East Asia, particularly Indonesia. Member of Research Group on Burma–Thailand Railway.

Hank Nelson. Senior Fellow in Division of Pacific and Asian History, Research School of Pacific Studies, Australian National University. Has written a number of books and articles on the war, including *Prisoners of War: Australians under Nippon* (with Tim Bowden), which is the most comprehensive survey of the experience of Australian POWs of the Japanese.

Tom Uren, ex-POW. Distinguished sportsman (boxer) before the war. Captured in Timor; worked on Thai end of railway. After the war a long term member of the Australian parliament and of the Whitlam and Hawke cabinets. Memoirs to be published soon.

Aiko Utsumi. Associate Professor at Keisen Women's University, Tokyo. Historian specialising in the history of Japan's relations with Asia. Author of many books and articles (in Japanese) on war topics, including war responsibility, the war crimes trials and Koreans in the war. Founding member of Research Group on the Burma–Thailand Railway.

Yi Hak-Nae, Korean. Was conscripted into Japanese Army in 1942 as *gunzoku* (civilian auxiliary) and sent as POW camp guard to Thailand; known then by his Japanese name as Hiromura Kakurai (or among prisoners as the Lizard). Was sentenced to death as a war criminal by Australian military tribunal at Singapore in 1947, but reprieved to 'life' sentence in prison. Leading figure in movement to demand compensation from the Japanese government for Koreans who suffered for the role they once played for Japan.

1

Introduction

Gavan McCormack and Hank Nelson

Between November 1942 and October 1943 a force of about 60 000[1] prisoners of the Imperial Japanese Army (at least 13 000 of them Australians)—together with a much greater (but still unknown) number of labourers conscripted from nearby countries throughout the South-East Asian region—was mobilised to construct a railway over a stretch of 412 kilometres from Kanchanaburi in Thailand to Thanbyuzayat in Burma. Much of the route lay through dense jungle. The Japanese forces in Burma were then in desperate need of supplies, the sea route south of Singapore was vulnerable to Allied attacks, and imperial headquarters in Tokyo decided that construction of the line was a military necessity. The line was built. Japan's first large-scale multinational engineering and construction project was successfully completed, but the cost was horrendous.

Many died in the construction process, including 12 000 POWs (2800 of them Australians) and a much greater number of South-East Asians, either from exhaustion, overwork, beatings and ill-treatment, or from malaria, cholera, dysentery and other diseases—diseases that nearly all would have survived had there been adequate food and medicine. The survivors have carried the physical and psychological scars of the experience ever since.

In August 1991 six of the surviving Australians, a Korean who had been employed as a POW camp guard on the railway, and a group of historians—both Australian and Japanese (all of them of a younger generation)—gathered to try to reach back across the intervening years to understand what happened then and why. Historians rarely (perhaps too rarely) compare their notes and the public records available to them with the memories of those who participated in the events. This book is about the

1

Map 1.1 The Burma–Thailand Railway

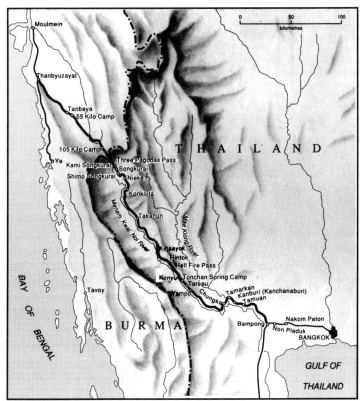

process of remembering (and forgetting) as much as it is about an actual railway.

The seminar had its origin when Gavan McCormack told Hank Nelson about the group of historians in Japan who had been researching and writing on the railway and whose challenge to their society over the way in which war-time events were commonly handled in broad and benign generalisations had led to their being harshly criticised. (After the seminar one of the Japanese received death threats from right wing groups in Japan.) Contact between Australians and members of this Japanese group, and exchange of materials and ideas, seemed highly desirable; the August seminar was the result. Although the quiet seminar rooms of the Coombs Building at the Australian National University (ANU) are the scene of some 500 academic meetings every year, few have had the tension, diversity, and engrossing anecdote and argument of this meeting.

No attempt was made to attract a broad audience: the meeting was advertised only within the university in the normal way of seminars. There was no requirement to register, no fee to pay. Participants included staff

2

from the university and the Australian War Memorial, as well as Australian and Japanese media representatives.[2] Small subsidies from the Australian War Memorial and the ANU's Research School of Pacific Studies covered necessary expenses.

In 1981 Hank Nelson wrote a brief note about the importance of prisoner-of-war (POW) experiences in Australian history. In 1982 he and Tim Bowden began the research and interviewing that resulted in the radio documentary series and the book *Prisoners of War: Australians under Nippon* (ABC, Sydney, 1985). Historians often research a topic, present their findings in a well-travelled seminar, publish something, and move on to another subject; but Hank Nelson never stopped working on POWs. Public activity, rather than academic research or debate, kept directing him back. Old soldiers continued to publish their reminiscences, some from major presses and many privately printed. The Australian media periodically seized on an issue: were Australian workers on the railway fed human flesh (no), and were Australian POWs used in medical experiments (yes). New memorials were erected and dedicated: a section of the railway was opened to the public at Hellfire Pass and at Duntroon the Changi chapel was reconstructed and a plaque commemorating the prisoner nurses was unveiled. Films and books drew on the experiences of the prisoners. Nelson retained close contact with some of his first informants. He grew to wonder about the power of particular narratives and the impact of such experiences on particular lives. In addition he became more convinced of the importance of the POW experience in Australian history: it raises issues that are central to Australian self-perceptions about Australian behaviour in war, Australian treatment of and attitudes towards ex-servicemen, Australian relations with Asians, Australian egalitarianism, and what Australians choose to remember of a brutal experience.

Gavan McCormack has taken a different track to the subject. Whereas nearly all the Australians have written strictly within an Australian tradition, using almost only Australian sources, he approached it as a Japan scholar with a special interest in modern Japanese history. Over many years of visiting and studying in Japan, he had built close contacts with historians there who were struggling against the organised forces of collective amnesia in an effort to have the nascent industrial superpower Japan confront and come to terms with its past. Though international attention on the occasion of the fiftieth anniversary focused on Pearl Harbor, for Australians the bombing of Darwin, the Kokoda battle and the construction of the Burma–Thailand Railway were no less momentous experiences. After 50 years it seemed to him time to try to bridge the gap between Japanese and Australian perceptions and understanding of the railway. His ability to understand Japan and to interpret and translate Japanese nicely complemented Nelson's understanding of the Australian experience of the war.

The six Australian ex-POWs who spoke at the seminar had had a varied experience of life before they entered the army. Tom Morris had been a schoolboy at Gunnedah High School, New South Wales, in 1940. Early in 1941 he went to a neighbouring town, claimed to be twenty-one and enlisted. He was in fact seventeen. By contrast Sir Edward Dunlop was established in his professional career. Born in 1907 he had studied pharmacy and then graduated in medicine from Melbourne University in 1934. After service in the peacetime militia he was commissioned as a captain in the Royal Australian Army Medical Corps. In 1938 he went to England for postgraduate training and was made a Fellow of the Royal College of Surgeons. He was a specialist surgeon at a leading London hospital at the start of the war. Having enlisted in November 1939, he served in the Middle East, Greece and Crete before he became part of the returning Australian force diverted to the Dutch East Indies, and disaster. The other ex-prisoners, David Barrett, Hugh Clarke, Dick Gilman and Tom Uren, were closer to the average age of Australian troops, who were in their mid twenties.

Hugh Clarke's prewar experiences were similar to those of many who joined the 8th Division. He sat for the public service examination in 1935, left school, and as a fifteen-year-old began looking for a job in Brisbane. After working as a shop assistant and a hat seller, in October 1936 he was given a place as a clerk (on probation) in the records section of the Public Curator's Office. He had the security of a government job so desired by his parents, but soon he was studying part-time to matriculate and to escape the search for files. In 1939 he was appointed a cadet surveyor with the Queensland Main Roads Commission. He heard the declaration of war on a portable radio in a tent near Maryborough, and realised that it probably meant the end of clearing a line of sight during the day and studying maths at night. Having completed 3 months' compulsory training in the militia, he was transferred to the Brisbane office and the 'dreary work' of plotting contours. In mid 1940 he said, 'Bugger this', and joined the Australian Imperial Force (AIF). He was twenty when he enlisted and twenty-two when he was captured. He was close to the most common age of the 8th Division, and like three-quarters of them he was single.[3]

About one-third of all Australian POW deaths were on the railway. It was the common and disastrous experience of Australian prisoners but for some it was just one among many extraordinary events in their 3½ years of imprisonment. Tom Uren was captured on Timor, worked on the wharf there at Kupang, went by ship to Surabaja, crossed Java to Jakarta, and was again sent to work on the docks. In mid July he was shipped to Singapore, and after 2 weeks he went by train to Thailand and the work camps on the railway at Konyu and Hintok. One of the fittest of the survivors, he was sent to Japan on the *Byoki Maru*, the sick ship, a battered rebuilt merchant ship, which made slow and hazardous progress to Moji. He worked in copper and lead smelting plants on Kyushu, endured air raids, saw the mushroom cloud rise above Nagasaki, and was liberated into a defeated Japan. Hugh

Clarke's experiences were a similar amalgam of thousands of miles of travel and diverse experiences.

Dick Gilman and Tom Morris were unusual in that both were among the minority of prisoners retained on the railway to work on maintenance and to cut wood for fuel. David Barrett, who had served in the 2/9 Field Ambulance and been captured in Singapore, went to the Thailand end of the railway with 'L' Force. One of the last groups to leave, 'L' Force was made up of medical officers and orderlies. Barrett went back up the railway after the end of the war to help locate graves. Sir Edward Dunlop too stayed in Thailand after the main construction phase of the railway was over. At the end of the war he was at the major hospital for survivors at Nakom Patom.

The seminar benefited greatly from the participation of Aiko Utsumi, a Japanese historian of war and of Japan–Asian relations, who has devoted much of her life to resisting official Japanese 'forgetfulness' over the war and to championing the cause of truth in the historical record (Chapters 8 and 11). She has been the central figure in establishing an international network of researchers on the Burma–Thailand Railway. Yoshinori Murai, another member of that network and a specialist in the social history of South-East Asia, reported on the often neglected role of the South-East Asian labourers (*romusha*) in the railway construction (Chapter 7).

Even after (nearly) 50 years, the seminar convenors were uncertain whether the passions aroused by the memory of those events could be contained within the seminar setting. They agreed to allow the participation of a Korean, Yi Hak-Nae, who, aged nineteen in 1943, had been conscripted into the Japanese forces and sent as a POW camp guard to the railway. He wanted to come to apologise for his role then and to make peace with the Australians. In the event the Australians, including Sir Edward Dunlop, who in his diary described Yi as a 'proper little bastard',[4] received him generously. He was able to leave Australia saying that 'the weight of nearly half a century has been lifted from my heart'. His brief statement is included (Chapter 10).

Gavan McCormack analysed the process of attribution of responsibility for war crimes in the postwar war crimes trials held by Australia (Chapter 9). His was the unusual experience for a historian, analysing on this occasion long-forgotten trial records, of speaking to an audience that included several men who had played key roles in the events before the courts in 1946 and 1947, and one man who had then been sentenced to death by an Australian court. The tension was palpable as these events were recreated from court records, and the astonishment, even shock, of the Australian soldiers as they learned for the first time some of the extraordinary twists in the judicial settlement of the railroad issue was plain.

In Australia the Burma–Thailand Railway experience is generally well-known. It is accepted as a central part of the modern Australian experience, and with the publication of David Malouf's 1990 novel *The Great World*[5] it seems also to have entered deeply into the national mythology. Hank Nelson suggested the significance of the railway in particular lives and in the national history of Australia (Chapter 2). Four of the Australian ex-prisoners, Tom Morris, Hugh Clarke, Dick Gilman and Tom Uren, spoke straight from their own experiences (Chapters 3 to 6). Morris had written down his moving and graphic account of a hospital where he had worked in Burma; the others used notes, and the record here retains something of their respective conversational styles and their reactions to the audience and the occasion. David Barrett added a history of the Australians' claim for compensation—practical evidence of history's impact on the present (Chapter 12). Sir Edward Dunlop reflected on his experiences and on the preceding speakers' words (Chapter 13).

However, the purpose of the seminar was not always well understood. Over a month later the campus newspaper, ANU Reporter of 25 September 1991, printed a summary of Hank Nelson's talk and emphasised the comparisons that he had made with death rates among other POWs (Appendix B). The ANU Reporter story was picked up by a journalist working for the Murdoch newspapers and spread widely. The careful comparisons became: 'BURMA RAIL HORRORS "BLOWN OUT"'. Japanese atrocities against Australian POWs on the infamous Burma railway have been blown out of proportion, a leading historian has claimed'.[6] Hank Nelson had not said that atrocities had been exaggerated. Much of his talk had been in fact a detailing of the horror in the memory of Curly Heckendorf, who had been with 'F' Force, the group suffering the highest death rate on the railway. The newspapers' quote marks about 'BLOWN OUT' indicated a quote, but it was a term not used by Nelson. Various spokesmen for ex-servicemen condemned ivory-towered academics, angry citizens wrote to editors, and some troubled ex-prisoners wrote to Nelson and assured him that people had suffered and died in great numbers. Those who were determined to correct Nelson had no idea that he had spoken from a prepared typed paper, that among his audience had been ex-POWs, or that they had accepted his summary as a fair account of what they remembered only too intensely. Eventually letters of correction from Nelson were published, and Tom Morris, one of the ex-POWs at the seminar, spoke and wrote to one of the ex-service organisations pointing out the distortion in the newspaper reports. The seminar was, he said, 'first class'; the Japanese had been left in no doubt about the atrocities; he sympathised with those Japanese historians trying to inform the Japanese public about the railway; and while he was not persuaded that the former Korean guard Yi Hak-Nae was innocent, he thought that there was a chance that Yi had been treated harshly.[7]

Ironically, in Japan the shadows of war loom larger over the contemporary superpower as the actual war recedes into history. Reality denied asserts itself in new and unexpected ways. So great are the efforts devoted by bureaucrats and politicians to denying or concealing from citizens the record of aggression and brutality that distrust remains deep among Japan's neighbours. Nearly 50 years after the events occurred, responsibility has still not been fully recognised nor restitution made. Meanwhile the movement among former victims of Japanese aggression to seek compensation from the Japanese government (or in some cases Japanese corporations) has gathered force.

Between 1990 and early 1992 the following actions for compensation were launched:

1 The Queensland Ex-POW Reparations Committee, on behalf of more than 10 000 claimants and with the blessing of the federal body of the Ex-POW Association, in April 1990 lodged its claim with the United Nations Human Rights Commission for an apology and $500 million compensation (discussed in Chapter 12 by David Barrett).

2 On 12 November 1991 a group of six former Korean conscripted workers for the Imperial Japanese Army who had been tried and punished as war criminals after the war, plus the family of one man who had been executed, launched a suit in the Tokyo district court. They claimed that they had unjustly been made to bear the war responsibility of Japan (including that of the Japanese emperor) and sought compensation. Yi Hak-Nae was one of this group. (On the Australian war crimes trial of Yi, and others, see Chapter 9 by Gavan McCormack.)

3 In December 1991 a group of 35 Korean women who had been seized by force or deception from villages and schools in Korea during the war and sent by the Imperial Japanese Army as sex slaves to the various war fronts (including Thailand and the railway construction zone) launched an action in the Japanese courts for apology and compensation ($200 000 each). Independent researchers published irrefutable documentary evidence of official responsibility, and the Japanese media variously estimated the numbers of Korean women involved at between 100 000 and 200 000. The Japanese Prime Minister then had to admit responsibility (though his predecessors had consistently denied it) and during a December 1991 visit to Seoul Mr Miyazawa made a formal apology. The question of compensation remained to be settled.

4 In October 1991 the Taiwan Federation of Former Japanese Soldiers and Bereaved Families filed suit seeking unpaid wages from the war and the return of the savings they had deposited in military post offices.

5 Another group of survivors of Chinese workers (or their families) who had been sent as slave labour on engineering and construction sites at Hanaoka in northern Japan under Kajima Construction Company sought compensation (approximately $50 000 for each worker or worker's family) from that company.

6 In December 1991 and February 1992, several groups of former South Korean soldiers and employees of the Imperial Japanese Army, numbering 35 and 1100 respectively, filed suits for compensation in the Tokyo district court.

7 In August 1990 suits for compensation (approximately $100 000 each) were launched by a group of 21 Koreans who had been forcibly taken to do wartime labour in the coal mines on Sakhalin (then a Japanese colony) and abandoned when the war ended. (A total of 43 000 Koreans had been sent to Sakhalin.)

8 Koreans who had been taken during the war as forced labour to work in the Mitsubishi Heavy Industries plant at Hiroshima and there been subjected to the atomic bomb launched an action for compensation.

9 In October 1991 a group representing some 23 000 Indonesians who had served as wartime soldiers under the Japanese demanded compensation amounting to about $800 million in unpaid salaries.

10 Finally, early in 1992 a bill was introduced in the National People's Congress in Beijing demanding $236 billion reparations for wartime damage suffered by Chinese civilians.

In the courts, parliaments and newspapers of Japan, China and Korea, the question of responsibility, evaded, treated as settled, or set aside for 50 years, has therefore become a major issue.

At the same time further details have slowly emerged, including not only the stories of the massive ill-treatment of women throughout occupied Asia, but also: the use of slave labour in construction projects (on which see Chapter 7 by Murai); the massacres of Koreans on Sakhalin immediately after the end of the war (and the increasingly likely proposition that a general massacre of prisoners was also planned); the widespread human experimentation on prisoners by Japanese scientific and medical units, with apparently the active co-operation of Japan's leading universities and hospitals; and the use of chemical warfare against China, accompanied by the buildup of massive secret stockpiles of chemical weapons, which have continued to kill and maim Chinese civilians ever since. In China, mass graves of wartime Japanese atrocity victims were still being discovered as late as September 1991. In the overall balance sheet of wartime issues remaining to be settled, the claims by Australian and other ex-POWs form a small, but obviously important, part.

Throughout Japan small groups of conscientious citizens work in co-operation with individuals and groups in neighbouring countries, striving even after so many years to clarify the question of war responsibility, to secure compensation for the victims of Japanese militarism, and to ensure that an objective understanding of their history is passed to a new generation. Until Japan settles its wartime accounts, they argue, Japanese government talk of the overseas despatch of Japanese troops, whether as part of a United Nations contingent of some kind or not, is premature.

From an Australian perspective it is sometimes difficult to distinguish between these small groups of conscientious Japanese citizens struggling, often at considerable personal cost, to have their country face up to its past, and the much more powerful political and bureaucratic forces arrayed against them. The latter include, for example, the members of the former Railway Regiment who every year gather around the former Burma–Thailand Railway locomotive kept at Yasukuni Shrine in Tokyo as a memento in order to celebrate the successful completion of their task. The sensational treatment in the Australian media early in 1992 of the antiwar Japanese film maker who was accused in a national newspaper of 'ransack[ing] graves of Death Railway victims' illustrated this combination of confusion and irresponsible chauvinism on the part of sections of the Australian media.[8]

Only a few dozen kilometres of the line built by Tom Uren and his mates survive; the rest has been pulled up, sold or slowly swallowed by jungle. But the line is not forgotten. The crimes committed in order to build it should be understood. This book tends to suggest that bureaucratic rigidity, blindness and insensitivity were at least as much at the root of what happened as individual cruelty or brutality. The extraordinary Australian involvement with Japan in those South-East Asian jungles needs to be better understood, both in Australia and in Japan, as does the broader international context within which the events occurred. We hope that the publication of this book, on the fiftieth anniversary of the construction and in both English and Japanese, will serve these ends.

Notes

1 55 000 was the official target. It was exceeded, and the real figure might have been as high as 68 000.

2 See articles by David Jenkins in Sydney Morning Herald, 21 and 23 August 1991, and by Yoshihisa Masuko in *Asahi Shinbun*, 23 August and 17 and 19 September 1991.

3 Hugh V. Clarke, *The Broke and the Broken: Life in the Great Depression*, Boolarong, Brisbane, 1982.

4 E.E. Dunlop, *The War Diaries of Weary Dunlop: Java and the Burma–Thailand Railway, 1942–1945*, Sydney, Nelson, 1986, p. 189.

5 David Malouf, *The Great World*, Chatto and Windus, London, 1990.

6 *Sydney Telegraph*, 25 September 1991.

7 Magazine of the 2/19 Battalion Association, December 1991.

8 *The Australian*, 23 March 1992. Subsequent articles in the same paper on 25 March and 3 April effectively retracted the original false and sensational story, but offered no apology to the Japanese film maker concerned.

2

Measuring the railway: from individual lives to national history

Hank Nelson

I will start with a particular soldier, and try to put his experiences into context, and then look more broadly at what happened to Australian prisoners in the war, and how Australians have chosen to remember the experiences of the prisoners of the Japanese.

The particular soldier I want to talk about is Erwin Heckendorf. He does not sound like an Australian; but he was one, and he looked like one, and he talked like one.[1] Other Australians, who called him 'Curly' or 'Heck', made him sound like one. The Heckendorfs, originally from the German–Polish border, had been selectors in the Riverina district of New South Wales in the 1880s, and Curly's father, John, who was born in Australia, was from the last generation able to speak German.[2]

Curly was, he said, pro-Australian and pro-British.[3] Later generations of Australians were to puzzle over the fact that most of the men of the 2nd Australian Imperial Force (AIF) could be both 'bigoted' Australian and British. But the Australians of the 1930s were taught that they were British; they celebrated their Britishness; and the distinction that they knew—at cricket, in accents, in attitudes, in national aspirations—was with the English. Their Australian and British identity also reflected the basic demographic structure of Australia: at the 1933 census just 2 per cent of the population had been born outside Australasia and the British Isles. For a nation of immigrants, Australia in the 1930s was remarkable in its uniformity.

Curly Heckendorf was educated at the little one-teacher bush school of Galore near Lockhart in the Riverina, and he left his father's wheat and sheep farm for just two years while at The King's School, Parramatta. He went back to the farm with three years of secondary education. In 1938 he joined the militia, the Light Horse, and he trained with them, not because

10

he expected a war, but because other young men of the district joined, and he liked the group activities. That militia training made him different from most young Australians who enlisted for overseas service, for most of them had no previous military training. Heckendorf was different, too, because he was older: he was thirty-three when he enlisted, whereas the most common age for men entering the infantry battalions of the 8th Division was twenty, and the average age was about twenty-five. They were younger than those who enlisted immediately war was declared and sailed to the Middle East in the 6th Division. But in all units of the 8th Division there were men in their thirties, men who remembered the First World War and who had wanted it to last long enough for them to go.

When Heckendorf filled out his enlistment form he said that he was a 'station hand'. He was more than that, but he did not want to risk being rejected by being classified in the reserved occupation of 'farmer'. He had no doubt that when he came home he would go back to farming. When others are asked what they hoped to be after the war, they give the practised answer, 'A returned soldier'. Most hoped to travel and survive, not with decorations, but with all their limbs and some pride in what they had done. Although few were unemployed on enlistment, many were young enough still to be students or trainees or testing themselves in the labour market. For them the postwar was uncertain: they looked to the army and the government to provide the occasion and the opportunity for a better life. Like three-quarters of the men enlisting in 1940, Heckendorf was unmarried;[4] and like the other young men of small close communities he was given a 'send-off'. '[T]hat was the normal procedure': the church, tennis or cricket club brought people together for speeches, tea, cake, a present and a farewell.

At his camp in the Wagga Wagga showgrounds Heckendorf thought that he was training to be a reinforcement for the 7th Division in the Middle East. He just seemed to be doing a lot of marching over well-known country, so when a team arrived calling for volunteers for a new battalion soon to be sailing for overseas, he put his name down. Formed at the end of 1940, the 2/30th trained on the high tableland country of Tamworth and Bathurst under the direction of the demanding, efficient, egotistical F.G. (Black Jack) Galleghan.[5] Curly applied to join the intelligence section; and although he had little formal education, he got into the final selection. Then he was told that he could stay as batman to the intelligence officer, Lieutenant George Clarke. Curly said that he had not joined the army to be a batman, and he ignored the boots Clarke left for him to clean. Eventually his countryman's skills at finding his way through bush won him a place in the intelligence section.

Few armies would have tolerated Private Heckendorf's indifference to his officer's boots. In another incident at Bathurst, Black Jack called a special parade at night, but there was a popular show on at the Salvation

Army, and the men 'jacked up'. They went to the Sallies and left an empty parade ground. The 2nd AIF was overwhelmingly an army of civilians. It was volunteer; and while individual men coveted rank and privilege, most men carried with them beliefs about independence and equality from the streets, the bush and the 1st AIF. They had values that were aids to survival, but not necessarily advantages for prisoners who were expected to be obedient and subservient.

At Bathurst all three battalions of the 27th Brigade—the 2/26th from Queensland, the 2/29th from Victoria, and the 2/30th—came together. They trained for war in the desert of North Africa and Europe: the intelligence section was supplied with records and a gramophone to help them learn German, Italian and French. At the end of July 1941 the battalion entrained for Sydney. Heckendorf threw a card addressed to his parents onto the platform of a country station. Somebody picked it up, and the people at home learnt that he was on his way overseas. In mid August the 27th Brigade disembarked in Singapore in flooding warm rain.

By the end of 1941 the 8th Division was in defensive positions to the north of Australia: two brigades, the 22nd and 27th, were in Malaya, and the three battalions of the 23rd Brigade were in Timor, Ambon and New Guinea. Early in January 1942 troops returning from the Middle East to defend Australia were diverted to the Dutch East Indies, and nearly 3000 men were left in Java. About 25 000 Australians were deployed in precarious locations, for reasons that were flawed, and without chance of reinforcement or evacuation.

When he went into battle Heckendorf had been in the army for nearly two years, longer than most, but the 8th Division units had been formed in mid 1940, and nearly all troops had had eighteen months of army life before they went into action. Nearly all the Australians who became prisoners of war (POWs) were conditioned to the discipline, style and values of a unit, and an army. They had formed friendships with particular men who were in the same hut, and with whom they went on local leave, played sport, yarned and swapped home news. Most of them thought that in the long period of training, building camps and garrison duties, they had been neglected by politicians and senior commanders.

Curly Heckendorf encountered the cruelty of war after he was instructed to force Malay and Chinese civilians from a battle area, and to smash and burn all their possessions. It was, he said, 'heart-rending' to shove families, struggling with a few possessions, into the pitiful stream of people crowding the road south. When Australian ground troops first fought the Japanese in the Second World War Heckendorf was with the 2/30th headquarters nearly five kilometres behind the Australian ambush positions on the Gemas road in western Malaya. After contact was lost with the fighting troops, Heckendorf 'was more or less volunteered' to go forward in charge of three men to investigate. They moved through Allied and enemy troops to look on the blasted Gemencheh bridge, and a confusion of broken bicycles and broken Japanese soldiers.

In the retreat south Heckendorf was again cut off behind the Japanese forward troops, and for a second time made his way round and through the shifting entangled front lines. By the end of January Heckendorf was a sergeant and, with the rest of the Australians, was back on Singapore Island. The 2/30th was on the western edge of Singapore city at the surrender on 15 February. Heckendorf had been in intermittent fighting for a month and had been recommended for an operational award: the 2/30th had carried out one of the few significant actions against the Japanese and had suffered some 80 dead or missing in action. Heckendorf could join the columns marching to Changi with some satisfaction that in defeat he had been an effective soldier. In all, 1789 Australians had died in battle in Malaya and on Singapore, and units in the toughest fighting had suffered casualties as high as any Australians in the Second World War; the men from the *Perth* had been through intense aerial attack and naval battles in the Mediterranean; and some units captured in Java had previously fought in the Middle East; but many men had been on the east coast of Malaya, been held in reserve or recently arrived on Singapore, and had scarcely been in battle.[6] John Lane of the 2/4th Machine Gunners had arrived in Singapore just three weeks before the surrender, spent time under aerial attack, often shifted position in confusion, and never fired a shot.[7] In Rabaul, Ambon and Java some men regretted that they had fought so briefly and ineffectively.[8]

Many Australians went into battle with a burden of high expectations—expectations that came from the record of the Anzacs in the First World War and from their own propaganda about the inadequacy of the Japanese as soldiers. Many of them went into prison believing that they had been let down by the Dutch or the British and denied the chance to demonstrate their worth as soldiers. Whereas in the Middle East the 6th Division had had the chance to replace officers and NCOs who were killed, wounded or seemed inadequate or incompetent in battle, most 8th Division units went into prison with few changes in rank. Essentially, the men who had been appointed officers on the formation of battalions in 1940 still held their positions in February 1942. They were school teachers, bank and insurance clerks, salesmen and lawyers: men who had lived close to drill halls and had the education and the time to take militia exams. Many had served together in the same militia units. Some of them were excellent officers, but when they failed there was the chance that the men would see them as the privileged who had never earned their positions. Heckendorf, who had been promoted and commended in battle, was an exception. Other Australians who marched into prison camps felt that their training and ability had been wasted. They were resentful, they looked for someone to blame, and they hoped yet for the chance to prove themselves good soldiers—or just to demonstrate an aggressive independence.

13

Within seven weeks, from the fall of Rabaul on 23 January to the surrender on Java on 12 March 1942, over 22 000 Australians became prisoners of the Japanese. All the men deployed to the north, except those who escaped in small boats, those few who trudged southward from Rabaul and those on the New Guinea mainland, were casualties. More than a division had been lost. It was by far Australia's greatest wartime disaster: more Australians were prisoners than were to die in action in six years of fighting in Europe and the Pacific. The units came from all over Australia— the 2/40th Battalion, the only infantry battalion to be raised completely in Tasmania, had surrendered in Timor—and few communities were untouched by news of the successive surrenders. By any simple accounting the imprisonment of 71 women of the Australian Army Nursing Service, 354 men from the Royal Australian Navy (RAN), 373 from the Royal Australian Air Force (RAAF) and over 21 000 from the army was a significant event in Australian history.[9]

In those first weeks in Changi the prisoners saw little of the Japanese. The Australians made their own adaptation to the rice diet, confinement, scrounging and improvising. Curly Heckendorf joined one of the work parties shifting the top of Bukit Timah hill for a Japanese shrine. He and the other prisoners soon learnt that if they worked hard the Japanese increased the daily quota, and that, while some guards could be sidetracked into long discussions or English lessons, others would fly into a rage and hit with whatever was close at hand. Curly had the tailboard of a utility flung at him, and he was lucky it missed; and he saw an Australian react instinctively, hit a guard and suffer a prolonged brutal bashing in retaliation. He heard a lot of talk about what happened to other prisoners, including the killing of some. After a year of imprisonment, Heckendorf knew a fair amount about his captors, and what they expected from him, and might do to him. He had learnt much about a prison economy: he had sold stolen petrol to the Chinese, and negotiated loans with fellow prisoners. Although he had lost weight, and suffered from the dietary deficiency diseases of skin rash on the scrotum, 'happy feet' and failing eyesight, he knew few men who had died, and he had reasonable hopes of survival.[10] When he was selected to go on 'F' Force to a rest camp somewhere 'up country', paid for previous work and issued with food for the first day's travel, he 'almost liked [his] Jap masters as their truck convoy pulled into the camp'. Galleghan in his farewell 'exhorted his troops to always remember that they were soldiers in the full tradition of the Anzacs'.[11] Jimmy Webster on his bagpipes played them out of Changi, and they left Barrack Square singing 'Waltzing Matilda'.

'F' Force was about 7000 men, half Australian and half British. It took twelve trains to shift them north. The Australian contingent was dominated by 651 men of the 2/30th. With Curly Heckendorf were three other members of the intelligence section, crowded in goods wagons. Knowing that their

Japanese occupation money would be of no use in Thailand, they traded generously with 'boong vendors' whenever they could. The unaccustomed diet of fresh fruit soon had its effect, and those railway station monuments to imperialism were turned to vast lavatories as first one man, and then all, squatted along the platforms under the surprised gaze of guards and Malays. After five nights on the train and almost no food on the last two days, they arrived at Bampong, struggled two kilometres under heavy packs to a camp, and were told that they would be marching that night, and for many nights. Men left behind from previous trains told them to sell everything not easy to carry. The Japanese ordered no trading with the Thai, but throughout the day frantic exchanges were negotiated behind all possible cover as men sold clothes, boots, blankets, collections of cigarette cards, books and other things hoarded through a year of imprisonment. As they marched that night in the pitch dark they realised that the Thai traders were moving with them, and more trading and thieving by both sides were done on the move.

On the second night Curly was put in charge of six yak carts, hired to carry heavy gear. He spent the night perched on the load, armed with a heavy stick, fighting off sleep and belting the hands of the Thais who walked alongside carrying wicker-handled blazing torches and waiting for their chance to plunder the packs.

The march settled to a pattern. During the day the men crawled under bushes, strung ground sheets between trees, dug hip holes and tried to sleep. Refuse and excreta of previous work parties fouled the ground, and as many of the men with diarrhoea could not reach the crude lavatories, they camped, Curly said, on their 'own dung-hill'. For the first few days traders set up stalls selling eggs and gulamalacca, but soon the prisoners were beyond paddy fields, villages, even timber cutter camps, and food was short. Sometimes guards would sell a little extra food, probably stolen from the rations. They began marching at about nine at night, rested for a few minutes in each hour and arrived at the new camp 12 hours later. They rested every fifth or sixth night. They covered about 25 kilometres a night, often blundering into each other or falling on slopes or log bridges in the dark. Heavy awkward cooking equipment and the pannier of medical supplies travelled up and down the line as men took 10 minute turns on the carrying poles. Men, inadequately fed and unfit after 5 days in the train, soon began dropping back: they never reached the front group at the hourly rests, and just trudged ceaselessly. The fittest men carried extra packs and supported mates. Officers who protested were bashed, but they did get permission for some of the most exhausted and disabled to drop out. After a week it began to rain. On 17 May, after 20 days on the track, they had covered over 300 kilometres and arrived at Shimo (Lower) Songkurai. It was a 'rotten camp': four bamboo skeletons of huts stood between a steep hill and a swamp, bushes drooped under the weight of masses of flies, and maggots crawled in the latrine trenches dug beside each roofless floorless hut. One 2/30th man who had lined up with them in the morning died of cholera in the afternoon. 'And then it Bloody Rained and Rained.'[12]

The men had tried to keep up on the march: unit members wanted to stick together; they hoped for the promised better conditions at the end, and they were fearful of what would happen to those left in the desolate camps along the way. But over a quarter of the men failed to reach Shimo Songkurai, and those who assembled on 17 May were close to exhaustion. Within a week 30 had died of cholera. The Japanese demand for labour on the railway was relentless, and the men who struggled to the quarries, cuttings and embankments were forced to work beyond the endurance of the fittest. They left camp in the dark, worked 7 hours before the midday meal, worked to dark, walked for an hour back to camp, and 10 hours after they had eaten at midday they ate again. The basic rice ration, which had started at over 20 ounces (560 grams) a day, was gradually cut to 11 ounces (310 grams) for working men and 9 ounces (250 grams) for those in hospital. The numbers of sick and dead increased. Dysentery and malaria killed weakened men. After a month only 200 men were fit enough to work from a camp of 2000. As the monsoon and the traffic of Japanese troops heading for Burma destroyed the road, it was almost impossible for rations to reach the prisoners. Men carried 18 kilogram packs over mud tracks, and the work parties on the road laying corduroy and carrying gravel on bags slung between poles knew that they had to get trucks through or they would starve. Prisoners worked in desperation and despair, driven both by brutal guards and by the need to survive.

Heckendorf was ill with fever from the first day, and then suffered malaria, dysentery and ulcers, and like everyone he had beriberi. His weight, normally 13 stone (83 kilograms), fell to 6 stone (38 kilograms) by early July. He worked on the railway and the road; but because he was sick, and perhaps because he was older, he was told to work in the dysentery ward. That and the allocation of four M&B tablets (sulphonamides) were, he thinks, critical in helping him to survive Shimo Songkurai.

At the end of July, the Japanese began shifting men out of Shimo Songkurai, some to other nearby 'F' Force camps and several hundred sick to a hopelessly inadequate hospital at the 50 kilo camp in Burma.[13] Indian labourers, including some women and children, were moved into one of the empty huts. Soon they were dying of cholera, and to the Australians it seemed that some of the sick were being burned before they were dead: they would hear them screaming. Sick Indians hoping to escape would crawl under the Australians' hut, and the Australians would have to force them out with sticks. It was, Heckendorf said, 'ruthless and cruel. It was like poking rabbits out of a log'. At the end of August, Heckendorf and the last of the Australians left Shimo Songkurai for the gentler camp at Naka (Middle) Songkurai, the rains eased, and the food supply increased slightly. Curly Heckendorf travelled on the new railway from Songkurai to Kanburi in November, went to Bangkok, and was shipped to Singapore in December. He was one of the first of the railway workers to arrive back at Changi. Only one of the four men from the intelligence section had died on the railway, but over 1000 other Australians and 2000 British on 'F' Force, over 40 per cent, had died within a year.[14]

Through 1944 Heckendorf was back at Changi. He did some work on the aerodrome, and at the end of the war he was at Adam Park camp, Singapore, working in Japanese vegetable gardens. He returned to Australia, married, worked his wheat and sheep farm, and died in the Lockhart area on 3 June 1991.

Over 13 000 Australians worked on the railway. It was the common and dominant experience of Australian POWs. Relative to the total number of Australian prisoners, more Australians had worked on the railway than prisoners from other major combatant nations. They were shipped from Timor and Java, so all three brigades of the 8th Division and troops diverted from the Middle East passed through either Thanbyhuzayat or Bampong. More Australian POWs died on the railway than anywhere else. Over one-third of all prisoner deaths were on, or an immediate result of, the railway.

From December 1942 to October 1943 General Wakamatsu Tadakasu was head of the section of the General Staff controlling transport and communication, and he inspected 'a portion' of the Thai end of the railway. He told the Tokyo war crimes court why so many prisoners had died on the railway:

> The causes were endemic diseases and unfavourable weather. The construction outfit did not have a proper commissary service. There were not enough trucks, and the truck road which was built in April parallel to the railroad, suffered bridge wash-outs and could not be used for some time. It was intended to be used during the raining season, but this proved to be difficult and prisoners and other workers had a very difficult time as a result. Because there were not enough trucks, it was thought necessary to employ more personnel, and because more personnel were employed, the food situation became more difficult.[15]

Wakamatsu told the truth: men died from disease and malnutrition. The Japanese army did not have the material or organisational capacity to feed the workers, and the wet season compounded the problems of supply and increased the rate of sickness. The relatively high death rate among Australians was mainly because so many of them worked at the highest camps on both the Burma and Thai sides of the railway. There the physical conditions were harshest, the demand for 'speedo speedo' was most intense, and the long supply line, finally dependent on the backs of exhausted men, was most likely to break or be diverted. But there was also much that Wakamatsu did not choose to put in his sworn statement.

17

Many prisoners died in some of the lower camps where barges could operate through most of the year, and where Thai traders would sell food if given the chance. Over 600 British and Australian prisoners died in less than 4 months in the hospital in Burma at the 50 kilo camp, where the problems of supplying medicines and food were not acute.[16] It was simply that the Japanese did not distribute the rations available. Wakamatsu omitted the deaths resulting directly from violence, and from forcing men to work in excess of their capacity. He did not take into account the variation in the death rates at the most distant camps, and one of the factors was the efficiency and compassion of the Japanese and Koreans in command. Lieutenant Fukuda and the Korean guard, Toyama (Toyoyama), were blamed by the Australians for turning Shimo Songkurai into a camp of relentless work and punishment. By contrast, when they shifted to Naka Songkurai they were under the benign rule of Lieutenant Wakabayashi, called Rockabye Archie, 'as much a gentleman as Fukuda was a sadist'.[17] From July 1943 Fukuda and Toyama were in command at Kami (Upper) Songkurai, which soon had the highest death rate: 60 per cent for the Australians and 80 per cent for the British—at least three times the rate in other camps.[18] The loose control increased the chance of local guards indulging their idiosyncrasies. The overall Japanese commander of the prisoners, Colonel Banno, was old, carried in a sedan chair and ignored by nearly everyone. At least conditions were reasonable at Nieke, close to his headquarters. Where other prisoners who took the train north were officially passed from the command in Singapore to that in Thailand, 'F' Force remained nominally under the Japanese command in Singapore. This left both the Japanese and prisoner officers without any line of appeal against excessive brutality by particular guards or engineers.[19]

The prisoners were victims, but they influenced their own fate. Although British prisoners were less fit when they arrived at Bampong, the British death rate on 'F' Force, twice that of the Australians, shows that the Australians were better organised, had greater group strength, and therefore were better able to carry out basic sanitary work, build huts, cook and distribute food efficiently, and share work loads. Among the Australians there were differences between groups, and officers and medical staff varied in their ability and willingness to stand between the prisoners and the Japanese, and to compel or persuade the men to act in their own best interests.

Heckendorf, who had the advantage of being with a group dominated by his own 2/30th, generally praised the officers. Major Bruce Hunt, the medical officer, was he said a:

> fantastic man. He took bashings from the Japs, and took abuse. They'd come along, and want to pull men out of hospital, and take them to work. He'd try and stop them. And he was a fanatic for hygiene.

But a minority of officers, Heckendorf said, 'took the least line of resistance'. Many men resented the officers' higher pay and readiness to take privileges, although they were not compelled to work. When the men first arrived at Shimo Songkurai the officers took the one small section of a hut that was roofed. When another hut was roofed, they 'kicked the men out of that and moved in there'.[20] Men in the ranks where death was so common have found it difficult to accept the differences in the statistics.[21] In the 2/30th Battalion 310 died as prisoners, nearly all on the railway. Not one 2/30th officer died as a prisoner although 39 of them were on the railway. It may be that the Japanese were more likely to die on the railway than Australian officers.[22]

It was a condition of being a prisoner that men had little control over where they went or what they did; but if a prisoner on his way to the railway could have made choices, this is what we can now say with hindsight he should have done: he should have gone to the Burma rather than the Thai end; he should have stayed at lower camps rather than ones close to the Three Pagodas Pass; he should have avoided work gangs in the 'speedos' when hours were at their longest and work heaviest; he should have selected effective and humane Japanese officers and Korean guards; he should have made sure that there was an efficient interpreter; he should have joined a coherent and disciplined group; he should have checked that the NCOs knew when to oppose, divert or compromise with the Japanese; if he could not be an officer he should have made sure that the officers were prepared to stand between him and the Japanese, keep the cooks efficient, guard the stores and maintain the camp; and he should have tested the competence and force of personality of the doctor.

The railway distorted or ended the lives of over half of the Australian prisoners of the Japanese, but it was not necessarily the worst place to be. In all wars prisoners are vulnerable immediately after capture. The victorious troops have been frightened, they may not have eaten or slept for a long time, they have had friends killed, and they may believe that the enemy has previously been guilty of barbarism. Prisoners are a burden to forward troops who have no stores for them, no transport, no gaol and no guards. Most armies are guilty of shooting newly captured troops, and many Australians died within 2 weeks of surrendering. At Tol on New Britain, 160 men were killed after they were captured;[23] at Parit Sulong 110 Australians and about 40 Indians were massacred in the aftermath of the battle,[24] and more were probably killed in western Malaya; about 150 men were executed after the battle at Laha on Ambon;[25] many of the patients and staff at the Alexandra Hospital on Singapore, 280 in all, were killed, but it is uncertain how many were Australians;[26] other executions on Singapore included the shooting of fifteen Australians near Bukit Timah;[27] and 21 Australian nurses were marched into the sea and shot at Banka Island.[28] The total number executed soon after capture is significant: perhaps 8 per cent of all prisoner deaths—too many to be accounted for by isolated incidents involving ill-disciplined renegade troops. The number of prisoners executed has often been under-estimated because only those who entered prison camps and had their names entered on rolls have been counted. Execution was a terrible threat and a real danger, but once in an established camp it was a minor cause of death. For example, on Ambon seventeen were executed while 370 died of disease and malnutrition.[29]

Two major camps had much higher death rates than 'F' Force: Borneo and Ambon.[30] After the removal of most officers about 2000 Australians and 500 British prisoners remained at Sandakan on North Borneo. Two years later at the end of the war only six Australians from that 2500 were still alive. Out of 528 prisoners on Ambon in October 1942, 121 lived to reach Australia.[31]

The other great danger for Australian prisoners was travel by ship. Over 10 000 Allied prisoners died when Japanese transports were sunk.[32] In the worst incident involving Australians, 849 POWs and 200 civilians captured in Rabaul died on the *Montevideo Maru*. Another 543 were drowned or killed when the *Rokyu Maru* was sunk. In all about 1600 Australian POWs died at sea.[33]

This is an approximate accounting of deaths of Australian prisoners (as a percentage of total prisoner deaths):

- 35 per cent died on the railway;

- 23 per cent died in Borneo;

- 20 per cent died at sea;

- 9 per cent died on Ambon (including those who died after capture at Laha);

- 13 per cent died in Japan, Java, Malaya, New Guinea, Timor, Sumatra, Singapore, etc.

Two factors are outstanding: the railway, Borneo and drownings account for over three-quarters of deaths; and on Singapore, numerically the most significant location, there were few deaths. Omitting those who died soon after they returned from the railway, less than 5 per cent of Australian prisoner deaths were on Singapore.

Nothing in their history had prepared Australians for the numbers of prisoners or the exhausting work and mortality in the prison camps. But when the death rates of Allied prisoners are placed in the context of the treatment of prisoners in modern warfare, the Japanese indifference to prisoner welfare is not exceptional. American POWs probably had higher death rates in Korea and Vietnam than in Japanese camps. Germans and Russians on the eastern front in the Second World War were twice as brutal to prisoners as the

Japanese were to European prisoners. Prisoners of the Turks in the First World War were more likely to die than European prisoners of the Japanese in the Second. The worst atrocities by the Japanese in the Second World War were in China (including Manchuria) and Russia. Prisoners in the Iran–Iraq war had an appalling life—for the time that they sustained life. To point out that several countries have been guilty of atrocities and criminal neglect of prisoners is not to excuse the Japanese—or anyone else.[34]

Australians have attempted to explain the behaviour of their captors. In the official history of the Korean War Phillip Greville says:

> The overriding reason for this brutality was the concept of superiority to all other peoples that was inculcated by the Japanese Army, a feeling that was reinforced by the Japanese army doctrine that considered it was dishonourable to be taken prisoner. Prisoners of war had no rights or status other than that of slaves to the Emperor.[35]

To this list are often added the assertions that the Japanese had long resented their treatment by white races; that they were determined to humiliate the one-time lords, *tuans* and masters in the eyes of Asians; and that, confronting Europeans, they felt inferior and compensated with outbursts of violence.

While there is some truth in these claims, they are inadequate as explanations. They assume that the Japanese were exceptionally brutal to their prisoners and that therefore there is some peculiar characteristic to be explained—but as there is nothing extraordinary in the Japanese record, it is not necessary to look for anything exceptional. They assume that the Japanese were particularly contemptuous of surrendered soldiers—but while that may be true, civilian men and women, who were clearly non-combatants, were not better treated than Australian soldiers. Men and women Anglican missionaries were executed in Papua, and over 30 Australian civilians were murdered in Kavieng.[36] They assume that European prisoners were more harshly treated than Asians—but it was better to be a captured European soldier on Singapore than to be a Chinese soldier, and it was much, much better to be a European soldier in a work camp than to be an Asian labourer. Apart from the appalling number of deaths among Asian workers on the railway, some Asian workforces shipped to New Guinea by the Japanese from China and South-East Asia had death rates of 80 and 90 per cent.[37]

Australians claim to have seen differences in the behaviour of particular Japanese. First, they say that the fighting soldiers were more considerate of prisoners than were those Japanese, Formosans and Koreans in the guard units. They were at times, but it was the front line troops who were responsible for the wanton killing of hundreds of newly captured men and women. Secondly, they claim that the Japanese navy, trained in the British tradition and grateful for the honour given to those Japanese killed in the

21

Sydney Harbour raid, were friendly in brief encounters, and sometimes ready to make concessions on crowded transports. Brigadier C.H. Kappe, the senior Australian officer on 'F' Force, wrote of the sailors on the ship that took survivors from Bangkok to Singapore: 'the crew did all in their power to make conditions comfortable, their courtesy to the Commander and his Hdqrs being outstanding'.[38] Again there are exceptions: the navy was in control at Ambon where three-quarters of the prisoners died, and after the war Vice-Admiral Tamura was held responsible for atrocities on New Ireland and executed. There are no simple generalisations about Japanese behaviour.

The Japanese justified the building of the railway by pointing to the realities of war. They had an army in Burma to supply and reinforce, and it was their only force able to exert real pressure on the Allies. By 1943 the American submarines were making it impossible for the Japanese to use the long sea route south of Singapore: either the Japanese abandoned their army in Burma and their capacity for offence, or they built the railway.[39] In these circumstances the Japanese demanded sacrifices from their own troops, and they regarded the prisoners and the Asian labourers as expendable. While there was a horrifying ruthlessness in the policy, there was rationality.

On Borneo it is possible to presume that the Japanese had real fear of invasion and of an uprising of prisoners, and that they were acting within a policy that said, under such circumstances, 'not to allow the escape of a single one, to annihilate them all'.[40] There was then a very weak rationalisation for the terrible killings at Sandakan and on the march to Ranau—but it did exist.

On Ambon there did not seem to be any rationality, weak or ruthless. In the last year on Ambon the prisoners were worked to death on useless projects, and they were starved when there was food available. Those of us who are outside Japanese culture look for rationality, for an excuse, and see neither.

Australians are generally aware of what happened to the POWs under the Japanese. In popular consciousness Changi and the Burma–Thailand Railway are probably as evocative as Kokoda and Tobruk, and just on a lesser rank than Eureka, Gallipoli, Phar Lap and Bradman.[41] From within months of their return to Australia when Rohan Rivett used his journalistic skills to produce *Behind Bamboo* in 1946, to the books of reflection written 50 years after enlistment, there has been a flow of autobiographical writing by ex-prisoners of the Japanese.[42] At least 45 personal reminiscences have been published, and many more have been written just for private circulation. The ex-prisoners of the Germans, or any other groups of ex-servicemen, have not been so prolific. The books of the ex-prisoners of the Japanese have been successful, and there continues to be a market, with Arneil and Dunlop going through several editions and some of the successful earlier books being reprinted. Sympathetic biographies and unit histories have extended the list of books expressing the perspective of those who were there.[43]

The experiences of the prisoners have gone into popular and serious imaginative writing. The playwrights John Romeril, in *The Floating World* first produced in 1974, and Jill Shearer, in *Shimada*, 1989, both have ex-prisoners shifting between past and present. One of the central characters in the ABC's popular serial drama *GP* is an ex-prisoner; the feature film *Blood Oath* was a major production with international release; and several novelists (Randolph Stow, Nicholas Jose and David Malouf) of a later generation have tried to penetrate the minds of the ex-prisoners.[44]

Much of the writing has been by or about individuals. It has been concerned with describing an overwhelming experience and the impact of that experience on a life. Some of the writing has been excellent, but there has been little research about the ex-prisoners by academics or by others who might generalise about the experiences and show how those experiences have influenced Australian images of themselves and the way they see others. The experiences of the prisoners have been seen as momentous events in the lives of individuals, but not as yet in the history of the nation.[45] Jeffrey Grey's *A Military History of Australia* may be taken as a summary of informed opinion. He says: 'The survivors of the Eighth Division . . . went into a captivity the deprivations and brutality of which had little equal anywhere else during the Second World War'.[46] Grey has continued the error that what was unprecedented for Australians was extraordinary elsewhere, and by giving the 22 000 prisoners just two sentences he has effectively omitted them from Australia's military history. If the successive surrenders and the experiences of the prisoners have had no impact on Australia's military history, then that muting of momentous events must be explained. Given that the taking of so many prisoners was the single most distinguishing fact of the Second World War so far as Australians were concerned, that the experiences of the prisoners have been kept alive by radio, film and writing, and that Australians have been so preoccupied in the postwar period with their relationship with Asia, it is surprising that this intense violent encounter between so many Australians and Asians has not been placed in a broader context and stimulated deeper reflection.

Notes

1 Interviewed 19 January 1990 by Hank Nelson. The tape is in the Keith Murdoch Sound Archive, Australian War Memorial.
2 Bill Gammage, *Narrandera Shire*, privately published, 1986, has background on the Heckendorf family.
3 Don Charlwood, *Marching as to War*, Hudson, Melbourne, 1990, p. 193 and elsewhere, writes of the attitudes of his generation.

4 I have based these statistics on a survey of three battalions of the 23rd Brigade. The files for individual soldiers are held in the Central Army Records Office, Melbourne.

5 A.W. Penfold, W.C. Bayliss and K.E. Crispin, *Galleghan's Greyhounds: The Story of the 2/30th Australian Infantry Battalion 22nd November, 1940 – 10th October, 1945*, 2/30th Battalion AIF Association, Sydney, 1979. Stan Arneil, *Black Jack: The Life and Times of Brigadier Sir Frederick Galleghan*, Macmillan, Melbourne, 1983.

6 The 2/20th Battalion had suffered 327 dead before they went into captivity (Don Wall, *Singapore and Beyond: The Story of the Men of the 2/20 Battalion Told by the Survivors*, 2/20 Battalion Association, Sydney, 1985, pp. xv–xviii). The 2/29th lost 275 killed or missing in battle (*A History of the 2/29 Battalion—8th Australian Division AIF*, 2/29 Battalion AIF Association, Sale, 1983, p. 212). By comparison the 2/2nd Battalion, which fought in North Africa, Greece, Crete, Papua and New Guinea, lost 187 dead (Stan Wick, *Purple over Green: The History of the 2/2 Australian Infantry Battalion 1939–1945*, 2/2 Australian Infantry Battalion Association, Sydney, 1978, p. 378).

7 John Lane, *Summer Will Come Again*, Fremantle Arts Centre Press, Fremantle, 1987, p. 37.

8 I have previously written about some of the attitudes of Australian prisoners of the Japanese: 'Travelling in memories: Australian prisoners of the Japanese forty years after the fall of Singapore', *Journal of the Australian War Memorial*, no. 3, 1983, pp. 13–24; *POW: Prisoners of War: Australians under Nippon*, ABC, Sydney, 1985 (the ABC radio documentaries of the same name were produced by Tim Bowden, who recorded most of the interviews); ' "A bowl of rice for seven Camels": the dynamics of prisoner-of-war camps', *Journal of the Australian War Memorial*, no. 14, 1989, pp. 33–42.

9 Most figures are from Gavin Long, *The Final Campaigns*, Australian War Memorial, Canberra, 1963, p. 634. The total Australians killed in action, died of wounds and missing presumed killed in the war against Germany was 9372. Those killed in the war against Japan (excepting those who died or were killed as prisoners) numbered 9470.

10 The Australians on Singapore had very few deaths in the first year. No Australians suffered the equivalent introduction of the Death March from Bataan to Camp O'Donnell, which killed so many Americans and Philipinos and left the survivors weak from the very start of their captivity (Donald Knox, *Death March: The Survivors of Bataan*, Harcourt Brace Jovanovich, New York, 1981).

11 Arneil, *Black Jack*, p. 119.

12 Heckendorf kept notes and he later wrote some of them up. His account of the march ends with these words.

13 Albert Coates called it 'a dirty depot for depositing the dying'. Nearly 2000 were sent there, including men from camps other than Shimo Songkurai (Albert Coates and Newman Rosenthal, *The Albert Coates Story: The Will that Found the Way*, Hyland House, Melbourne, 1977, p. 116).

14 Two published diaries of Australians on 'F' Force are: Stan Arneil, *One Man's*

War, Alternative Publishing Co-operative, Sydney, 1980; and James Boyle, *Railroad to Burma*, Allen and Unwin, Sydney, 1990.

15 R.J. Pritchard and S.M. Zaide, eds, *The Tokyo War Crimes Trial*, Garland Publishing, New York and London, 1981, vol. 6, pp. 14, 635–6.

16 Coates and Rosenthal, op. cit., p. 116, and evidence in *Tokyo War Crimes Trial*, vol. 5, pp. 11, 403 ff. Coates mentions that a nearby Japanese hospital was 'lavishly supplied'.

17 Penfold et al., op. cit., p. 311.

18 Captain J.F. Hardacre, 'The story of 'F' Force', typescript, Australian War Memorial, p. 116. Hardacre says, 'It is hard to understand why such a great discrepancy existed in the issue of rations in the different camps, since all were under the same administration', p. 109.

19 James Bradley, *Cyril Wild: The Tall Man who Never Slept*, Woodfield, Fontwell, 1991, p. 48.

20 Heckendorf transcript, Australian War Memorial, p. 112.

21 Note how Arneil (*One Man's War*, p. 189) carefully presents the figures: ORs 1065 deaths, Officers 3.

22 *Tokyo War Crimes Trial*, vol. 3, pp. 5, 568. The Japanese claimed that the Japanese death rate was about 7 per cent. Their other figures on the Allied and conscripted labourers were wrong.

23 Lionel Wigmore, *The Japanese Thrust: Australia in the War of 1939–1945*, Australian War Memorial, Canberra, 1957, pp. 410, 669.

24 Wigmore, op. cit., p. 247. James Bradley, op. cit., p. 71, quotes Wild as suspecting that in another massacre some 200 Australians and Indians were killed.

25 The Japanese on trial spoke in detail about how the executions were carried out: *Tokyo War Crimes Trial*, vol. 6, pp. 13, 929–41; and Australian War Memorial 54, 1010/9/18, Report on the Laha action.

26 *Tokyo War Crimes Trial*, vol. 3, p. 5401.

27 Statement by one of the survivors, L. McCann, Australian War Memorial 54, 1010/4/98. One other survivor, although at the time each thought he was the sole survivor, was Fred Airey: Australian War Memorial 54, 1010/4/2; and *The Time of the Soldier*, Fremantle Arts Centre Press, Fremantle, 1991, pp. 122–8.

28 Statement by Sister Vivian Bullwinkel, Australian War Memorial 54, 1010/4/24. Bullwinkel also gave evidence in *Tokyo War Crimes Trial*, vol. 6, pp. 13454 ff.

29 There are two books about the prisoners on Ambon: Joan Beaumont, *Gull Force: Survival and Leadership in Captivity 1941–1945*, Allen & Unwin, Sydney, 1988; and Courtney Harrison, *Ambon Island of Mist: 2/21st Battalion AIF (Gull Force) Prisoners of War 1941–45*, privately published, Geelong, 1988.

30 There were also small camps, such as Rabaul after the shift of all Lark Force men, where the death rate was over 50 per cent.

31 Details in Nelson, *POW: Prisoners of the Japanese*.

32 Sumio Adachi, *Unprepared Regrettable Events: A Brief History of Japanese Practices on Treatment of Allied War Victims during the Second World War*, Studies of Cultural and Social Science, no. 45, National Defense Academy, Japan, 1982, p. 274, lists shipping losses.

33 Don Wall, *Heroes at Sea*, privately published, Sydney, 1991.

34 One factor that should be taken into account when considering death rates in different wars is the changes in the medicines generally available. This is complicated by the emergence of new strains of malaria resistant to the most common suppressant drugs during the Vietnam War, but generally there should be declining death rates over time.

35 P.J. Greville, 'The Australian prisoners of war', p. 533, in Robert O'Neill, *Australia in the Korean War 1950–1953*, vol. II, *Combat Operations*, Australian War Memorial, Canberra, 1985.

36 A.J. Sweeting, 'Civilian wartime experience in the Territories of Papua New Guinea', appendix p. 685, in P. Hasluck, *The Government and the People 1942–1945*, Australian War Memorial, Canberra, 1970.

37 J. Griffin, H. Nelson and S. Firth, *Papua New Guinea: A Political History*, Heinemann, Sydney, 1979, pp. 82–3.

38 These may have been merchant seamen.

39 Wakamatsu also refers to the railway opening up the possibility of tungsten mining 'needed in munitions manufacture' (*Tokyo War Crimes Trial*, vol. 6, p. 14635).

40 *Tokyo War Crimes Trial*, vol. 6, pp. 14, 726, from the instructions sent to Taiwan on 'extreme measures'.

41 This is a guess. I would like someone to do a survey.

42 The books are listed in Nelson, *POW: Prisoners of the Japanese* and *Journal of the Australian War Memorial*; Rohan Rivett, *Behind Bamboo: An Inside Story of the Japanese Prison Camps*, Angus & Robertson, Sydney, 1946.

43 In addition to the unit histories already noted, two other unit histories that include considerable detail are: R.W. Newton, *The Grim Glory of the 2/19 Battalion AIF*, 2/19th Battalion Association, Sydney, 1975; and R. Connolly and B. Wilson, eds, *Medical Soldiers: 2/10th Australian Field Ambulance 8 Div. 1940–45*, 2/10 Field Ambulance Association, Kingsgrove, 1985.

44 Randolph Stow, *The Merry-go-round in the Sea*, Macdonald, London, 1965; Nicholas Jose, *Paper Nautilus*, Penguin, Ringwood, 1987; and David Malouf, *The Great World*, Chatto and Windus, London, 1990. Malouf acknowledges the influence of the radio series, *P.O.W. Australians under Nippon*, produced by Tim Bowden and first broadcast by the ABC in sixteen parts in 1984, and the series stimulated others to write.

45 Beaumont is an academic who has written about a group, and she carefully tests what happened to the prisoners against generalisations about survival and AIF behaviour—but she is not, and does not claim to be, trying to assess how the prisoners' experience has fed into Australian attitudes. Catherine Kenny's, *Australian Army Nurses in Japanese Prison Camps*, University of Queensland Press, Brisbane, 1986, is also primarily concerned with the experience of individuals and the group.

46 Jeffrey Grey, *A Military History of Australia*, Cambridge University Press, Cambridge, 1990, p. 169.

3

Memories of the Burma–Thailand Railway

Tom Morris

In his unpublished memoirs John G. (Tom) Morris has an eloquent passage in which he explains how he rehearsed his arguments to be allowed to enlist under age; but his father gave the abrupt reply, 'Why the hell would you want to do a damn fool thing like that?'[1] Tom then used his reserve argument: he reminded his father that he himself had enlisted under age in the First World War. His father declined to give his written consent, but gave Tom his support—if Tom could wangle admission without parental agreement. Tom convinced recruiting officers and doctors that he was twenty-one, and at seventeen became Private Morris, paid 5 shillings a day (50 cents). Later Tom's father also enlisted, and for a second time served overseas. Every boy with Tom in fifth year at Gunnedah High School in 1940 served overseas.

It is difficult for foreigners and later generations of Australians to understand why free men should have been so ready to volunteer. Nearly all those who became prisoners of war (POWs) enlisted from mid 1940 to early 1941—after the 'phoney war' was over and before Australia was under immediate threat. Their sense of obligation to respond to distant events was strong. They enlisted for what looked like a hard, long, distant war. The battles were brief and hard, and after the guns ceased firing the war was long and terrible.

My involvement in the construction of the railway began at Thanbyuzayat on 1 October 1942. In the beginning our daily quota of spoil, be it rock or soil, was 0.5 cubic metres per man per day, quickly rising to 3.6 cubic metres. By April 1943 the hours of work had increased to the extent that work parties left camp at 7.00 a.m. and often did not return until 2.00 a.m. the following morning. A short rest of 3 hours was usually followed by more of the same. Our *yasume* or rest days ceased, and at one stage in 1943, the railway workers spent 12 weeks straight without a rest day.

The middle of 1943 saw me at the 75 kilo camp. Although this camp had the advantage of a small stream running through it, there was the considerable disadvantage of its being in a highly endemic fever belt. The sick rate was very high, deaths occurred at an alarming rate, and the brutal treatment of both sick and fit men gathered momentum. The big 'speedo' push was about to take place, as the gathering clouds and the daily showers heralded the approaching monsoon rains.

The huts in this camp were of the usual atap and bamboo, but for the first time they had two-tiered bunks to conserve space and materials. The available ground area was rather limited by the topography of this small valley. The food was of poor quality and considerably below the quantity specified by the Japanese in the official ration scale. The one small scrawny beast, less the goodly portion that the Japanese kept for themselves, did not go very far among 2000 men. Numerous items were unavailable. Medical supplies were almost non-existent.

Not only were the Japanese and Koreans in this camp among the most brutal we encountered, but they were probably the most inefficient. This inefficiency led to considerable duplication of work for the hard-pressed POWs. It was not uncommon to build an embankment and then remove half of it, to dig a cutting and then fill in a portion of it, all because of incorrect survey levels.

Sick parades were held each morning by the Korean orderly room staff, and sometimes the engineer staff joined in. Many seriously ill POWs, including those in the so-called hospital, were sent out to work in spite of protests from our doctors and officers, who were regularly bashed while trying to ease the burdens of both the sick and the men on the working parties.

The Japanese now introduced a system where the 'light sick'—men suffering from malaria, dysentery and tropical ulcers—were forced out, supposedly to do a half day's work, which was often extended beyond this period. This classification of 'light sick' should not be misconstrued. Many were suffering from diseases to such an extent that, under normal conditions, they would have been classified as seriously ill.

While I was recovering from malaria, dysentery and a small tropical ulcer on my foot, I was forced out from the hospital on the half-day working parties. These were mainly pick and shovel teams on embankments and cuttings. On some occasions I was detailed to work with the Japanese engineers on bolting the platform supports on the railway bridge that crossed the nearby stream. This was a task that I both feared and detested, as these engineers were a particularly vicious lot: unpredictable, demanding and

Tom Morris in Gunnedah, NSW, April 1941.

brutal. They thought nothing of striking a prisoner with the first thing that came into their hands: bolts, hammer or a length of timber—not a pleasant experience while 6 metres above the ground.

Then the rains poured down. On 11 May 1943 all the camp, except those classified too ill to march, into which category I now fell, were moved to the 105 kilo camp. This march of 30 kilometres was done at night in pouring rain, by men who had already completed a hard day's work. As well they had to carry all their gear, while the Boy Bastard spurred them on by firing rifle shots over their heads. Major Charles Green described the 105 kilo camp as the worst camp on the Burma side of the railway. How fortunate I was to miss it, I learned later.

Shortly there occurred an outbreak of cholera in both the POW and the adjacent Burmese huts at the 75 kilo camp. Fortunately we had been given cholera shots a few weeks previously. The Japanese, because of their dread

29

of cholera, seemed to provide inoculation against this disease quite willingly. (I might add that it was not the result of their compassion for their POW slaves, but out of their own terror of contracting the disease.) As there was only one medical orderly in the hospital, I volunteered to act as a medical orderly in the cholera section—an act that was to remove me for the next 10 months from any further part in the railway construction. It was, however, the beginning of a nightmare that still haunts me even today.

As a result of a visit by Brigadier A.L. Varley and Lieutenant-Colonel Nagatomo, it was decided to move Colonel Albert Coates and the remnants still at the 75 kilo camp back to the 55 kilo camp, where a new 'base hospital' to cater for 2000 patients was to be established for the deluge of sick expected from the camps north of the area. The 55 kilo hospital was actually an abandoned railway camp consisting of eight large and one small atap-roofed bamboo huts. Of the 1800-plus patients more than 500 had large tropical ulcers, usually on the legs. The remainder suffered from a combination of malaria, dysentery, smaller ulcers, beriberi and general debility.

The monsoon was in full swing. It not only broke early, but it was to be the longest and wettest recorded up till that time. The torrential rain, falling day after day, for weeks on end, was something I had not experienced nor would I ever again experience. There was no respite for the poor devils slaving away on the railway. Not only did they have to meet their daily quotas of work to keep the line construction on schedule, but they also had to repair the bridges and embankments washed away by the raging torrents, which only a couple of months earlier had been mere rivulets or dry streams. Additionally, exhausted POWs had to make the daily trip back to the 100 kilo camp from the 105 kilo camp to carry the camp's rations of rice and what little else was available. Soaked to the skin, bare-footed, this exhausting trip through mud 30 to 45 centimetres deep took a terrible toll on them.

Let me take you through the two most depressing sections of this so-called hospital: the dysentery and main ulcer wards.

I worked in the dysentery 'death house' from July to December 1943. In the centre of this gloomy, isolated hut, there was a 'thunder box' in the centre aisle, but few patients were capable of making their way to this offensive-smelling container. For those bedridden patients on their bamboo slats, with nothing more than a rice bag or a worn thin blanket beneath them, there was neither incentive nor medicines to help them on the road to recovery. We had no bedpans, no facilities for bathing patients, no soap or disinfectants, and no special diets. The only medicine we had was Condy's crystals and ground charcoal. Yet the Japanese had the gall to call it a hospital. For bedpans we used tin cans, old mess tins, half coconut shells and troughs or pots made from large bamboo. Toilet paper was the large leaves from nearby trees. The Japanese would not concede that amoebic dysentery was one of the main diseases in this camp. Dr Higuchi, the Horse Doctor, refused to allow the words 'amoebic dysentery' to be

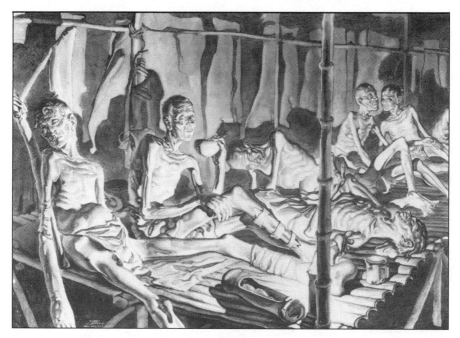

Murray Griffin, Hospital ward, Thailand railway, *1946, brush and brown ink and wash over pencil heightened with white, 35.1 × 51.2 cm. Australian War Memorial (25104).*

entered on the death certificates, insisting that it was only 'hill diarrhoea'. Eventually a microscope was procured, and Higuchi could no longer deny the presence of amoebic parasites. We still did not get any emetine and our patients continued to die.

In the main ulcer ward the patients were packed three deep, head to foot, with barely enough room for the orderlies and doctors to pass between their frail miserable bodies. As in the dysentery ward there were no beds and they had to lie on the hard bamboo platforms. For the desperately ill amputees beds of rice bags slung on bamboo poles allowed a small degree of comfort, as well as easing access to them. There were no sleeping draughts or painkillers to help these poor unfortunates through their agonies. The stench from this ward was indescribable. Bandages were made from rags, clothing and the bottoms of mosquito nets—not that we had any nets to ease the malaria problem. These putrid cloths were washed and used over and over again to cover ulcers, which often extended from knee to ankle, with bone and tendon completely exposed.

The sad part of this sorry story is that, where proper food is available, the condition is easily cured without serious complications. Apart from our dietary deficiencies, the high rate of tropical ulcers could be attributed to the fact that most men had no footwear or protective clothing. Even minor abrasions became infected, and the ulcers spread with incredible rapidity. Once the infection reached muscle, its progress of infection and destruction was even more rapid.

The only truly beneficial medication was iodoform, which was available only in minute quantities. Yet at the 105 kilo camp Commandant Hoshi had a supply of this powder, which he used to sell to ulcer patients in return for their few valued possessions such as watches, rings or fountain pens. Many substitute medicines were tried in the ulcer ward at the 55 kilo camp—Eusol, salt solution, raw salt packed into the wounds, lysol, hot rice poultices, ointments using axle grease as a base, Condy's crystals—and at one stage maggots were intentionally introduced into these great festering ulcers. Daily curettage, using a curette or a spoon as a substitute, was another heart-rending form of treatment, again without any form of sedation or painkillers. It was not unusual for 80 to 100 patients to have their ulcers scraped and gouged in this manner each day. It was pathetic to hear the screams of those poor souls, whose shattered nerves could no longer stand the strain of even seeing the doctor approach with the curette in his hand. Yet Colonel Coates, in his evidence at the Tokyo War Crimes Trial in 1946, said, 'At the 55 kilo camp I had the opportunity to visit a jungle hospital for Japanese troops, and found it lavishly supplied with drugs and medicines of every kind'.

Of the 110 major amputations of legs carried out by Colonel Coates at the 55 kilo camp, only 40 survived. The remainder died through gangrene and/or the added complications of dysentery, malaria and inadequate diet.

Food was basically boiled rice and thin watery stew. Being a camp of mostly non-workers, we were on half rations. The Japanese also had an inexplicable custom of weighing us each month and then issuing rations based on the combined weight of all the inmates. The less we weighed, the less we received, with obvious compounding results.

The Japanese refused to allow us to buy food to supplement our diets. Even though our midnight traders were able to contact Burmese willing to sell some of their small skinny cattle, our request for official permission to purchase them was refused. The clandestine nocturnal ventures by this small POW group did allow small quantities of meat to reach our cookhouse unofficially. Being a camp of sick, therefore non-workers, we were not paid by the Japanese. Perhaps this attitude is best reflected in an incident at Tamarkan, Thailand, in 1944. The Japanese suddenly announced that our canteen could no longer buy meat, sugar and salt. The reason given was: 'Under the Geneva Convention, you should get these things from us. If you have to buy them, it means we are not giving you enough. If we stop you from buying these things, therefore, it means you are getting enough'.

In spite of all this, some patients recovered sufficiently to hear those dreaded words 'Fit for duty'—that is, fit as defined by the Japanese—and so returned to the agonies and horror of a further period on the railway at the height of the monsoon. For many it was a death warrant.

At last the monsoons dried up, the railway was completed, and the influx of patients from the work camps fell to a trickle. Finally, in December 1943 the 55 kilo hospital was closed and the surviving POWs transferred to Tamarkan, Thailand. Approximately 430 bodies remained in the nearby cemetery.

There was a vast improvement in our rations in Thailand: for the first time we were adequately fed. There was also a vast improvement in our treatment by both Koreans and Japanese. Historians have suggested that improvement was due to worldwide reaction to the high death rate among POWs in 1943. They have also noted that by 1945 the Japanese had reverted to their previous callous indifference, and the death rate soared once again in all areas where POWs were held.

Throughout 1944 work parties were sent back up the railway for repairs and maintenance. Relatively fit when despatched from Tamarkan, many were to return within a few short months, carried in on stretchers, so weak and emaciated that they were often unrecognisable even by their closest friends. These parties, even though the railway was operating reasonably efficiently at this time, met the same brutality, lack of food and medical supplies that we had all experienced throughout 1943.

A stroll through the Kanchanaburi War Cemetery, with its 6844 head-stones, is a lesson in the history of the railway. Each headstone helps to document precisely the tragedy that it encompassed:

1942: Only occasional death dates.

1943: A noticeable increase between January and April, followed by an horrendous increase from May to December.

1944: A tapering off from January to April. The period May to December again reflects the sharp increase in deaths among the maintenance groups on the railway as they experienced a pattern of treatment similar to that of the 1943 'speedo' period.

1945: A further tapering off in the period January to April, with a sharp increase between May and August.

Of the 3771 graves in the Thanbyuzayat War Cemetery in Burma, almost 3000 result from deaths during 1943.

The Japanese had repeatedly told us: 'We will build this railway no matter what the cost to you. It will be built even if it is over the dead bodies of each and every one of you'. They certainly tried hard to live up to this statement. People often say to me: 'Why don't you forget all about the railway. After all, it happened nearly 50 years ago. It surely is time to forgive and forget'. My response is always: 'I cannot and will not forget.

Nor will I ever forgive my generation of Japanese and Koreans. I no longer hate them, but I still have no respect for them'.

As a POW I could understand and accept the hard work, the poor food, the withholding of our mail (I received two letters in October 1944, my first and only POW mail), the primitive accommodation and the constant aggravation of being face to face with our unpredictable and brutal captors for 24 hours a day. That was part of the price for being a POW. What I cannot forget or forgive is the inhumane brutality and total disregard for the welfare of our sick and dying POWs. Nor can I forget the withholding of our medical and Red Cross supplies, which were held in Japanese stores adjacent to our camps—supplies that were often purloined by both Japanese and Koreans for their own use. During my period on the railway—23 months—I did not receive one individual Red Cross parcel. In May 1944 I participated in the sharing of one American Red Cross parcel between six men. Through the period October 1942 to August 1945 I was in ten camps along the railway line. In that time there was not one death in any of those camps of a single Japanese or Korean, from starvation or disease. That speaks for itself.

The Japanese were surely aware of their responsibilities towards their prisoners. Otherwise, why did they produce propaganda films such as that at Thanbyuzayat Base Hospital, Burma, in late 1942 or early 1943? The canteen was stocked with items not previously seen by POWs. A lorry was brought in laden with vegetables, but when the top layer was removed nothing but empty crates lay underneath. A clothing issue of shorts, jackets and boots was made to a large number of prisoners. The shelves in the RAP were filled with bandages, drugs and medicines. After 2 days of rehearsals the film was shot, the phoney vegetables, the medical supplies, the clothing and boots were all taken back, and things returned to normal.

I make no apologies for the horrors of Hiroshima and Nagasaki. Instead I contemplate the treatment handed out by the Japanese to the civilian populations in the countries they occupied in the South-East Asian area:

- the Nanking massacre in 1938: 200 000 in 6 weeks;

- the unknown, but estimated 90 000, Asian labourers who died in Burma and Thailand in the construction of the railway;

- the massacre of civilians in the Philippines, especially in Manila, in 1945: total unknown, but thought to be in excess of 100 000;

- the massacre of some 6000 Chinese in Singapore in 1942.

To these add the deaths of 26 000 POWs. Finally, reflect on the plans, now well documented, for the extermination of all remaining POWs, set for late August 1945. In terms of casualties, Hiroshima and Nagasaki were small by comparison. Having set the ground rules, Japan had no justification to claim foul play, horrible though the bombings were.

At the Tokyo War Crimes Trial in 1946, Tojo, the former Japanese Prime Minister, said:

> Since the end of the war I have read about the inhumane acts committed by the Japanese Army and Navy. Such acts are not permissible in Japan; the character of the Japanese is such that they believe Heaven nor Earth would permit such things. It will be too bad if people in the world believe that these inhumane acts are the result of Japanese character.[2]

My only comment is: actions speak larger than words.

In my 1983 memoirs I used an old anonymous quote: 'Those who forget the past are bound to relive it'. To the Japanese nation I say: 'Those who ignore the past will live to regret it. It is time that you told the truth by putting back into your history books at least the basic facts of your atrocities. At least your younger generations will then have the opportunity to come to grips with it'.

In recent discussions with a colleague at the Australian War Memorial, relative to this matter, he said, 'What better place to start than the perusal of the 1010 series of War Crimes Statements provided by POWs after their release. These statements should be compulsory reading for every group of Japanese visitors to the War Memorial'. Perhaps that is impractical, but the evidence is there if the Japanese are really serious about telling their population the truth of one aspect in their war against Australia of 1941–45.

Let us make a visit to a railway maintenance camp, 1945, somewhere near the Burma–Thailand border. Among this group were Australian POWs. The Japanese worked them mercilessly; beatings were the order of the day; many had no footwear. Among them was VX 19728, Private John Edward Durkin, 2/2nd Pioneer Battalion aged about forty. One day he went out to work and collapsed. The next day he was sent out again, assisted by his mates. On the third day he lagged behind the work party, and when they arrived at the line he was missing.

The next day the Japanese assembled the group and, through an interpreter, told them that Durkin must be wandering somewhere in the jungle and that he would have no chance of survival. They wanted to find him so that they could nurse him back to health. Several days later Durkin was brought into the camp. He had a rope around his neck held by a Japanese guard, who followed behind him, hitting him with his rifle butt as he stumbled along. He was tied to a post. Over the next 3 weeks he was kept there, allowed a little rice and water and to visit the latrine. When he slumped down, he was often kicked to his feet again. One day he was told by a guard, 'You sleepo. Sama sama all men', and he pointed to the cemetery.

Durkin was led away by a small party of Japanese, some carrying rifles and bayonets. POWs who tried to see what was happening were forcibly turned back. Hoarse cries were heard soon afterward. When the Japanese party returned, Durkin was not with them. That afternoon, when a burial party went to the cemetery, there was a grave nearby, the earth newly filled in. After a lapse of a day or so, the Japanese returned a bundle of ragged clothes, which were identified as Durkin's. They said they were no longer needed.

What is the significance of this story, you might well ask. The date of death on Private Durkin's headstone in the Thanbyuzayat War Cemetery is: 14th August 1945. That was the day Japan agreed to surrender to the Allies.

Notes

1 A copy of Tom Morris's personal memoirs, *A Soldier's Reflections Forty Years On*, written primarily for his family, has been placed in the Australian War Memorial.
2 Ibid. Part 4, p. 20.

4

Of elephants and men

Hugh Clarke

Hugh Clarke has been one of the most prolific of the writers of the ex-prisoners of war (POWs), and one of the best. His novel The Tub *is an imaginative reconstruction of the life of a group of men on the Burma–Thailand Railway. When Hugh Clarke is mentioned to other POWs they shake their heads and say, 'But a bit of a troublemaker on the line'. It is not clear what they mean by that, but it is a common reaction of fellow POWs:*

My first association with the Burma–Thailand Railway began in Changi in early March 1943. We were told that there was a better land far away. Where we were going, we would be better fed and the climate would be better, and we should be sure to take plenty of sporting gear. I was enlisted into 'T' Battalion, a group of 500 artillery men, all Australians; and 'T' Battalion in turn was part of 'D' Force, a total of about 5000 prisoners, half British, half Australian. We were put on board a train, and after 5 days and 5 nights we got off at Bampong, which is on the Singapore–Bangkok main line about 50 kilometres south of Bangkok. We were searched and promptly put onto another train, which was a flat top. It was a wriggly sort of line, obviously only recently laid, and we then began to suspect that we were up here to work on a railway. We were taken to Kanburi, now called Kanchanaburi, and there the line stopped. We got off the train, and the guards we had with us promptly disappeared! They no doubt had been told to take us to Kanburi, and that was it.

Due to some mistake no other guards turned up to collect us for about 4 days. We thought, 'Hullo, they can't feed us. They've dumped us here'. So we promptly set about building humpies and trading with the Thais. Very soon a sort of marketplace was set up. They had these signs 'Flying Eggs'. What they meant was fried eggs, but they were flying eggs. We promptly sold whatever we could: we had watches and pens. We thought, 'This is great. We're going to settle down here'. But after about a week the new guards turned up, and they promptly set about beating us up just to let us know who was boss. They put us on trucks and drove us up into the mountains. Eventually we arrived at a place called Tarso, where there were British and Dutch prisoners.

As we entered this camp nobody said 'Goodday' or 'Hello'; they were totally dispirited; half of them looked like skeletons. A lot of them were very badly stricken with beriberi, carrying their testicles that were the size of footballs in their hands. We thought, 'This doesn't look too good. This isn't the land of Utopia at all'. We slept there that night, and the next day were taken back south—we walked.

We were put in the charge of about 200 Japanese engineers headed by a Lieutenant Sumi, who spoke fairly good English. We were set to work building an embankment the height of a large table, which was not a bad job. Sumi prevented his men from bashing us, and in 2 weeks we finished the job. He said, 'Well, I'm very pleased with you Australians. You work well. Tonight we're going to have a feed and a concert'. So his men dynamited the river we were camped behind, and we went in and caught a lot of fish and brought them out. We lit a big bamboo fire. The Japanese lined up on one side of the fire and we lined up on the other, and the concert began. The first song the Japanese sang was 'My Blue Heaven' in Japanese. We said, 'That's not a Japanese song'. So there was a bit of a dispute about that. Then they sang 'She'll Be Coming round the Mountain' in Japanese. So we sang the same song, but with different words. I do not know how it all happened, but the words we were singing were 'They'll be flying in formation when they come', then 'They'll be dropping thousand-pounders when they come'. Sumi, who understood English very well, got very upset. He started belabouring the people nearest him, and all of his men joined in. We got a hell of a hiding, and they threw all the bloody fish in the river. That ended that part of the job.

The next job was at Wampo. I think most people who have been there will remember Wampo. It was a tremendous viaduct, which ran into a big embankment. We were marched to this camp. They were already dynamiting the track, and we were showered with stones and debris as we walked through the bamboo. The Japanese in charge of that camp was called the Black Prince. Again, the British in this camp were in a very bad shape—they all had beriberi, they were skeletons, and very few of them were fit to work at all. We were promptly put to work. At that stage the line had travelled further north from Kanburi, and it was held up by the embankment that had not been built. The Black Prince, or the Black Bastard as we renamed him, said, 'You'll work on this non-stop until it's finished'. So we went to work.

Hugh Clarke in the ring on the deck of the Queen Mary *on the way to Singapore, 1941.*

We worked for about a week for about 18 hours a day. Then one particular day he said, 'You go to work today and nobody comes home until the embankment is finished'. The job was digging and carrying. The embankment must have been about 24 metres or more high. Two men dug out mounds of earth, and then two men carried it on a bamboo frame, using a stretcher made out of bags. We just filled this up with dirt and walked up this tremendous embankment. We worked continuously. Men were dropping and being beaten and getting up again. I think that we worked 36 hours straight—and we finished it.

When we got back to camp we were allowed to sleep for a day, and then we marched north, back to Tarso. We left 100 men behind. We had quite a few people in our group aged about thirty or forty, and these old ones all stayed behind. We walked for 2 days, up to Tarso, then through Tonchan, another camp. It was 25 April 1943, Anzac Day, and we were marching. Around midday we stopped, and our guard said, 'Well, this is your camp, when you build it'. The place was called Konyu Three. Half of us were allowed to start building the camp, cutting bamboo and building frames for the tent flies we had brought with us. The other half were taken out to the job site, which was about 100 or 200 metres from where our camp was being built. The Japanese engineer said, 'Well, this is the job. You're going to dig down—', he used metres, I think he said, 'Forty metres'. We said, 'This is bloody silly. How are we going to do that?' A truck turned up with some tools, and we started drilling.

The Burma–Thailand Railway

I became a hammer and tap man. That meant working in pairs: one with an 8 pound (3.6 kilogram) hammer and the other with three drills of different sizes. The biggest was a metre long; there was another about two-thirds of a metre long, and then a smaller one. So we started drilling the rock. At first they said, 'One metre finished—go home'. The bigger men with us did this by about two o'clock, and they would pack up and go home. Then after a few days it was, 'Two metres finish—go home'. Some men were still getting home before dark. Then it became, 'Three metres finish—go home'. And you were really flat out doing that. We would all drill a metre hole. The engineers would plug it with dynamite, get six or seven of us out and give us a cigarette. We would light a cigarette each. We would have to light four or five fuses and then go for our lives up into the bush before the charges blew. And that was the pattern of life.

After a while another work party came. We got a group of 200 fairly elderly Malayan volunteers. I remember one fellow, a Professor Silcock from Raffles University. They lasted no time. Another group came and joined us: about 600 men of 'H' Force under another famous doctor, one of Weary Dunlop's colleagues, Kevin Fagan. From then on it became a 24 hour a day job, with 'H' Force providing the night shift. This was good for me because I was taken off the hammer and tap and put in charge of a group of twenty 'light men'. Our job was to go out at twelve o'clock with axes, cut down bamboo and drag it down into the cutting. At six o'clock we would come back, have a cup of rice, and then go back and start lighting the fires. As well as the bamboo fires we had some carbide lights, and some bamboo containers filled with dieseline with hessian wicks. We had elephants helping to drag logs down, but the Burmese drivers soon got cholera and died.

This was coincidental with the arrival of the monsoon. As the monsoon set in, it just started to rain. The sky came down until you could almost touch it, it was so low. We just had incessant rain. The camp turned to mud, our boots rotted off, our clothes rotted off, the tent flies rotted away, so we slept almost in continuous rain. That became the pattern of life. Men started to die, particularly in 'H' Force. I think that cholera must have taken half of them in no time. Of course we had other things like malaria, dysentery and ulcers. Our boots had gone, and the track we walked down to Hellfire Pass, as it is called now—we just called it the Cutting—was also used by the elephants. When the elephants' drivers died, the Japanese tried to take charge of them, but the elephants would not be in it. In fact one Japanese was belting an elephant one day, and it just picked him up in its trunk and hit him against a tree. What the elephants were doing was carrying containers of water, which were used with the hammer and tap. The water was poured into the hole to get the mud out. When you drilled down about half a metre, the drill became clogged with mud, so you used a length of wire with the end flattened like a spoon to get the dirt out. The elephants would

Elephant used in construction work on the railway.

never get off the track, which meant that prisoners with no boots had to get off among the thorns and scratch their ankles—and of course the scratches turned into ulcers.

Then another group arrived. By this time the cutting was down to about 12 or 15 metres. They were 'U' Battalion under Major 'Roaring Reg' Newton. The Japanese in charge of them [Sergeant Hiramatsu] had been highly decorated in Manchuria and wasn't a bad bloke. The Tiger looked after Newton's mob, who arrived looking very fit. We thought they were giants, because we had all shrunken away. Nobody smiled, and things were really bad; but then 'U' Battalion came, and things improved a bit because the Tiger would not allow the engineers to bash *his* men around. He would go down into the cutting and say, 'Well, you don't do this sort of thing'.

We had very little sense of humour, but I remember one humorous incident. In the tent fly I was in, about eight men had died of cholera out of about twenty. 'Bluey' Linnane, who died in 1990, had a very big nose. He was glooming about something, and he made the remark 'I wouldn't cut off me nose to spite me face'. Quick as a flash Tom Carroll, another man

The cutting at Konyu—Hellfire Pass.

from Toowoomba who was in the tent, said, 'By Christ, Blue, if you did I wouldn't mind it full of rum!'

Then we got a compressor, and Japanese jackhammer men. But the compressor had a leaky radiator, and instead of fixing it the Japanese took me off the lights and I had to work with another bloke walking backward and forward, filling this leaking radiator up with water. They put three elephants on the carrying—walking backward and forward to keep filling this leaking radiator on the compressor, instead of putting a bit of chewing gum or something on it and fixing it. But that's the way the Japanese worked.

By this stage there were only about 67 of our original 400 left, plus 'H' Force, whose numbers were dribbling away all the time. Then they brought up a team of, I think, Argyll and Sutherland Highlanders—anyway, the major in charge of them wore a kilt. Our officers were not at any stage allowed to go near the railway line. Major Quick was in charge of 'T'

Battalion, and there were four other officers, but none of them was allowed to go near the railway. This Scot, when told that he was not to go near the railway, said, 'I go where my men go'. So on the first day they started work he went down to the railway, and of course he did not last long because the engineers were very nasty people. One, Itchinoi, was a de-ranked officer—Battlegong, the Mad Mongrel, Mussolini—I can see them all still. When this Scot bloke turned up in a kilt, they all took to him, throwing rocks at him, and he was last seen disappearing along the railway line with his thin little legs going along under his kilt.

About this stage I got fairly crook, and Dr Parker, our doctor, said, 'I think you've got appendicitis, we'd better get you out'. He sent me down to a place called Konyu on the river. So I walked down—they never bothered sending guards with you—to this place on the river. The Japanese in charge was a medical orderly called Doctor Death; I do not know his real name.[1] His only prescription was a wooden sword; if you went near him, you got a hiding with the wooden sword. That's the only treatment I ever got from him.

There was also a big cholera ward under the control of Doctor Death. One day I was preening myself on how we were getting plenty of vitamins and food, and Doctor Death decided to move the cholera patients up to Hintok. So myself and a man named Sam Parsons were given the job of carrying one patient on a stretcher. It was wet. We were walking along the river, falling over logs, until we tipped this bloke out into the mud. He struggled to his feet and said, 'Bugger this. I'll walk'. So we and he walked. Finally we arrived at Hintok, and that is where I first saw Weary Dunlop.

There were a lot of Tamils and other Asians in this camp, remnants of bigger groups who had vanished or been buried. So they were there, we were there, and there was also a Korean guard we called the Mad Mongrel, who was fairly partial to Thai whisky. When he got drunk, he would go round at night and get you out. The tent fly I was under was on an embankment about twice as high as a table. The Mad Mongrel came round one night, got us all out and lined us up facing the edge of the embankment. He was very athletic and very tall, and he walked along the back of us, and one by one he kicked us each in the back of the neck and kicked us over the embankment! This was his form of entertainment when he got drunk.

There was a Japanese camp at the top of the rise, and their rations used to come up quite regularly by barge. The Tamils and other Asians who were in the camp with us used to form a line carrying the rations up the hill to the Japanese camp: big baskets of pomelos and dried fish and pumpkins. There would be a guard at the front and a guard at the back. We found that if we got halfway up the narrow track when a barge came in, and hid in the bushes, and waited till we were in the middle of the carrier line, we could just rush in, grab a couple of pumpkins or a fish, and then dash into the bush on the other side and down. In about 3 weeks we found that our health was improving because we were getting better rations—and I suppose the poor Tamils used to get a hiding, when they got up the top with the empty baskets.

After a few weeks at Hintok ulcers on my feet and legs earned me a trip on a barge south to the hospital camp at Tarsoa. From then on I felt reasonably safe until about June 1944, when I was included in a draft of prisoners selected to do further work for the emperor in Japan. Many others were doomed to remain in Thailand for further work on the line and to face the ever-present prospect of death from disease, malnutrition, dysentery, malaria, and ultimately from Allied bombs.

Notes

1 Doctor Death, Corporal (later Sergeant) Okada Seiichi, was later convicted of war crimes and sentenced to 10 years in prison.

5

Joining the railways

Dick Gilman

Dick Gilman, like Tom Morris, was on the Burma end of the railway, and like Tom he stayed on the railway, whereas most workers were moved out when construction was completed. There is a great irony in Dick Gilman's life, for when he entered the Australian Foreign Affairs Department after the war, his first appointment was to Burma. Burma looms large in his life.

Since Hank Nelson has given the story of a country boy who enlisted in the 8th Division of the Australian Imperial Forces (AIF), it might be of interest to you if I speak briefly of my own experience as a city boy who enlisted.

When Germany declared war, a lot of young Australians immediately felt that they should go to the help of the Mother Country. Many of us thought that it would be a wonderful life up in the clear skies attacking enemy planes. I was one who put my name down for the Royal Australian Air Force (RAAF) at age twenty. But they took so long to train us. It was not until the evacuation from Dunkirk that we patriotic young men realised that the war was getting serious. So some of us decided we'd not wait for the rather flamboyant life in the air force; we would join the army. This was seen as a mistake, because the army was regarded the lowest of the three services, but I joined the army and trained in both Sydney and Dubbo. In our final camp in Dubbo, I met the woman who is my present wife, and we had an understanding. We decided that it would not be wise to marry, since my future was uncertain. She has always alleged that I should have married and given her a child before I embarked; but we didn't marry, and it was 5 years from that time until she saw me again.

Gunner Richard Gilman, portrait before the storm.

We trained in Malaya for almost a year. We were called by some of the popular press the Glamour Boys, because while the 8th Division was training in the jungles of Malaya, some of our men were dying in the Middle East and in skies over Europe for the air force. One of our commanders said to us, 'Well, we don't know whether the Japanese will actually strike—it's uncertain. However, if they do strike, we'll clean them up and then go over to the Middle East and do some real fighting.' That was the atmosphere when we were waiting for the Japanese onslaught in Malaya.

The circumstances of life on both the Thai and the Burma side of the railway have already been covered. I would like only to recite one anecdote, which shows the difference between the fighting soldiers on either side and the guards and the engineers, who were, after all, not fighting men. We were working in Burma on an embankment that ran alongside a bullock track over which the Japanese were taking military supplies. They were desperate to build the railway because their motor transport was making very little progress over these rough tracks. They were also taking their troops by foot along this rough bullock track. It was raining heavily, and there was a very slippery and muddy slope. We stood watching the troops pass by. We saw a group of young soldiers; they looked no more than about sixteen or seventeen—tiny fellows. They were pushing their field gun up the incline but were not making very much progress. The gun kept slipping back, and the officers and NCOs kept forcing them with the aid of rifle butts or sticks. A group of us who were gunners also, and who knew something about manhandling field pieces, quite impulsively hopped in and pushed the gun. It was a most extraordinary experience, because it was simply impulsive. I think much has been spoken of the camaraderie between opposing forces. We know that in the First World War the Germans and the Allied soldiers met on occasion on Christmas Day and exchanged pleasantries while the war stopped. We also know that the Australians very much respected the Turks at Gallipoli. I am suggesting that there is a great difference between fighting soldiers and non-combatants.

Continuing my personal story, on returning at age twenty-six to Australia, I decided that it would be a good idea to join the public service, and I joined Foreign Affairs. But in order to reach diplomatic staff one required a degree, so at age twenty-six I became a student at the Australian National University (ANU). Along with the seventeen year olds and eighteen year olds there were a lot of ex-servicemen who were going back to school, and I was lucky enough to be under Manning Clark, who taught as a junior lecturer in Australian history. When I did join the diplomatic staff, I went to Burma for my first posting. I took my wife and my two young children on a very pleasant sea voyage, which had no resemblance to the trip I had made some 5 years earlier in a Japanese hell ship from Singapore to Moulmein, where with Tom Morris we started to build a railway at a place called Thanbyuzayat.

I am simply an amateur historian, but I love history, and I want to touch on Dr Aiko Utsumi's theme that we, as historians, must do more. What Aiko is doing in Japanese schools is to try to interest the young in what has happened in the Pacific War, but I feel that it is not all that well covered in Australian schools. I would like to see much more attention given to history in school curricula. I say this, remembering that my own generation took very little interest in the First World War. We knew that our fathers had fought in it: my father was in France, where he was gassed. These men had all the horror of trench warfare, but we knew only, on Anzac Day perhaps, that there had been a war. So I do not think really that this lack of knowledge is due to any particular fault in the Japanese education; I think that this applies also to our own. It is inevitable that each succeeding generation is occupied with its own affairs and does not pay a great deal of attention to the past. I congratulate Aiko on what she is doing and hope that we can do much more ourselves.

Hugh Clarke kindly asked me to write a small piece in his book *A Life for Every Sleeper*. I happen to be one of those—very few of us—who was at the joining of the railway. The work had been done; the embankments had been built; the building of the railway was coming to conclusion. I was what we called a specialist: I was a rail layer. I had to drive dogspikes and do things like that. We were regarded as the experts, so we had to be there, along with some Dutch and others, for the actual joining of the two sections of the rail. For those of our men who died in camps along the railway it was a memorial, and to all of us it was a great relief. Many of our own men did not know what a dramatic, but also humorous, occasion it was.

There were signs of consternation and doubts among the Japanese engineers as the time for the joining of the railway lines being pushed forward from Burma and Thailand drew nearer. It was rumoured that in departing from the original British survey the Japanese had taken a number of short cuts and miscalculated to the extent that the lines approaching from the two directions instead of meeting would, if not redirected in good time, pass one another leaving a gap of some hundreds of yards between them. It was never really established that such a catastrophe was likely to occur, but it was noted by prisoners on both sides of the railway that the Japanese engineers seemed to be ordering some sudden changes in the direction of the embankments and the lines over the last several kilometres of their course prior to their joining near the Three Pagodas Pass.

As the day for the joining of the lines came closer there was an air of expectancy and excitement among the Japanese and the prisoners alike. For the Japanese engineers and guards it signalled the completion of a momentous undertaking and a sense of fulfilment of a mission which would bring them merit in the eyes of the Emperor and the acclaim of their countrymen as well as advancing the strategy of their High Command for an assault on India mounted from Burma with equipment and troops moved across the railway from Thailand.

For the prisoners it spelt disbelief that a project which they had often thought impossible could have been achieved and utmost relief that their travail was almost over. In recent months a time limit and target date had been imposed by the High Command in a bid to complete the rail link before the more extreme monsoon conditions made the task more difficult and to accelerate plans for an offensive into India from northern Burma. The engineers and guards had responded to the 'speedo' order with fanatical zeal, intensified by their fear of dire consequences and loss of face should they fail to complete the task on schedule. For the prisoners, that 'speedo' had involved more brutality from the harassed and short-tempered guards and engineers, and more insistence by the Japanese camp commanders that quotas on the work parties would be maintained no matter how weak and disabled were those individuals who were declared by the Australian Camp medical officers to be unfit for work.

Joining the railways

For the men actually laying the sleepers and rails as they came up on railway bogies over the completed line from the supply base in Burma, the pressure became almost intolerable as the time for the joining of the lines came closer. The onset of the monsoon rains was intensifying and the line-laying prisoners toiled interminably in mud and slush on the newly built embankments. Having walked through heavy rain some ten kilometres from their camp to the railhead the prisoners would wait sometimes for hours until new supplies of sleepers or rails came forward. As these supplies were irregular and unreliable the men would sometimes be kept on the job for shifts from twenty-four to thirty hours with their only nourishment a plate or two of rice carried out to them from the camp by their no more fortunate fellow prisoners. Lacking sleep, and weakened for want of food and by the heavy work of manhandling sleepers and railway lines which were pinned to the sleepers by dog spikes driven in by heavy sledge hammers, the prisoners toiled in a dazed, almost unconscious state. Oblivious to the mud under their feet and the driving rain the men would be utterly exhausted as they waited for the next supply of sleepers and with the already laid and dog spiked rails pillowing their heads. With the rain falling steadily on their upturned faces they would fall into a heavy sleep having posted one of their number, in rotation, as a lookout to warn them of the approach of the next consignment of sleepers and rails lest the wheels of the railway bogies sever a row of heads. Release from these nightmare conditions was eagerly contemplated.

Except for the nationalities involved and the costumes being worn, the scene on the day of joining of the line resembled a western movie in the Hollywood tradition. There was the same air of expectancy as the two teams of line layers approached one another from the two directions; the clanking of hammers upon metal as dog spikes were driven into the sleepers; the puffing locomotives coming up to the railheads from both directions; the shouting and posturing of the dignitaries responsible for the successful completion of the railway. The Japanese senior officers looked awkward and self-conscious in their small caps and over-large jackboots. A military band played airs which seemed not a little off-key to the prisoners with their western-type musical orientation. Of necessity almost, there had to be a film to record the event for propaganda purposes both at home in Japan and in the Japanese-occupied countries in east and south-east Asia within what the Japanese Government described as the 'Greater East Asia Co-prosperity Sphere'. The producers and directors of the film were scurrying about looking important and, at the same time, embarrassed and self-conscious in their too new looking military uniforms which, as civilians, they had probably been obliged to wear in this military zone.

The film makers' plan was to use the prisoners in a line-laying scene to fit the last and joining section of rail into place and to drive home the dog spikes pinning the rail to the sleeper. When the time came to select the bit-players for this scene, the film men viewed the gaunt, skinny and near-naked prisoners with evident horror. How could these bony and under-nourished specimens as they stood barefooted and clad only in

G-strings or lap-laps, be depicted on film as fit and contented men happy to be a part of the all-conquering Japanese Army and be working for the glory of the Emperor? The answer was found in part by the property department which provided 'costumes' for the several dozen prisoners who were hand-picked for the final line-laying scene. These men were fitted out with Japanese shirts, shorts and black sandshoes. These film stars, as they were immediately dubbed by their comrades, suffered a good deal of ribald chaffing as they were called 'pansies' or even less complimentary names.

The cameras rolled, the band played a suitably triumphant air, and the selected prisoners—having been once rehearsed—performed their last line-laying rite. They carried the rail on their shoulders to the final remaining gap in the line, dropped it to the ground with a resounding bang, manhandled it into position on the sleepers, and drove home the dog spikes with a practised skill.

As the last spike was ready to be driven a most important but self-conscious looking senior and overweight officer of the Japanese Army came forward and was presented with a heavy sledge hammer to perform the symbolic driving of the last spike. Panting with the weight of the hammer this portly dignitary aimed a feeble blow at the head of the spike which he missed completely and gave the rail a resounding clang instead. Bracing himself and looking quite dismayed at his own clumsiness, the officer took a much shorter grip of the hammer and managed to drive the spike a fraction into the sleeper to be finished off by a lithe engineer who leaped to his assistance.

For the prisoners the whole episode of the joining of the lines near the Three Pagodas Pass was both farcical and pathetic. While they could not but smile at the antics of the Japanese as they enacted the final scene with so many Hollywood trimmings, their thoughts were on the futility of the 'achievement' and upon the tragic and unnecessary deaths of so many of their comrades.

For the prisoners, the line-laying ceremony had one remaining element of fun. Those of their number who had been selected and suitably costumed to take part in the final scene were prone to rejoice and swank their new shirts, shorts and footwear. Ironically, they were not even allowed to retain these small offerings as payment for their services. To the accompaniment of cheers and jeers from their mates the 'film stars' were deprived of their bounty by an unsmiling Japanese quartermaster and his staff who walked down the line of dandified prisoners collecting their uniforms in large bags and leaving the men standing bare and exposed-looking in their G-strings.

The ceremony was capped for the Japanese engineers and guards by a celebration dinner in which, judging from the sounds of revelry, generous portions of saki were served. For the prisoners there was little but anti-climax following the ceremony. They did however receive an extra ration of rice, which they were glad enough to have.[1]

Notes

1 First published in Hugh Clarke, *A Life for Every Sleeper: A Pictorial Record of the Burma–Thailand Railway*, Allen and Unwin, Sydney, 1986, pp. 57–61.

6

Journeys in captivity

Tom Uren

Tom Uren is one of the best-known ex-prisoners of war (POWs), having been in the Australian parliament for 31 years and either opposition spokesman, or minister responsible, for environment, local government, housing and urban development. From 1969 to 1987 he was part of the leadership of the Australian Labor Party. As a nineteen year old, just before he transferred to the 2nd AIF, he fought for the Australian heavyweight title. He was one of those who made that progress across Australia—going by rail through Broken Hill to Terowie in South Australia, to Alice Springs on the Ghan, and then from Alice Springs in motor and rail trucks to Darwin— to join Sparrow Force to sail to Timor. So he too became part of the group of Australians making the initial engagement with South-East Asia.

Prior to leaving Sydney on that great venture, I had never travelled further north than Newcastle, further south than Port Kembla or further west than Katoomba. I went right up through the heart of the country to Darwin, and of course on 8 December 1941 embarked for Timor. My experience took me briefly through Timor, Java, Singapore, on to the Burma–Thailand Railway, back down to Singapore again, then to Japan for the last 12 months of the war. In those days the only travel people were Cook's, and I always say that I got the Cook's tour. I served briefly in the camps of Tarso, but reached Konyu, then Hintok Mountain camp, Hintok River camp and Kinsayok on the railway line. I walked into Konyu camp on 26 January 1943. Weary Dunlop was the commander of that camp, and I remained under Weary's command until June 1944, when I left Tamuan for Japan. We spent most of our time in Hintok Road camp. Our visiting Korean, former guard and now friend Yi Hak-Nae, served in that period with us.

Many of our group under Weary were Middle East veterans, because Weary had of course served through the Middle East. That group were the great heroes, who were shanghaied and put into Java, put into trucks and made to look like a division, so that they would attract a million Japanese to try and take the island because of the enormous forces involved. They were sacrificed. Now there were also Singapore people there under Weary, plus many of the 2/40th Battalion and the associated troops that I was a part of, and there were also some called the Empire Star Group. The *Empire Star* people had forced themselves, it is said, onto the last ship out of Singapore. They were accused of forcing women and children and nurses off so that they could take their places. When they got to Java they had to make up their minds whether or not they would stay and fight the Japanese. An old Englishman once said to me, 'Tom, you can never judge a Welshman until you've eaten a bag of flour with him'. The Welsh used to come across in the 1930s and take the employment, particularly of the Londoners. They would work for a lower wage, and there was a class difference between the Londoners and the Welsh. I now have a saying that you can never judge a man until you have eaten a bag of rice with him. When we started eating our bag of rice in the camps, some people looked marvellous, but by the time they got down to the bottom of the bag they were not too good at all; you would not give a beer bottle top for them. On the other hand, some of the young people from the *Empire Star* came through and were magnificent, though they did not look very good when they started. All they needed was security and leadership, and Weary of course gave both.

I was on the hammer and tap, drilling rock, as my comrades were. I happened to be with a very wise guy, an old worker, a cane cutter, named Harry Baker. He had lost one of his forefingers cutting cane. In one thing he educated me. He said, 'Tom, don't bust your guts, just take your time. Don't be in a hurry to finish'. It was a skill to hold the drill, and he would hold the drill, and I would do most of the swinging with the 8 pound (3.6 kilogram) Plum hammer, letting the weight on the head do the work. I would work on the hammer most of the day. We started off having to drill 80 centimetres a day; we finished up having to do 3 metres; then they would work us all day. But we had it easy compared to those who had to clear away the rock. Some of those people worked up to 20 hours a day, when you take into consideration the 5 to 6 kilometres they had to walk from the camp to go to the site where they worked, and then to get back home again at night. You had to get through the bush, and particularly in the wet weather you would slip, your feet would go completely from under you, and you would fall down. It was so agonising, so painful.

There were 500 of us in camp under Weary's leadership. As I have written in my book:

Our doctors were quite remarkable fellows, combining medical ingenuity with leadership and comradeship. They often had to improvise because of the primitive conditions in which we lived. They worked, like all of us, as part of a team. It was that collective spirit which was fundamental to our survival.[1]

Weary had with him two other remarkable doctors: Arthur Moon and Ewan Corlette. I have been a tough politician in my time, but I have always found it very difficult to get stuck into the medical profession. The Labor Party would be harsh, but I have always found it very difficult to criticise. I remember cutting my wrist, and my tendons hung down on the hand. I watched Dick Parker, another doctor, pull the tendons together and sew them. How he looked after me! And with the doctor was a team of assistants. When I got amoebic dysentery, I experienced their compassion—it was just remarkable. So I get sentimental when I talk about Weary, but also about other doctors. I gave an example of the collective spirit they fostered in my maiden speech to parliament on 26 February 1959:

> I should like to relate an experience I had during the war. I was a prisoner of war at a place called Hintok Road Camp on the Burma–Siam Railway. Our commanding officer was Lieutenant-Colonel Weary Dunlop. He was a remarkable man in many ways. He was not only a great doctor, but also a great soldier. We were known as 'Dunlop Force'. As honorable members probably know, the Japanese made our officers and medical orderlies an allowance. The non-commissioned officers and men who worked on the railway were also paid a small wage. This was a sham kept up by the Japanese to save face under the Geneva Convention. In our camp, the officers and medical orderlies paid the greater proportion of their allowance into a central fund. The men who worked did likewise. We lived by the principle of the fit looking after the sick, the young looking after the old, and the rich looking after the poor. A few months after we arrived at Hintok Road Camp a part of 'H' Force, all British, arrived. They were about four hundred strong. As temporary arrangements they had tents. The officers selected the best, the non-commissioned officers the next best, and the men got the dregs. Soon after they arrived, the wet season set in, bringing with it cholera and dysentery. Six weeks later, only fifty men marched out of that camp and of that number only about 25 survived. Only a creek separated our two camps, but on one the law of the jungle prevailed, and on the other side the principles of socialism.[2]

I said that experience—and the impression it left on me—was one of the reasons why I argued philosophically as a socialist, and why I talk about myself today as a collectivist. It was the collectivism that Weary really bred in us. By the way, I also say in the book that, although the Australians tended to have a higher rate of survival than prisoners from Britain and other countries, not all Australian camps were like ours. Our survival rate was due, basically, to Weary's leadership.

Tom Uren, the contender.

I will never forget meeting Weary soon after I was elected to parliament. My wife Patricia's brother was also a POW. We met at the London Hotel in Melbourne. We were having a cup of tea, and Weary started talking about the Labor Party. I looked up and said, 'Colonel, you've degenerated due to your environment'. Anyway, I love him.

The people that died at Hintok—we used to have to walk over them every morning when we went to work. They were just corpses laid out. It was really a moving experience, and it does not leave you. Cholera is probably the most frightening thing I have ever encountered.

I want to mention two things: Asian conscripted labourers and my attitude to the Japanese. First of all, if you think we Australians had a raw deal, you should look at the history of the Asian forced labourers. Unfortunately not enough has been written about them. We all lived on springs and in the country surrounding those springs. When we camped on a spring we would be organised. The Asian labourers would come up and just surround a spring. They had no latrines: they used to excrete where they were; they'd wash with one hand and eat with the other. In the wet season conditions were at their worst, for cholera is water-borne, and they died in thousands.

Secondly, if I had been asked at the end of the first 2½ years of my life as a prisoner, I would have exterminated *every* Japanese on the face of the planet. But in the last year of the war I went to Japan. I worked with indentured Korean labourers, I worked with old Japanese workers, and I saw the compassion of a human being to a human being. I had only one Red Cross parcel in my years as a prisoner, and I found myself sharing it with those Japanese. I myself developed in that period a great deal. It was growth in compassion, and you will find that in all my arguments and all my thrust. People say to me, 'Do you hate the Japanese?' And I say, 'No, I don't hate the Japanese, but I hate militarism and I hate fascism'. I have fought them all my life, and I will continue to fight them. I am fighting as much as anybody: I am fighting Bill Hayden; I am fighting Bob Hawke; I am fighting those Americans who want to remilitarise Japan and make Japan take a more active role in world affairs. Recently I had to challenge Hayden, saying that he was interfering in the internal affairs of Japan, seeking Japan to change its constitution to become a world military power. Everybody should challenge those who advocate it. Already Japan, *without* being a world military power, is spending 39 billion US dollars each year on the military.

Tom Morris has gone the closest to describing the actual conditions in a POW hospital. Nobody can tell you the stench of an ulcer ward. You have got to be there; you have to smell it. The suffering, and the way that people suffered, and the real brutality of militarism and fascism—it really was a killing experience. You cannot describe that, but I give you these cold figures. In the last war, 550 000 Australians served in all theatres of war, and 19 000 were killed in action—that is, 3 per cent. Even with those dreaded Nazis, 8000 Australians were taken prisoner with them, and 7700 came back; in other words 3 per cent remained in another place. With the Japanese, 22 000 Australians were captured either in Malaya, Singapore, New Guinea or the Dutch East Indies, but only 14 000 came home; 8000 perished, or 36 per cent—twelve times greater. But it did not end there. Because of the barbarous treatment and the conditions under which they had lived, between 1945 and 1959 ex-POWs of the Japanese died at four times the rate, or 400 per cent more, than other veterans who had served in the same theatres of war. Between 1959 and now they died at a 20 per cent higher rate. There has now been a study made comparing our conditions with those of other servicemen.[3] Over 7 per cent of our people had cholera, with almost none of this disease among other veterans. Hookworm—35 per cent with us, 7 per cent with other veterans. Leg ulcers—61 per cent with us, 12 per cent with other veterans. 'Happy feet'—49 per cent as compared with 4 per cent.

The only government that gave POWs any special treatment, and it gave it to prisoners of both the Germans and the Japanese, was the Whitlam government, of which I was a cabinet minister. We gave them free medical, free hospital, free dental and free optical treatment. But to my surprise these benefits were gradually eroded in the period under Malcolm Fraser and then butchered to some extent under Bob Hawke. The government changes did not affect me personally because I was always reasonably fit, but some of my mates would tell me, 'We're getting a pretty raw deal from your government'. They spelled out some things, so I started making speeches in 1988 after the real cuts in 1987. They were so arrogant, if I can use the word, in the Veterans' Affairs Department that they did not even have separate files for our POWs: they integrated them among all veterans. When I made my first speech in 1988, things started to change a little, and then gradually we got some of those benefits returned. We had wiped the limits off dental treatment, and certain disabilities were recognised as automatic. If a veteran had a wife and an income, he was having to pay half the Medicare levy; now we're back to the position where we don't have to pay a Medicare levy.

But there are two injustices that need to be fixed. Firstly, the Japanese POWs suffered more than any other group of Australians in the Second World War. If they have left work or turned sixty-five, that should not put a bar to their getting the TPI (Totally and Permanently Incapacitated veteran status, and associated benefit). I have argued with the government that, if they qualify in illness to get the TPI, they should get it irrespective of whether they have left work or whether they've reached the age of sixty-five. Secondly, until 1987, if you died from your war-caused injuries, you could die at no expense in a nursing home. That was wiped away, and I believe that it should be reintroduced. A former Japanese POW should have the option: if he wants to live in a nursing home, he should be able to stay there free of charge. The least the nation can do for our veterans is allow them to spend their last days without economic stress. Paradoxically, the two enemies against us are the Veterans' Affairs Department and the top brass of the Returned Services League (RSL). The real reason is that they will not accept a group of people; each individual has to prove his own case. I concede that some of our POWs had it lighter than others; but 83 per cent on the record had beriberi, for example, and beriberi has many other implications for people's health.

We have got to get stuck into politicians, because politicians and governments are the only ones who can send people to war. It is politicians and government—our own government—that have to give justice to these POWs.

Notes

1 Tom Uren's autobiography is currently being written.
2 Parliament of Australia, *Hansard Parliamentary Debates* (House of Representatives), 26 February 1959, pp. 358–61.
3 Alison J. Venn and Charles S. Guest, 'Chronic Morbidity of former prisoners of war and other Australian Veterans', *The Medical Journal of Australia*, vol. 155, November 18 1991, pp. 705–12 reviewed 48 studies of prisoners and war service and long-term health; see also Owen Dent, Bruce Richardson, Sue Wilson, Kerry Goulston and Catherine Murdoch, 'Post-war Mortality among Australian World War II prisoners of the Japanese', *The Medical Journal of Australia*, vol. 150, April 3 1989, pp. 378–82.

7

Asian forced labour (*romusha*) on the Burma–Thailand Railway

Yoshinori Murai

In November 1990 the remains of more than 700 people were dug up from a sugarcane field at Kanchanaburi in Thailand. These remains were assumed to be those of ex-*romusha*, because some local people testified that the place had once been the site of a camp of Asian *romusha*. Witnesses testified that they had seen Japanese soldiers throwing dead bodies into holes dug in the ground. Most seemed to have died because of diarrhoea or malaria after working very hard as slaves.[1] This news again calls attention to the Burma–Thailand Railway and to the cruel treatment meted out by the Japanese Army to Asian *romusha* as well as to Allied prisoners of war (POWs).

'*Romusha*' is still a disgusting word among South-East Asian people, particularly among the elderly. This word reminds them of the harsh, severe and sad experiences under Japanese military occupation. An Indonesian dictionary contains the following entry: '*Romusha* means forced labour, namely persons who were forced to work heavily during Japanese occupation.'[2]

This word '*romusha*' and its nightmarish memory are still handed down from generation to generation in South-East Asia. A junior high school textbook of the history of Indonesia says of *romusha*:

The people who suffered the most painful experience during the Japanese occupation were Romusha. They were forcibly worked by the Japanese for the construction of military facilities such as airports, fortress, railways etc. Most of them were recruited from the rural area. They were made up of the uneducated people or those educated at most only in elementary school. At first they were induced by sweet words. But if this invitation was unsuccessful, in the end they were forced to be Romusha. Densely populated Java was able to supply many labourers . . . Hundreds of thousands of Romusha were sent to the outer islands of Java. Some of them were sent abroad to countries such as Malaya, Burma and Thailand.[3]

Although the *romusha*'s experiences under Japanese occupation were miserable and terrible enough, until now little research has been done by the Japanese, mainly because of a lack of a feeling of responsibility towards Asians. At the same time documents have been lacking, having possibly been destroyed by the Japanese Army or concealed by the Japanese government up to now. But fortunately two interesting researches done by Japanese scholars are now available: the one is Kurasawa Aiko's interviews with eighteen Javanese former *romusha*;[4] the other is Professor Yoshikawa Toshiharu's recent report on the Burma–Thailand Railway.[5] Professor Yoshikawa discovered many official documents of the Supreme Command of the Thai National Army at the National Archives in Bangkok.

Military background of the need for *romusha*

There might be an inevitable (though never justified) reason for the Japanese Army's cruel treatment of *romusha*. The aims of Japanese invasion towards South-East Asia were:

1. acquisition of natural resources like oil, rubber, tin, and so on, which were hard to secure because of the American, British, Chinese and Dutch blockade as a result of Japanese expansionism and invasion of China; and
2. to cut off the supply route of the Allies to the Jiang Jie Shi (Chiang Kai-shek) government at Chongqing (Chungking).

On 20 November 1941, just before the war, the Outline of Administration in the Occupied Areas of the South was decided at the co-ordinating meeting between the imperial headquarters and the government. The outline prescribed the main purposes of the Japanese Military Administration in the occupied area as:

1. restoring public order;
2. rapid acquisition of important natural resources for national defence;
3. self-support in each occupied area.

The basic policy of the Military Administration, included in that outline, deserves close attention: 'For the acquisition of important natural resources and for the self-supply of the occupied area, the army should force the local people to endure the heavy burden needed'.[6] Some Japanese ultranationalists still continue to say that the purpose of Japanese occupation in Asia was 'the liberation of Asian colonies and people from the iron chain of the white people'. But this position becomes completely untenable when one reads the basic policy of the Imperial Army cited above, or even more so when one considers the real situation of local people such as *romusha*.

After the middle of 1943 the war situation deteriorated for the Japanese Army; it set up the Absolute Defence Sphere, and more and more *romusha* came to be needed for constructing military facilities. The Burma–Thailand Railway was keenly needed for occupying Burma efficiently, cutting off the Allied supply route to Chongqing and carrying out the Imphal Operation (invasion of India). But Thailand was an independent country and not an enemy country for Japan. Also, in Thailand it was very difficult to procure the huge amount of labour needed for the construction of the railway. Because of this Allied prisoners and *romusha* from Malaya, Indonesia and Vietnam were brought to this rash and absurd construction.

Number of *romusha* on the railway

After the completion of the railway (February 1944), Japanese Railway Headquarters built a cenotaph near the bridge over the River Kwai in memory of the POW and *romusha* victims on the Burma–Thailand Railway. The memorial address for the victims was written in six languages: Japanese, English, Thai, Vietnamese, Chinese and Malay (note that there was no Dutch, no Burmese, no Tamil). The Malay text says: 'Paying our respects to the souls of Moslems who worked here. Al'lah rewards you.'

At that time no one knew the exact number of victims, and unfortunately even now the numbers cannot be estimated with certainty. Hiroike Toshio, a staff officer of the 2nd Railway Headquarters and an initial planner of the railway, has estimated the total number of *romusha* at about 200 000 (at the peak period about 80 000).[7] It would be difficult to calculate the exact number of *romusha* because so many of them, particularly Thais and Burmese, ran away from their camps and so many died. Also, some *romusha* brought their families with them, which may have confused the Japanese. Moreover, the Japanese may have paid very little attention to the numbers of dead and runaways.

The figures for Japanese, POW and *romusha* as shown in Table 7.1 are those reported by the Kanchanaburi prefectural police office (15 September 1943) and the governor of Kanchanaburi prefecture.

In this table the category of Chinese possibly includes both Thai and Malay Chinese. It was very difficult to recruit Thai *romusha* because Thailand was an independent country, so the Japanese asked the Thai Chinese Association of Commerce to recruit Chinese *romusha*. But this recruitment was not so successful because the work conditions were not at

Table 7.1   Number of Japanese, POWs and *romusha* on the Burma–Thailand Railway, 1943

Workers	15 Sep. 1943	27 Sep. 1943	25 Nov. 1943
Japanese	20 158	24 764	25 423
POW	27 790	41 570	32 820
Romusha	42 770	67 480	52 079
Chinese	12 000	22 910	9 075
Malay	26 300	40 570	36 954
Mon	1 600	1 600	2 050
Burmese	2 870	2 400	4 000

Source: Yoshikawa Toshiharu, 'Tai ni totteno Taimen tetsudo' (The Burma–Thailand Railway from a Thai point of view), manuscript, 1991.

all attractive. From 15 July until 31 August, 12 968 Thai Chinese *romusha* were to have been received by the Japanese, but only 5641 reached the Kanchanaburi camp: others ran away en route.

Among *romusha* in Thailand the biggest group was Malay. But this group probably included Malaysian, Javanese, non-Javanese–Indonesian, Malay–Indian and Vietnamese. It is almost impossible now to know the percentage of these ethnic groups.[8]

Thai *romusha* and *romusha* in Burma are not included in this table. The number of Thai *romusha* is unknown. For the construction of the railway between Nong Pladuk and Kanchanaburi about 5000 *romusha* were registered (September and October 1942). In Kanchanaburi prefecture about 700 *romusha* were hired by the Japanese (October 1942). On 18 December 1942 Thai *romusha* and some policemen attacked the Japanese military base of Ban Pong. After this Thai people became very reluctant to become *romusha*.[9]

In Burma also it is difficult to estimate the number of *romusha*. One Japanese source gives the figure of about 70 000,[10] but this may represent a significant underestimation. According to Tanabe Hisao,[11] a Japanese specialist on Burma, the Burmese government estimate of the total number of *romusha* recruited within 3 years was 177 000. Among them only 91 836 reached Thanbyuzayat (Burma Base camp). A lot of Burmese escaped on the way to Thanbyuzayat and from the camp because of low wages and heavy work. At least 30 000 *romusha* were estimated to have died.

Among the *romusha* recruited from Thailand, Burma, Malaysia, Indonesia and Vietnam, Burmese, Chinese and Javanese made up comparatively large ethnic groups. We can roughly estimate the total number of Asian *romusha* as more than 200 000. Hiroike has estimated the *romusha* victims on the railway at about 33 000,[12] but we do not have any reliable evidence to support this figure. In Burma alone more than 30 000 *romusha* are said to have died. Clarke has estimated the dead at 70 000.[13] These numbers show that the construction of the Burma–Thailand Railway was truly cruel for the *romusha* as well as for the POWs.

Recruitment of *romusha*

Many people have testified to the fact that they were abruptly taken to some place by local officials and forced to 'consent' to become *romusha*. In many cases they never knew where they were brought or what they should do. One Indonesian testified as follows:

> Sadin was recruited at Kuningan, West Java. He was asked to work for only two weeks at Cirebon near Kuningan. But one day while he was working at Cirebon he was sent secretly by boat with his 1,500 colleagues to Tanjung Priok, port of Jakarta. From Jakarta, Sadin and other Romusha were brought to another big ship which went to Malaya. Sadin was sent to Thailand. The Japanese were so cruel as to bury alive Romusha who were seriously ill and could hardly work. We could no longer put up with this cruel treatment. One day Romusha rose against the Japanese. But this uprising was easily suppressed. Fortunately Sadin was able to escape from the Japanese. In November 1959, fourteen years after the war ended he was able to come back to his home thanks to Indonesian Government support.[14]

Java was the biggest supplier of *romusha* because of the densely populated character of the island and the fact that it was not directly attacked by the Allies. It is estimated that more than 2 million people in Java were recruited as *romusha*. This means that more than 8 per cent of the labour force (the population aged between fifteen and forty years of age), and 17 per cent of the mobile (recruitable) population, became *romusha*.[15]

At the initial stage of the Japanese Military Administration in Java, *romusha* were recruited by the ordinary administrative bodies, but after people came to know of the terribly bad treatment of *romusha* it became difficult to recruit them in this way. Because of this the Japanese organised a new system of recruitment and advertisement in line with vertical administration: Romu Kyokai (Labour Association). In each province of Java a central body of Romu Kyokai was organised. Pyramidal organisation of Romu Kyokai from province down to prefecture, district and village was supposed to work efficiently. To try to gain a better image for the *romusha*, new words were used. These included *pradjoerit pekerdja* (worker soldier) and *poeradjoerit ekonomi* (economic soldier). But people already knew the true fate of *romusha*.

The final responsibility for recruitment was loaded onto the shoulders of village officials, who were forced to choose some villagers as *romusha*. Usually *orang kecil* (small people) such as landless agrarian labourers, uneducated people in the rural areas and petty traders, beggars and unemployed in the city were chosen as *romusha*. Sometimes the method of false invitation was utilised. Thus one young man in Jepara prefecture (central Java), on the way to market to sell agricultural products, was persuaded to 'study abroad'. He had been educated for only 3 years in elementary school. He promptly agreed to the proposal and registered his name. Then he was sent to Tanjung Priok as a *romusha* by ship together with several thousands of colleagues.[16]

Romusha worked for the construction of agricultural infrastructure, airports, railways, air-raid shelters, trenches and so on. They also worked in arms factories and at coal mines. They were sent to outer Java islands like Sumatra, Sulawesi, British Borneo, Papua New Guinea, Malaya, Singapore, Indochina, Thailand, Burma, Andaman Islands and Guadalcanal. Kasmijan Yosoprapto, a railway technician, was sent to the Burma–Thailand Railway as a technician. According to him, about 15 000 Javanese *romusha* went to Thailand with him in March 1943. After completion of the railway they had to continue to work; they cut trees for the fuel of trains.[17]

By the estimation of the Japanese Army, about 270 000 *romusha* were sent to outer Java and abroad. But this figure does not include the number sent before April 1944, which means that it does not include *romusha* who worked on the railway and were sent before then. The number of *romusha* sent from Java to the railway is still not clear. However, one thing that is clear is that most of them were not able to go back to their homeland until the end of the war. It is estimated that, among 270 000 *romusha* sent to outer Java and abroad, only 70 000 were able to go back home before the end of the war.

Treatment of *romusha*

According to a provision of the Japanese Labour Regulation, *romusha* were organised into *han*, which consisted of 25 *romusha*, *kumi* consisting of four *han*, and *buntai* consisting of five *kumi*. The biggest organisation was a *kutai*, which consisted of 1000 *romusha*. Some of the provisions in the regulation were as follows:

* *Romusha* are to be provided holidays to a maximum of 10 days.

* When *romusha* die, they are to be buried courteously.

* The work hours per day are 10 hours from 9:00 till 19:00.

* Three holidays a month are to be allowed.

* Daily wage: ordinary *romusha* 1 baht (= 1.6 yen), headman of *han* 2 bahts, headman of *kumi* 2.5 bahts, headman of *buntai* 3 bahts, headman of *kutai* 3.5 bahts.

- Wages of the sick and wounded are fully guaranteed.

- For deceased Malay and Javanese *romusha* 15 bahts a month will be provided to the family left behind.

- Allowances for overtime work, night work, homecoming and so on are to be provided.

- Five hospitals will be built, the capacity of each to be 2000 beds.

The real situation of *romusha* was very different.

Matsui Yayori recently reported on the experience of Malay Chinese *romusha*:

> From Seremban in Malaysia, 780 Romusha were sent to the railway construction. Among them only 49 Romusha were eventually able to go back home. Son-likkai (Malaysian Chinese, seventy-five years old) was abruptly taken to the Japanese military office on his way to go shopping to the market. He was forcibly taken to the train without anything but what he stood up in. He was given a registered number as Romusha, No. 669. In his group, Malays were in the minority (only two or three per cent), Chinese and Indians were in about equal numbers. They went to Kanchanaburi by train or truck. From Kanchanaburi they walked up to Teimonta (Timontar) near the Thailand–Burma border. It took sixteen days, in the midst of the rainy season. On the way he saw many dead bodies of POWs. There were about 2,000 or 3,000 Romusha at Teimonta. Their work was cutting and sawing trees, digging, carrying rails and so on. They were forced to work heavily even at night and in the rain. They were whipped when they stopped to work. Every day their food was only dried sweet-potatoes [or cassavas?]. A lot of them died of malaria and diarrhoea. They were also often attacked from the air by the Allies. Some Romusha committed suicide. POWs came to bury the dead bodies of Romusha. Though they had contracted to the Japanese to work for only three months, Son-likkai and others worked for three years and eight months, and never received any wage.[18]

This kind of tragic experience of both *romusha* and POWs was very common, not only on the railway but throughout Japanese-occupied areas.

Tan Malaka, the famous Indonesian revolutionary, returned to Indonesia in 1942 after a long period of exile and hid in Bayah coal mine in western Java. He witnessed the miserable situation of *romusha*:

> About five or six kilometres from Bayah, along the coast, was a place called Pulau Manuk, which was feared by everyone, for few were the Romusha who emerged from that place uninfected by fatal diseases such as ulcerated boils, dysentery, and malaria. The Romusha were provided with insufficient food, very few medicines, and an inadequate nursing staff; in particular no care at all was given to the sick and dying. Every day along the Road from Pulau Manuk to Bayah one could see Romusha

covered with festering lesions, struggling to reach a marketplace or an empty building where they could stretch themselves out to await death. In all the towns along the road from Saketi to Jakarta the markets, roadsides, and empty yards were filled with living corpses.[19]

Unsettled problems

Son-likkai and his group consisting of 288 ex-*romusha* and their families are now requesting that the Japanese government pay their unpaid wages.[20] Another group of Indonesian *heiho* (auxiliary soldiers) also are now requesting the Japanese government to pay their unpaid and saved wages. The Japanese government always says that this kind of problem was solved by the war reparation treaties. However, the *romusha* contract with the Japanese Army may be viewed as a kind of personal contract, and these Asian people should still have the right to demand compensation for their physical and mental losses. The Japanese very often broke their contract with *romusha*, and such illegal acts should be compensated, even though a treaty has been signed by the two governments.

It is still very hard to make clear the whole and exact losses and damages suffered by *romusha*. While we continue to do research together with ex-*romusha*, we should also ask the Japanese government to open all relevant documents, data and materials.

Notes

1 *Mainchi Shimbun*, 20 November 1990 and *Ashai Shimbun*, 1 May 1991.
2 Tim Penyusun Kamus Pusat Pembinaan da Pengembangan Bahasa, *Kamus Besar Bahasa Indonesia*, Balai Pustaka, Jakarta, 1988, p. 753.
3 Department Pendidikan da Kebudayaan (ed.), *Sejaraha Nasional Indonesia Jilid III*, Balai Pus, Jakarta, 1977.
4 Kurasawa Aiko, 'Mobilization and control: a study of social change in rural Java, 1942–1945', PhD thesis, Cornell University, 1988.
5 Yoshikawa Toshiharu, 'Tai ni totteno Taimen Tetsudo' (The Burma–Thailand Railway for Thailand), unpublished resume, 1991, courtesy of Professor Yoshikawa.
6 Institute of Social Science, Waseda University, *Indonesia ni Okeru Nihon Gunsei no Kenkyu* (Studies in the Japanese Military Administration of Indonesia), Kinokuniya Shoten, Tokyo, 1959, p. 112. See also Nishijima Shigetada, Kishi Koichi, et al., *Japanese Military Administration of Indonesia*, Washington, US Department of Commerce, 1963.
7 Hiroike Toshio, *Taimen Tetsudo—Senjo ni Nokoru Hashi* (The Burma–Thailand Railway: Bridge Remaining on the Battlefield), Yomiuri Shimbunsha, Tokyo, 1971, p. 237. Hugh V. Clarke wrote that the number of 'Asian civilian labourers' was over 270 000: *A Life for Every Sleeper*, Allen & Unwin, Sydney, 1986, p. 49.

8   In the 4th Battalion of the 9th Railway Regiment, the percentage of these groups was as follows: Malay 67 per cent, Thai 8 per cent, Chinese 25 per cent. In a platoon of the same battalion it was: Malay 4.5 per cent, Indian 88.1 per cent, Thai 2.3 per cent, Chinese 3.4 per cent, Vietnamese 1.7 per cent (Hiroike, op. cit., p. 243).

9   Yoshikawa, op. cit., pp. 11–17.

10 Ota Tsunezo, *Biruma ni Okeru Nihon Gunseishi no Kenkyu* (A Study on the History of Japanese Military Administration in Burma), Yoshikawa Kobunkan, Tokyo, 1968.

11 A member of Taimen Tetsudo Kenkyukai (Burma–Thailand Railway Study Group). See also Tanabe Hisao, *Shi no Tetsuro—Taimen Tetsudo Birumajin Romusha no Kiroku* (Death Railway: Records of a Burmese Labourer on the Burma–Thailand Railway), Mainichi Shinbunsha, Tokyo, 1981, Japanese translation of Lin Yone Thit Lwin, *Yodaya-Myanma Miyhta-lan Kodwe Chwaydat Hmattan*, Duwun Sarpay, Rangoon, 1968.

12 Hiroike, op. cit., pp. 357–8.

13 Clarke, op. cit., p. xv.

14 Kurasawa, op. cit.

15 Total population of Java in 1944 was 50 420 000. Labour force population was 24 985 630, and mobile (recruitable) population was 12 497 815 (male 5 794 014. According to the survey by the Japanese military in November 1944, *romusha* were classified into six categories:

Heiho (auxiliary soldier)	15 271
Giyugun (volunteer defence army)	36 067
Jobi romusha (permanent *romusha*)	1 356 271
(female 450 998)	
Rinji romusha (temporary *romusha*)	738 844
(female 69 345)	
Ginosha (technician)	277 153
(female 12 605)	
Kinroshi (labour service)	200 085
Total	2 623 691

In the narrow sense categories three and four are the true *romusha* (see Goto Kenichi, *A Study on the Period of Indonesian Occupation by Japan*, Tokyo, Ryukei shoshd, 1989, pp. 83–9; and also see Kurasawa, op. cit.). But the experience of some *heiho* was almost the same as *romusha* (Fuke Yosuke, 'Asian people commandeered by the Japanese Army', *Gunjiminron*, no. 23, 1981, pp. 104–13).

16 Kurasawa, op. cit.

17 Ibid.

18 Matsui Yayori, 'Romusha wo Otte' (In Pursuit of Romusha), *Asahi Shimbun*, 2 May 1991.

19 Tan Malaka, *Dari Pendjara ke Pendjara II*, trans. Helen Jarvis, *From Jail to Jail*, Ohio University, Athens, Ohio, 1990, p. 157.

20 Matsui, op. cit.

8

Prisoners of war in the Pacific War: Japan's policy

Aiko Utsumi
(translated from the Japanese by Gavan McCormack)

On 14 August 1945 the Japanese government advised the Allied powers of its ratification of the Potsdam Declaration. Article Ten of the Declaration read in part: 'stern justice shall be meted out to all war criminals, including those who have visited cruelties upon our prisoners'. Of all Japanese war crimes, the Allies were particularly concerned about prisoner-of-war (POW) atrocities. The transcript of the Tokyo Trial (the International Military Tribunal for the Far East) tells us that 35 756 of 132 134 Allied prisoners perished: a death rate of approximately 27 per cent. This is extremely high compared to the death rate of about 4 per cent (9348 out of 235 473) among prisoners taken by the German and Italian armies.[1] Why did so many die? What was wrong with the Japanese government's policy towards POWs? Here I shall examine the Japanese Army's policy towards prisoners in the Second World War and also touch on the postwar BC-class war crimes trials.

Mechanism for POW administration

The Japanese Army launched into all-out war against the Allies—America, Britain, Australia and so on—with the army landing at Khota Baru on the Malay peninsula and the naval attack on Pearl Harbor in Hawaii on 8 December 1941 (7 December in the United States). At the cabinet meeting on 12 December, this war was designated *Dai Toa Senso* (the Greater East Asian War).[2]

Immediately following the commencement of hostilities, on 27 December, the United States announced its intention to observe the terms of the Geneva Convention with regard to Japanese POWs and internees, and requested Japan to do likewise with regard to American nationals. Japan had signed, but not ratified, this convention on 27 July 1929. On 3 January 1942 Britain, Canada, Australia and New Zealand followed suit. In response to these representations, on 29 January 1942, Foreign Minister Togo pledged that it would be applied, *mutatis mutandis*. Via the diplomatic missions in Tokyo of Switzerland and Argentina, he communicated the following points to the governments of the Allied countries:[3]

1 The Japanese imperial government has not ratified the 1929 international convention on the treatment of prisoners, and accordingly is not bound by the provisions of this treaty, but will provisionally observe the terms of this treaty in respect of the British, Canadian, Australian and New Zealand prisoners now subject to its authority.
2 So far as the provision of food and clothing to prisoners is concerned, the national and racial customs of the prisoners will be taken into consideration, on reciprocal terms.

Although it was the Foreign Office that received complaints from the Allies, the real power in the treatment of POWs was wielded by the Army Ministry. Once the war began, the POW Information Bureau (27 December 1941, Imperial Edict no. 1246) and the POW Management Division (31 March 1942) were set up within the War Ministry as a division of the Military Affairs Bureau, under the control of the Army Minister.[4]

The army's mechanism for handling POWs was as shown in Figure 8.1. I shall make several comments with regard to this, based on the evidence given by Tanaka Ryukichi at the Tokyo trials. Tanaka served as head of the Military Affairs Bureau in the War Ministry from 1940 until 1942, and was fully conversant with the various mechanisms and responsibilities of the ministry; he appeared in court as a witness for the Public Prosecutor. According to Tanaka, complaints and inquiries from the Allied powers were sent by the Foreign Office to the Army Ministry, the Ministry of Home Affairs, and the Navy Ministry. Within the Army Ministry they were sent first from the POW Management Division to the Military Affairs Bureau, and further to the POW Information Bureau. However, responses to complaints were formulated by the Military Affairs Section of the Military Affairs Bureau.

The POW Information Bureau had nothing at all to do with the control and supervision of POWs; its role was simply to collect information. This included surveying the detention, movement, release on parole, exchange, escape, hospitalisation and death of POWs, keeping cards known as *meimeihyo* for each prisoner, and handling prisoners' mail. The POW Information Bureau was a temporary bureau of the Army Ministry's external

Figure 8.1 Management structure for POW affairs

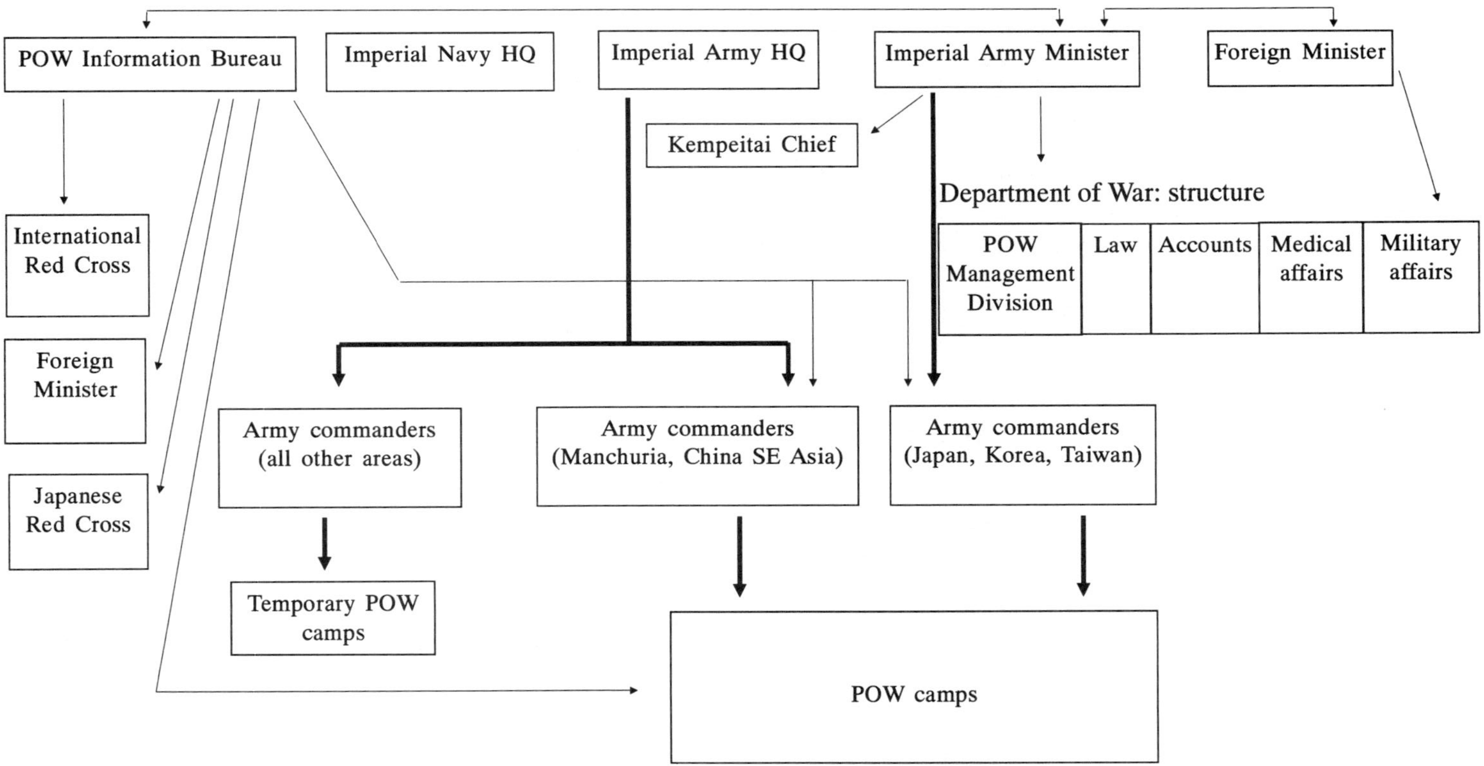

Note: Heavy lines indicate control; light lines indicate flow of information, inquiry, reference, etc.

bureau, set up under the jurisdiction of the Army Minister at the beginning of the war.[5] The POW Management Division handled all matters relating to prisoners. It was established as a result of the unexpectedly large number of captives taken in battle in the south: over 97 000 in the Malayan campaign, over 93 000 in the Java campaign, and 19 000 in Hong Kong and other areas, totalling 261 000.[6] In order to handle these large numbers, the POW Management Division mentioned above was established and a fundamental law dealing with the handling of POWs was prepared.

As already mentioned, Japan had not ratified the 1929 Geneva Convention, but had pledged to apply it *mutatis mutandis*. It had of course decided to be bound by the convention, as witness the fact that, prior to the Foreign Office's response, army and navy troops had been commanded by the government to apply its provisions.[7] In response to the large numbers of POWs taken during the southern campaigns, the Japanese government created a mechanism for handling them under the supervision of the Army Minister.[8]

Problems in dealing with POWs

The mechanism for handling POWs was put in place at the beginning of the war. However, the *Senjinkun* or Combatants' Code (issued on 8 January 1941 by the Army Minister), which was influential in forming the Japanese Army's attitude to POWs, was not changed.[9] Item Six contains the following words under 'Value honour': 'not survive to suffer the dishonour of capture'. Troops were taught that to be taken prisoner was a soldier's greatest shame. Not only soldiers but civilians too were bound by the appeal. Instructions with regard to POWs emphasised the kind of spirit represented by the Combatants' Code, not international law.

According to Otani Keijiro, 'In the Japanese Army there was not the slightest instruction on how to deal with prisoners. Such was assumed to be unnecessary since it was an iron rule that death should be chosen rather than suffer being taken prisoner'. For this reason men had no idea how to refuse to divulge military secrets under US Army interrogation, and when officers were made to work they complied without protest. They did not know that it was up to officers to decide for themselves whether they would work or not. Furthermore, even if made to do ordinary work, they could not be made to co-operate in army operations. Yet some Japanese prisoners co-operated positively, even when their work was clearly counter to the interests of the Japanese Army.[10]

As shown by the words 'expect death to be lighter than goose down' and 'the way of the samurai is to find death', Japanese instruction regarding capture was that it was better to choose death rather than life in captivity. This teaching went beyond being merely a matter of moral instruction: it was put into practice at the time of the Nomonhan Incident (20 August 1939) and the Sino-Japanese war. In the former the officers who were repatriated after being captured in Russia were court-martialled and later given revolvers and forced to commit suicide. According to *Nihon Kenpei Seishi* (Authentic History of the Japanese Kenpei):[11]

> The first exchange of prisoners occurred on 27 September 1939 when 97 prisoners from the Japanese side were exchanged for 88 from the Soviet side. Subsequently, another 32 from the Japanese side were exchanged for 204 from the Soviet side on 27 April 1940. The officers and men who were returned in the exchange were held at the Shintan Military Hospital about two kilometres outside Kirin (city), and after an immediate court martial the officers were each given a pistol and made to commit suicide, while the N.C.O.'s and men were put to work on tasks such as camp construction. However, not all the Nomonhan survivors returned. Quite a few officers and men remained in the Soviet Union, giving up the idea of return because of their shame at having been captured.

The NCOs were sent to the front and given the opportunity to die.

In the Japan–China war the treatment of soldiers taken prisoner was even harsher. During the Pacific War the Combatants' Code was spiritually binding on Japanese soldiers. To Japanese soldiers, capture was the ultimate shame, and they were taught to die rather than be taken prisoner. Since logically it was therefore impossible for Japanese soldiers to become POWs, they were not educated in what to do if taken prisoner. Moreover, the Geneva Convention was hardly mentioned at all in educating soldiers and civilian employees who worked in POW management. Rather, they felt strong contempt and antipathy for Allied POWs who had 'suffered the dishonour of capture'. A certain Japanese NCO reported wishing that POWs would die.[12] From officers the words 'You can kill as many POWs as you like' were heard often. Actually, the POW camps had no end of trouble with the units who set the POWs to work.[13] This attitude was one of the factors in atrocities against POWs in the field.

We may surmise the kind of social atmosphere that surrounded POWs in Japan in those days from reports such as that concerning one prison camp commandant who respected prisoners' rights in accordance with international law. As a result he was informed on as being a possible 'enemy sympathiser', resulting in a secret investigation by the Kempeitai.[14] In another incident a woman was reported to have said 'Oh, poor things' on seeing some American POWs, thereby causing a great stir and resulting in headlines of: 'Down with this cherishing of America! What is this "Oh, poor things" for American prisoners!'[15]

It was extremely difficult to respect the rights of prisoners and to treat them according to international law in the midst of cries of 'American and English devils'. It was difficult to procure food supplies for prisoners because many people were reluctant to sell, saying, 'We have no food for the likes of them'. Anti-POW sentiment was fomented among the populace.

Establishment of POW camps, and Korean guards

The treatment of POWs was first discussed at a meeting of bureau chiefs in the War Ministry in late April 1942, at which time the Army Minister, Tojo, ruled on the following two points:

1 All prisoners of war will take part in forced labour to help ease the labour shortage.
2 Prisoner of war camps will be established not only in the south but also in Japan, Taiwan, Korea, Manchuria and China. We will act so as to create in the peoples of East Asia, who have for many years been resigned to being no match for the white races, a feeling of trust towards Japan.[16]

The relevant units were notified of policy 1 in the name of Uemura Mikio, head of the POW Management Division and also concurrently head of the POW Information Bureau, on 3 June. Officers were not to work, but units were instructed that 'in view of the need to keep POWs healthy and of the present situation in Japan, which does not permit of even one person's leading an idle life, the central policy is that they too may be assigned voluntary labour according to their rank, function, and physical strength'.[17] Inevitably, this sort of central policy led to forced labour for officers of front line units, labour of sick prisoners and POW atrocities.

Because of the intellectual propaganda of policy 2, a policy of using white POWs was requested by colonies in Taiwan and Korea. A report, 'POW camp plans', was sent on 23 March 1942 to Army Minister Tojo in the name of Itagaki Seishiro, commandant of the army in Korea, in which this is clearly specified as one of the aims: 'We will use them as material for an intellectual propaganda exercise aimed at stamping out the respect and admiration for Europeans and Americans still secretly harboured by most Koreans, as well as to bring about recognition of the power of the Empire'.[18] On one occasion 998 white POWs sent from the Malay peninsula were made to parade before the public, which was said to be 'very effective'.

Not only that, but Taiwanese and Koreans were used as guards for these POWs.[19] Within Japan injured soldiers (those who had been wounded and were not assigned military duties) were often used. The aim was not just to supplement a deficient labour force but also, by using youths from colonies as guards for white prisoners, to foster a sense of respect for Japan and to bring about 'a sense of good fortune in being the subjects of the Empire' and a determination to see the Greater East Asia war through.[20] There were 3000 of these Korean guards despatched to POW camps in

Thailand, Malaya, Singapore and Java in August 1942.[21] Taiwanese guards were also sent to camps in Borneo and Rabaul. The presence of Korean and Taiwanese guards during such incidents as the mistreatment of Australian POWs on the railway and the Sandakan Death March was a result of this Japanese Army policy of personnel deployment.

Complaints about POW atrocities, and Japanese government propaganda

While the Japanese government had said that it would apply the Geneva Convention *mutatis mutandis*, there were many problems with the army's actual treatment of POWs. The Allied powers often tendered complaints about this treatment. Through Switzerland and other places, 134 requests were made for visits to POW camps, and a further 83 Allied complaints and inquiries were collected by the POW Information Bureau. Complaints were made by radio so frequently that Foreign Office officials 'could not remember them all'.[22]

The Japanese government continued to deny the veracity of these complaints, saying, for example: 'there is no truth in the rumour that POWs in the Shanghai camp have been assigned to duties directly related to the conduct of operations'; or with regard to food, 'the prisoners are given sufficient food to maintain health, just as are Japanese soldiers; but prisoners' food is further supplemented by aid packages'.[23]

In response to requests for visits to POW camps, within a week visits were permitted to camps in Japan proper, Korea, Manchuria and Taiwan, but requests were denied for camps in the 'south'. (Exceptions were sometimes made in Hong Kong, the Philippines and Thailand.)[24] However, there were problems with these visits: they were very short, Japanese guards were present during interviews with prisoners, and so on. The Geneva Convention had laid down that representatives of the International Red Cross and neutral powers could interview prisoners without witnesses.[25] In response to repeated complaints about mistreatment of POWs made through neutral countries and the Red Cross, the Japanese government not only investigated and responded; it also conducted counter-propaganda to the effect that prisoners were thankful to the Japanese Army for its treatment of them, through such agencies as the production of films and foreign broadcasts using POWs.

Tokyo Rose's broadcasts to the front (*Zero Hour*) and the broadcasts by groups of POWs to the western coast of America (*Hinomaru Hour*) are well-known;[26] but there were also broadcasts by POWs from Jakarta in Indonesia to Australia. One large-scale attempt at this sort of propaganda was the film *Calling Australia*, which portrayed the happy lives led by Australian POWs in Java. It took the form of an independent production by

Australian POWs and showed them playing tennis, swimming and frolicking in the water, hiking, playing cricket, chatting over a beer, and eating steak with every evidence of pleasure. The role of this film was to convey the message that Australian POWs were leading a pleasant life under the Japanese.[27] *Calling Australia* was produced under the supervision of the No.16 Army Special Squad at the opening of the northern Australia campaign in April 1943. The special squad also arranged:

1 propaganda for the overseas broadcast department, interception of Australian broadcasts, and strategic broadcasts;
2 exchange of information on POWs and internees, censorship of inquiries, questioning of crews of shot-down planes, debriefing of fellow Japanese repatriated on repatriation vessels;
3 preparation of anti-Australian strategy using POWs; and
4 sea-based intelligence and counter-intelligence operations.

When production was decided on in April 1943, POWs in Java were mobilised and filming was carried out over a period of approximately 6 months. The director was a Korean who used the name of Hinatsu Eitaro; he remained in Indonesia after the Japanese defeat, continuing his involvement in film production.

At the beginning of 1944, the completed film was previewed at Imperial Army headquarters in Tokyo. It seems that similar films were produced not only in Java but also in Korea, Manchuria and Japan itself.[28] At the time of the preview, they were all screened together. As *Calling Australia* was the best, it was decided to send it to all countries via Switzerland. After the war *Calling Australia* was used in a movie proving POW atrocities called *Nippon Presents*, which was screened at the Tokyo trials.[29]

Japan sent denials in response to the repeated Allied complaints of POW atrocities, and permitted visits by Red Cross representatives to POW camps within a limited sphere. Japan attempted to parry Allied criticisms by actively arranging radio broadcasts and films praising the Japanese Army's 'humane actions' in addition to this passive response.

A case of POW mistreatment: the Burma–Thailand Railway

The Burma Railway, which produced almost one death for every railroad tie laid, is also called the Death Railway. To build this railway 55 000 POWs and 70 000 Asian workers were used: 42 000 (among them 12 000 POWs) died—42 000 people died to build a railway 415 kilometres long. The Burma Railway sacrificed them at the rate of one person per sleeper.[30]

One hundred and thirty thousand, people were cast into the depths of the jungle. Naturally an elaborate supply line was set up. However, when the rainy season came, the River Kwai rose and it proved difficult to carry

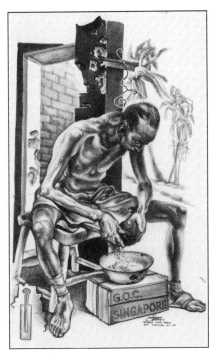

Murray Griffin, The scraper of
coconuts, *1945, brush and ink
heightened with white over pencil,
53.5 x 31 cm. Australian War
Memorial (25073).*

food supplies in small boats. Still more, the makeshift roads became muddy
quagmires, and transport of commodities by truck became impossible. The
carelessness of this supply system led to the death by malnutrition of POWs.
In evidence given by adjutants at the Thai POW camp headquarters, it was
reported that food and medical supplies with no means of transportation
were stockpiled in Bangkok.[31] The fault of the Japanese Army in neglecting
supplies led to the loss of many lives.

The construction of about 50 kilometres of roadbed around Hintoku,
155 kilometres from the railway's point of origin at Kanchanaburi, was
fraught with unparalleled difficulty. POW labour conditions worsened: even
at the Hintoku base camp, where cholera did not break out, 20 per cent of
POWs died[32] and further inland 3087 of the 7000 POWs died.[33] Rations
were restricted to 100 grams of rice per day for as long as a month, and
there was of course no other food. The calorie allowance of the Japanese
Army was less than that of the Europeans and Americans, but even compared
to Japanese army standards, 100 grams of rice a day were no more than
one-fifth.

The absence of food and medical supplies, and the fact that the Japanese were urged on to complete the railway for the Imphal campaign, led to the deaths of POWs. The work became progressively harder as their physical strength was exhausted, and the problem of hunger increased, so death was inevitable. However, a certain high-ranking staff officer in the Railway Unit told an officer in the POW camp, 'I don't care if they all die, so long as the railway is finished'. It was the task of the POW camps to provide the personnel requested by the Railway Unit. Of course, the men they provided included those who were sick, as the command from Imperial Army head-quarters to complete the railway took precedence over all else. Having been ordered to complete the railway on time in order to open the campaign, the Railway Unit requested the POW camps to supply a quota for the labour force, and the camps coerced prisoners into working. The inconsistency of the Japanese Army was passed further and further down the chain; such things as international treaties had little relevance at this level.[34]

The camp guards who whipped prisoners on with cries of 'Speedo! Speedo!' and forced sick men to work were held accountable after the war.[35]

POW atrocities and the BC-class war crimes trials

The Potsdam Declaration, which Japan ratified, contained a clause to the effect that war crimes, including POW atrocities, would be prosecuted. Perhaps because of this the following urgent telegram was sent from the head of the Tokyo POW camp on 20 August 1945:

> Personnel who have ill-treated POWs and internees or who are very much hated by them should at once be transferred elsewhere, or steps taken to conceal their whereabouts. Moreover, documents which it would not do to have fall into enemy hands should at all costs be destroyed after use.[36]

The telegram was sent to the armies in Korea, Taiwan, Kwantung, North China, Hong Kong and so on, as well as to the POW camp commandants in Malaya, Borneo, Thailand and Java for reference. Tokyo commanded

Table 8.1 Relative proportions of POW camp personnel and Kempeitai in war crimes trials (%)

Trial progress	POW camp personnel	Kempeitai
Cases prosecuted	16	27
Personnel prosecuted	17	37
Guilty verdicts	27	36
Executed	11	30

transfer and flight: an indication that severe reprisals for war crimes in POW camps were anticipated. It is not clear just how these instructions were executed; the telegram was not received by Korean civilians in military employ who were serving in the camps.

In the case of the Burma–Thailand Railway, where prisoners had clearly suffered mistreatment, 120 people were subsequently prosecuted and 111 found guilty, of whom 32 were sentenced to death by hanging. If we examine the numbers more closely, we see that many were connected with the POW camps: 69 of the guilty and 25 of those executed. The camps, which managed the POWs, were held much more responsible than the Railway Unit, which forced them to work. Nor was this attitude restricted to the case of the Burma–Thailand Railway. The BC-class war crimes trials conducted by the British, American, Dutch, Australian, French, Philippine and Nationalist Chinese governments also showed this tendency to try those who executed the orders and to designate the lower ranks as war criminals. The words 'war crimes trials' may call to mind the Kempeitai or secret police, and in fact many Kempeitai were convicted of war crimes, as Table 8.1 shows.[37] These figures reflect the gravity of the Allied view of the mistreatment of POWs.

Japanese troops had been taught to regard the command of a superior officer as a command from the emperor. At the trials the lower ranks—those without authority who carried out the orders—were punished severely, among them Korean and Taiwanese civilian military employees.[38] Such punishment of those without authority was beyond the comprehension of the Japanese soldiers, who did not recognise any possibility of refusing to obey orders.

There were also problems of inadequate interpreting, lack of lawyers and inexperience. There is a deeply held conviction in Japan that the BC-class war crimes trials were vendettas disguised as trials.[39] Procedural inadequacies engendered antipathy towards the judge countries rather than recognition of fault. The fact that the notes from the BC trials have been published and read shows how the Japanese regard these trials. A typical comment about those found guilty in the trials might be: 'People who were sacrificed in an unjust vendetta by those who flaunted their victory'. Others feel that 'It was war. What else could we do?'[40] This view that they had been 'victims' rapidly spread in Japan, including among those concerned with the war criminals, after the A-, B-, and C-class war criminals were returned to the jurisdiction of the Japanese government. The Senpan Jukeisha Sewakai (Association to Help Those Undergoing Penalties as War Criminals) was launched on 10 May 1952, with Fujiwara Ginjiro as chairman. Its founding statement said: 'There may be many views about war crimes, but [these men] went to war for their country and they are in a sense victims caused by the reality of defeat'.[41]

The following passage may be quoted from the memoir written by

Sanematsu Yuzuru, former naval staff officer at imperial headquarters and a former war criminal. He writes of his emotions when, on 22 October 1952, at the autumn athletic meeting at Sugamo Prison, the 'Hinomaru' flag was raised and the 'Kimigayo' anthem sung:

> I could not have been the only one who was unable to restrain my tears when, after more than four years living as a prisoner, for the first time at Sugamo 'Kimigayo' was sung and the 'Hinomaru' unfurled.
>
> Ah! Though the state perish, the rivers and mountains remain. Imprisoned as a sacrificial offering upon the defeat, with how full a voice now do I sing 'Kimigayo' to greet the national flag flying for the first time in years against this dark blue autumn sky! I am moved beyond words.[42]

Army Minister Tojo Hideki was hanged as a result of POW atrocities, and Uemura Mikio, head of the POW Management Division, was imprisoned. Many guard and camp commandants were also executed. However, this did nothing to solve the many problems in Japan's POW policy: the contradiction between international treaty and civil law; the mobilisation of people by government propaganda; the lack of awareness of human rights in dealing with foreigners; the lack of insight with regard to the results of the BC-class war crimes trials; the need for introspection with regard to the excuse that 'there was nothing else we could have done at the time'. The POW atrocities and the BC trials that resulted produced hardly any reflection by Japanese on the war. On the contrary, resentment against the judgments created the climate for the growth of self-justification.

As is clear from the recent plea by former Education Minister Fujio, strongly advocating a re-examination of 'The Historical View of the Tokyo Trials', new questions are being asked as to just what the Japanese were accused of at the Tokyo trials and the BC trials. In this context the point of view of the POWs and the Asian *romusha* labourers must be heard.

Notes

1 The judgment of the Tokyo Trial (Chapter 8 of Section B) contains the following entry on conventional war crimes or atrocities:

> The degree of atrocities and the results of inadequacy of food and medical supplies are demonstrated by a comparison of the death rate for prisoners in the European War and in the Pacific War. 255,473 men of the Allied Armies were held prisoner by the German and Italian armies, of whom 9,348 or 4 per cent, died in captivity. In the Pacific theatre, from the British and American armies alone 132,134 men were held prisoner by the Japanese, of whom 35,756, or 27 per cent, died in captivity.

The Australian Encyclopedia, 5th edn, Grolier Society of Australia, 1988, p. 3146, has the following entry:

The Burma–Thailand Railway

A large number of Australians became prisoners following the Japanese offensive in the early months of 1942. The total numbers captured between 1942 and 1945 by the Japanese were, by services, AIF 21 649, RAAF 543, RAN 324 [total: 22 516] . . . At war's end, 13 872 members of the AIF, 417 of the RAAF, and 237 of the RAN were recovered from Japanese prison camps. More than a third—7964—had died of disease, were killed or had drowned at sea.

2 The question of what to call this war is still debated in Japan. When the war began, the Liaison Committee of the imperial headquarters and government decided to call it the Greater East Asian War, which included the China Incident. This meant that the war in the China region subsequent to 8 December 1941 was included. On 12 December the Cabinet Information Bureau added a further explanation:

The term Greater East Asian War means the war for the construction of the new Greater East Asian order, and does not imply that the war zone is limited to Greater East Asia.

Within this appellation were included the two purposes of Japan's war as a war of 'survival and self-defence' and as a war for 'the construction of the new Greater East Asian order'.

The United States after the war, in the Shinto Shirei (Directive Concerning Shinto) of 15 December 1945, forbade this term.

3 POW Information Bureau, *Horyo ni Kansuru sho Hoki Ruishu* (Compilation of the Various Laws and Regulations Concerning Prisoners), Tokyo, November 1943, pp. 174–5.

4 The POW Information Bureau was set up in accordance with the Hague Treaty of 1911 and the Geneva Convention of 1929. The POW Management Division was set up under the Regulations for the Control of Prisoners (31 March 1942).

5 Evidence of Tanaka Ryukichi, 3 March 1947, *Kyokuto Gunji Saiban Sokkiroku* (International Military Tribunal for the Far East, Shorthand Record), no. 144, Yushodo, Tokyo, 1968.

6 *Asahi Shinbun*, 17 May 1942. If subsequent numbers are added, the total comes to about 350 000. Prisoners were in two categories. According to the Army Ministry's Outlines for the Treatment of Prisoners (*Horyo Shori Yoryo*) of 5 May 1942:

1 White prisoners are to be utilised for increasing the productivity of Japan and for military-related labour.

2 In the case of non-white prisoners, those not necessary to be detained should be released on oath and as much as possible made use of in their localities.

For this reason not all 261 000 became prisoners. After the war, according to the Japanese Army's 'Table on the implementation of prisoner handover', the number of prisoners handed over then to the US Army was 103 022, and there were an additional 90 527 civilians who had been held in military detention camps ('Horyo johokyoku no gyomu ni tsuite' [Concerning the

80

affairs of the POW Information Bureau], *Showa 21 nen Kobun Zassan* [Compilation of Public Documents of 1946], vol. 13).

176 805 prisoners were released under category 2. (See Adachi Sumio, 'Kokusaijin doho sai-ninshiki e no michi' [Path to a new recognition of an internationalist law and morality], *Ho to Chitsujo*, vol. 74, no. 5, September 1983, p. 25.)

7 Adachi, op. cit., p. 23.

8 There were 170 main POW camps, and 214 branch or sub-branch camps. Main camps in Japan were at Aomori, Sendai, Tokyo, Nagoya, Osaka, Hiroshima and Fukuoka; and main camps abroad were in Korea (Seoul), Taiwan (Taipei), Manchukuo (Mukden), Thailand (Bangkok), Malaya (Singapore), Philippines (Manila), Java (Jakarta), Borneo (Kuching), Hong Kong (Hong Kong city) and China (Shanghai and in the suburbs of Peking).

9 The Combatants' Code (*Senjinkun*) was drawn up around 1938 and was issued as a directive in 1941 when Tojo Hideki was Army Minister. Shimazaki Toson, Sato Sonosuke and Doi Bansui co-operated in the preparation of the final draft. See Otani Keijiro, *Horyo* (Prisoners), Kokusho Shuppan, Tokyo, 1978.

10 Otani, op. cit., pp. 45–6.

11 *Nihon Kenpei Seishi* (Authentic History of the Japanese Kenpei), Kenbun Shoin, Tokyo 1980, p. 778. This work was compiled by the national organisation of former Kenpeitai members. Otani, op. cit., denies this episode, but here we have relied on the more recently published 'Authentic History'.

12 The Korean civilian Auxiliaries (*gunzoku*) attached to POW camps in Java, Malaya and Thailand were given 2 months' training at Pusan West Gate Temporary Gunzoku Training Unit, but their training resembled that given to Japanese army recruits. It was a spiritual education based on the Imperial Rescript to Soldiers and Sailors and the Combatants Code. According to the testimony of the Korean *gunzoku*, not only did they receive no education on the Geneva Convention; they had never even heard of it (Utsumi Aiko, *Chosenjin BC-Kyu Senpan no Kiroku*, Keiso Shobo, Tokyo, 1982).

13 According to Colonel Yanagida Shoichi, head of No. 2 Section of the Thai POW camps for the construction of the Burma–Thailand Railway, one senior staff officer remarked: 'So long as the railway is completed, it does not matter if all the POWs collapse in the process'. Yanagida also remarked that the Railway Unit, which lost the right to free use of prisoners when the POW camps were set up, was very cold towards the commanders and staff of the POW camps, and relations between the two were bad (Yanagida Shoichi, 'Taimen tetsudo kensetsu no jisso to senpan saiban' [The reality of the Burma–Thailand Railway construction and the war crimes trials], mimeograph, 1954).

14 *Asahi Shinbun*, 3 June 1987.

15 *Asahi Shinbun*, 5 December 1942. (See Lewis Bush, *Clutch of Circumstance*, trans. Akashi Yoichi as *O Kawaiso Ni*, Bungei Shunjusha, Tokyo, 1956.)

16 Kyokuto Gunji Saiban Sokkiroku no. 144.

17 'Horyo taru shoko oyobi kashikan no romu ni kansuru ken' (Concerning work by prisoner officers and NCOs), *Horyo ni Kansuru sho Hoki Ruishu*, 1943, p. 225.

18 Kyokuto Gunji Saiban Sokkiroku, no. 146.

19 According to section 5 of 'Horyo shori yoryo' (Outlines for treatment of prisoners), contained in 'Nanpo ni okeru horyo no shori yoryo no ken' (Outlines for the treatment of prisoners sent to South-East Asia), 5 May 1942:

> In setting up POW camps, special units of Koreans and Taiwanese should be created to meet the need for their establishment and control.

(See *Horyo ni Kansuru sho Hoki Ruishu*, p. 168.)

20 Kyokuto Gunji Saiban Sokkiroku, no. 146.

21 On 17 August 1942, 804 of them left Pusan for Malaya and 1408 for Java, with an additional 804 leaving on 21 August 1942 for camps in Thailand. (Numbers from 'Nanpo horyo shujojo yoin no haken oyobi Chosenjin horyo shuyojo kaisetsu no ken hokoku' [Report on dispatch of staff to the South-East Asian POW camps and on the establishment by Koreans of POW camps].)

22 POW Information Bureau, 'Horyo ni kansuru kogi ni kanshi horyo joho oyobi horyo kanribu ga shochi shita kotogara o kiroku shiaru shorui no utsushi' (Documents recording the handling by the POW Information Bureau and POW Management Division of complaints concerning prisoners), 1945. See Kyokuto Gunji Saiban Sokkiroku, no. 148; and Utsumi, op. cit., p. 149.

23 'Documents' as in note 22, pp. 242–3.

24 Adachi, op. cit., pp. 28–9.

25 One of the reasons for postponing ratification of the Geneva Convention was this provision for meeting with prisoners without witnesses: in other words, 'military objections to being able to talk with prisoners in the absence of third country representatives'. (See Fukiura Tadamasa, *Kikigaki—Nihonjin horyo* [Oral History—Japanese Prisoners], Tosho Shuppansha, Tokyo, 1987.)

26 For details on Tokyo Rose see Masayo Duus, *Tokyo Rose*, Simul, Tokyo, 1987. On *Hinomaru Awa* see Ikeda Norizane (who was in charge of the programme), *Hinomaru Awa* (Hinomaru Hour), Chuo Koronsha, Tokyo, 1979.

27 The *Calling Australia* film is held in the Australian National Library. For details see Utsumi Aiko and Murai Yoshinori, *Shineashisuto Hyo Hyon no Showa* (The Showa of Cineast Hyo Hyon), Gaifusha, Tokyo, 1987.

28 The use of prisoners in making propaganda films occurred not only in Java but also in Japan itself, Manchuria and Korea. In Korea the film *Chosen ni Kita Horyo* (The Prisoners who Came to Korea) was made in 1943 by Chosen Eiga company.

29 Four-reel film shown before the Tokyo tribunal on 26 December 1946 as evidence of the Japanese Army's ill-treatment of prisoners. This film, made after the war in Australia, exposed the falsity of the film *Calling Australia*, which had been made by a unit attached to the 16th Army's staff office in Java, and complained of the reality of the Japanese Army's ill-treatment of prisoners. *Nippon Presents* (made by the Information Department of the Dutch East Indies government) contrasted the prisoners, who appear happily chatting, swimming, and playing tennis and cricket in *Calling Australia*, with the reality of prisoners reduced to skin and bone and vacant-eyed. The impact of this film on the judges was said to have been more profound than that of any oral evidence.

30 The Burma–Thailand Railway was constructed over 415 kilometres between

Kanchanaburi in Thailand and Tanbizaya in Burma; works commenced in November 1942 and finished on 17 October 1943. On average, 890 metres of track were laid each day. At the end of February 1943, an order to reduce the time for the project was issued, as a result of which the prisoners and labourers were made to work 10 hours a day with 1 day off in 10. This was known as the 'speedo' period. The situation of the prisoners as of April 1943 appears in the following:

Total numbers of prisoners working on the railway	49 766
Sick prisoners (Thai side)	19 892
Sick prisoners (Burma side)	11 982
Deaths (Thai side)	186
Deaths (Burma side)	20

A total of 7746 prisoners died in Burma and Thailand combined between January 1942 and August 1944. Overall deaths to completion were about 12 000. (See POW Information Bureau, 1945, tables 1 and 2.) However, according to the Tokyo tribunal judgment, '16,000 out of 46,000 prisoners died during 18 months' (Kyokuto Gunji Saiban Sokkiroku, p. 191). Overall victims are estimated at 42 000, but this is only an estimate, since there are no accurate figures on deaths of Asian labourers.

31 Interview with Yashiro Kameyoshi, former staff member of Thai POW camp, 2 September 1980.

32 Interview with Yi Hak-Nae (Lee Kakurai), former Korean guard at Hintok camp, 23 February 1978.

33 Between May 1943 and April 1944, of a total of 7000 prisoners (3666 Australians and 3334 British) on the Banno Section (or No. 4 Section Malaya POW camp, known among the British as 'F' Force), 3087, or 44.4 per cent, died (Hiroike Toshio, *Taimen Tetsudo* [The Burma–Thailand Railway], Yomiuri Shinbunsha, Tokyo, 1971, p. 158).

34 Hiroike, op. cit. See also Utsumi, op. cit.

35 Former prisoner Ernest Gordon wrote of the experience of the 'speedo' period in *Through the Valley of the Kwai*, London, Collins, 1972 (translated by Saito Kazuo as *Shi no Tani o Sugite—Kwai Shuyojo*, Otowa Shobo, Tokyo, 1976). There are hardly any records of the Asian labourers who worked on the Burma–Thailand Railway. See, however, the account of Burmese workers: Lin Yone Thit Lwin (translated by Tanabe Hisao) *Shi no Tetsuro* (Death Railway), Mainichi Shinbunsha, Tokyo, 1981.

36 Kyokuto Gunji Saiban Sokkiroku, no. 148.

37 Homudaijin Kanbo Shihosei Chosabu (Judicial Investigation Department of Secretariat of Ministry of Justice), *Senso Saiban Gaishiyo* (Outline History of War Crimes' Trials), Ministry of Justice, Tokyo, 1973, pp. 264–5.

38 Compared to 5379 Japanese, there were 148 Koreans and 173 Taiwanese. Broken down according to punishment, the figures are as follows (from Utsumi, op. cit., p. 120):

Death penalty	Japanese 148	Koreans 23	Taiwanese 21
Prison terms	Japanese 2690	Koreans 107	Taiwanese 147

39 This view is particularly emphasised in individual accounts, and the following,

written by B- and C-class war criminals held in Sugamo Prison in their movements to secure release, may be seen as typical: Sugamo Homu Iinkai (Sugamo Legal Affairs Committee), 'Senpan saiban no jisso' (The reality of war crimes trials), mimeograph, 1952, p. 852.

40 Utsumi Aiko, 'Chosen senso to Sugamo purizun' (The Korean War and Sugamo Prison), *Shiso*, vol. 8, no. 734, August 1985, pp. 151–2.
41 Mimeographed materials in possession of author.
42 Sanematsu Yuzuru, 'Sugamo purizun gokuchuki' (Sugamo Prison journal), *Sugamo*, Tosho Shuppansha, Tokyo, 1972, p. 60.

9

Apportioning the blame: Australian trials for railway crimes

Gavan McCormack

The question of war crimes and war responsibility in the Second World War has been considered in a substantial literature on the Nuremberg and related tribunals covering the war with Germany and Italy and the crimes of fascism and Nazism. A smaller literature covers the equivalent trials of the Japanese political and military leadership (the Tokyo trials or the International Military Tribunal for the Far East), and a much smaller literature again addresses the many 'minor' trials, or trials of 'conventional' war criminals, conducted after 1945 throughout the Asian and Pacific region. The Australian trials in that category have been studied least of all, and it now appears likely that they will become known through a fictionalised film account before they are properly studied.[1]

Australian war crimes tribunals were convened between late 1945 and 1951 at Darwin, Singapore, Hong Kong, Manus, Wewak, Labuan and Rabaul. Nine hundred and twenty-four Japanese officers, soldiers and civilians were charged with either B– or C– class war crimes: conventional war crimes or breaches of the laws or customs of war on the one hand, and crimes against humanity, especially non-combatant civilians, on the other. In 23 trials in all, 280 were found not guilty, 496 sentenced to various terms of imprisonment, 148 sentenced to death, and 137 actually executed, either by hanging or by firing squad.[2] Since the outcome of the much better-known Tokyo trials was seven death sentences and eighteen prison sentences, including sixteen for life terms, the lack of attention to the Australian trials is anomalous.

The general assessment of the Australian trials offered by David Sissons, who has written the only comprehensive, if very summary, account of them, rejects the notion that the trials were conducted in a spirit of vengeance, with 'proud victors exercising arbitrary judgement over the vanquished', and conveys an impression of an earnest and sincere attempt to see 'justice' done.[3] Other Australian commentators take a similar view (though Glenister notes an apparently high rate of conviction at the Singapore trials).[4]

Japanese commentators, by contrast, are unanimous in criticising the Australian trials as another expression of what has become commonly known as 'victor's justice'. Saburo Ienaga refers to the outcome of the trials in particular: 'The executions were more expedient revenge than careful justice'.[5] Awaya Kentaro asserts that, while the 'major' trials in Tokyo showed meticulous concern for the formal rights of the accused under Anglo-American legal procedures, and those trials were conducted in the full glare of publicity over a prolonged period in open court, the B- and C-class trials proceeded through trial, judgment and punishment in a very short time and without adequate legal procedures.[6] Utsumi, in her various writings, takes a similar view.[7]

Here I shall present a very preliminary consideration of the records of some of the trials, with particular reference to those involving Korean camp guards. The Burma Railroad trials conducted by Australia were held in Singapore between 26 June 1946 and 11 June 1947. The 23 Australian Singapore trials of a total of 62 defendants resulted in eighteen death sentences, eleven acquittals, and 33 sentences to varying terms of imprisonment.[8]

The Australian literature on the railway makes it clear that the worst phase was that which occurred in the period of 3 or 4 months from April 1943, especially after the heavy monsoonal rains, which that year commenced a month early, when the line was being constructed through the most remote, disease-infested jungle territory, in conditions such that the supply system broke down, when the machines did not work and had to be replaced by human labour, and where sickness, exhaustion and malnutrition wore down the workforce but military discipline and inflexible schedules remained adamantine. Some 65 000 POWs and 300 000 Asian labourers[9] were thrown at the tasks, in giant 'human-wave' tactics of a kind familiar a generation later from the Chinese development campaigns of the 1950s and 1960s. More than 12 000 of the POWs, including 2646 out of about 13 000 Australians, died, of disease, starvation and ill-treatment. Of the Asian labourers less than half eventually returned home, though exactly how many of them died and were buried along the line is still unclear; even in 1990 new mass graves were being discovered.[10] Even among the Japanese there are estimated to have been about 1000 casualties.[11]

The supervision of the motley labour force that was cast out of the POW camps and the villages of the region into the jungle was in large measure entrusted not to the regular Imperial Japanese Army but to camp guards (*gunzoku*, or literally civilian auxiliaries) recruited, in effect conscripted, in the villages and small towns of colonial Taiwan or Korea. These men were ill-trained, and they knew only the rigid, often brutal, discipline of Japanese militarism. They were totally ignorant of the almost diametrically opposite tradition of the Australians, of whom Hugh Clarke wrote:

> My generation had been brought up under the influence of the White Australia policy and considered ourselves superior. Our attitude to our captors had, at all times, been defiant and arrogant. We sabotaged anything we touched. We stole anything not nailed down or watched . . . We must surely have been an infuriating embarrassment to our captors.[12]

The railway 'relationship', commonly characterised as a simple one of a vicious enemy alien exploiting virtuous innocent captives, was therefore more complex: the 'enemy' was actually a structured hierarchy of exploitation and alienation. Ordinary soldiers were themselves deliberately bashed and brutalised as part of their training, but the Korean and Taiwanese civilian auxiliaries were inferior to the lowest Japanese private soldier; though constituting a part of the 'enemy' they were at the same time themselves victims, as much alienated, victimised and exploited as, on the other side, were the POWs and the Asian labourers. Since the Koreans and Taiwanese were deprived even of their names, as well as their language and culture, their humiliation was in a sense deeper, even if invisible to those whose role it was for them to 'guard'.[13]

Each of the six major camps along the line into which the workers were organised was commanded by a Japanese officer and several subordinates, with perhaps a small group of NCOs and 100 or more *gunzoku*, usually employed as guards but sometimes in various roles such as driver, clerk or even interpreter. The actual construction work was supervised by a corps of engineers from two Japanese railway regiments, who each day requisitioned the required labour force. When the issue of war crimes responsibility arising out of the railway construction was considered in Singapore after the war, however, it was the lowest ranks of the Japanese system, particularly the Korean guards, upon whom the heaviest retribution was visited (Table 9.1). Ironically, therefore, judicial responsibility increased as actual power in the Japanese hierarchy diminished. Those responsible for scripting and directing the tragedy—the planners, politicians, engineers and officers— by and large escaped responsibility. And not only did the emperor, at the apex of the whole structure, escape responsibility altogether, but, as Awaya notes:

> To put it most simply, one gets the strong feeling that even the political responsibility that should have attached to the war leaders was loaded onto the 'B' and 'C' class criminals, and eventually set aside altogether, as part of the inescapable price for 'preserving the imperial polity' (i.e. 'absolving the emperor from blame').[14]

The worst experiences were those of the detachments that had to march

Table 9.1 Burma–Thailand Railway—related war crimes trials for offences against POWs (Singapore)

	Guilty	Death sentences
Total	111 (33)	32 (9)
British and Australian trials only	64 (28)	16 (9)

Note: Figures in brackets for Koreans only.

Source: Utsumi Aiko et. al., *Tokyo Saiban Handobukku* (Tokyo Trial Handbook), Aoki Shoten, Tokyo, 1989, p. 117; and Utsumi Aiko, *Chosenjin BC-Kyu Senpan no Kiroku* (Records of Korean B- and C-class War Criminals), Keiso Shobo, Tokyo 1982, p. 197.

long distances into the most remote sections, there to tackle the hardest engineering problems, with supply lines that first stretched and then, under pressure of extreme weather conditions, virtually collapsed. Overwork to meet inflexible schedules, exhaustion, illness and ill-treatment combined to wreak their toll.

So developed the horror that lies at the heart of the modern Australian experience: the 'heart of darkness', which stamped its mark on Australian history no less deeply than did Gallipoli on a previous generation. However, the exclusive focus on the pain and anguish of Gallipoli, such that the other parties to that experience are depicted, if at all, as foils whose motivation and passions are almost irrelevant to the experience, is quite different from the case of the railway, in which contact with the enemy was direct, prolonged, and complicated by the bitterness of a relationship of racial inequality and prejudice in which the tables had suddenly been turned, and historic dominant–subordinate roles reversed.

Viewed now from a 50 year perspective, modern Japan's first great multinational construction venture has left little save jungle graves and memories etched with unforgettable bitterness in the minds of all who toiled on it.

The B- and C-class war crimes trials conducted by the Allied countries as a whole concerned mainly two categories of war crime: atrocities by the notorious Kempeitai, and ill-treatment of the POWs, with more than one-quarter of all guilty verdicts coming from the offences against the prisoners (Table 9.2). In the cases arising exclusively from the railway construction, while 25 of the 32 death sentences were imposed on the staff of the Thai POW camps, there were none for the Kempeitai and only one for the engineer detachments who actually supervised the work[15] though, as Weary Dunlop notes, 'In my experience, however, most of the brutality and actual violence meted to our prisoners was by the engineers'.[16] The British doctor Robert Hardie remarked that 'Even the Korean guards . . . were appalled

88

Table 9.2   Relative proportions of Kempeitai and POW-related offences in war crimes trials (%)

	Cases tried	Indictees	Guilty verdicts	Death sentences
Kempeitai	7	37	36	30
POW-related	16	17	27	11

Source: Utsumi Aiko, 'BC-kyu saiban' (B- and C-class trials), in Shukan Asahi hyakka, *Nihon no Rekishi* (125), *Gendai* 4, 'Tokyo saiban to jugo nen senso no sekinin' (The Tokyo trials and responsibility for the 15 year war), 18 September. 1988, pp. 120–4.

by the behaviour of the engineers'.[17] Major C.E. Green (of 'A' Force) described the engineers as 'sadistic morons'.[18]

The camp guards, exposed at the interface of the relationship between the Japanese system and the prisoners, bore a correspondingly heavy burden of the blame. The ratio of POW-related cases to 'war crimes', generally high, was even higher in the case of Australian trials: more than 60 per cent of Australian war crime indictments were for POW-related crimes.[19] The high priority accorded to crimes against nationals of the countries constituting the courts-martial, compared, for example, to crimes against the citizens of countries occupied by Japan, is a major plank in the case for seeing the trials as primarily 'revenge trials', not worthy of the name of trial in the proper sense.[20] It should be said, however, that in places such as New Guinea or Nauru, where Australia had been responsible for internal administration, many cases of atrocities against New Guineans, Chinese, Indians, Nauruans and others were heard.[21]

The case of Im Yong-Jun (Hayashi Eishun)

It is time to consider in a little more detail some of the Australian trials. Take first the case of Im Yong-Jun, a Korean known to the Japanese (and to the prisoners) by his Japanese name of Hayashi Eishun.[22] This twenty-five-year-old young man, third son of a Korean farmer, was recruited in June 1942, given 2 months' training at a camp in Pusan, and left Korea in September. Four and a half years later, in March 1947, he stood trial for his life in Singapore, charged with having 'inhumanely treated a Prisoner of War', thereby causing his death, in an incident that had occurred in '131 kilometre camp'. The trial, which lasted less than 2 days (on 10 and 12 March), concentrated on a brief incident late in the evening of 23 December 1943, when an Australian Lance-Sergeant, L.E. Whitfield, recently discharged from hospital after a bout of dysentery, and also very short-sighted, failed to rise to salute when a guard entered his dimly lit hut. He was thereupon allegedly set upon by the guard and kicked in the stomach. Whitfield died 12 days later, on 4 January, after having walked some distance to the 134 kilometre camp in the meantime. His death certificate recorded dysentery as cause of death.

As with virtually all the POW-related trials, the evidence was presented in the form of affidavits, whose authors were therefore not available for cross-questioning,[23] together with some medical evidence on the likely consequences of a kick in the stomach. A key witness for the prosecution was Major Sydney Krantz, a medical doctor of the Australian Army Medical Corps, who was said to have been called to examine Whitfield immediately after the assault. Major Krantz, however, swore affidavits for the court in which:

1 He referred to a Korean guard known as the Maggot, whom he said he knew well from having been in camps with him in several locations in Burma, including the Nieke camp on the Burma–Siam border. He described this man as 'a particularly nasty piece of work . . . harsh and brutal' whom he had on several occasions seen beating prisoners. However, he did not recall details of any specific incident, or the names of any prisoners who had been beaten. (affidavit of 15 April 1946)

2 He insisted that he did not at any time know a 'Sergeant' Whitfield (thereby contradicting evidence that he had been called to Whitfield's attention immediately after the assault and raising serious question about the medical opinion attributed to him that Whitfield's death was the result of injuries caused by the kicking. (affidavit of 6 December 1946)

No report about the alleged Whitfield assault was made either to the camp commander, Lieutenant Matsuzaki Minoru, or his offsider, Sergeant Shimojo Harukichi. Im (Hayashi) himself denied the alleged assault, though in court he admitted that he had once, at the end of September, beaten (slapped across the face with his hand) a prisoner who had uttered obscene and insulting words to him. His pretrial affidavit recorded a slightly different version, in which he recalled having slapped across the face a POW who did not salute properly when he entered a hut one evening where POWs were drinking tea. (A number of those indicted protested in court about these pretrial affidavits, which they claimed were signed under duress and often without clear understanding of their contents.)

All that is clear from the trial is that there was a Korean who was known as the Maggot, whose reputation was that of a brutal guard who beat prisoners without provocation. The question of whether Im (Hayashi) was or was not the Maggot was open to serious doubt, since the Maggot that Krantz knew was short, stocky, bandy-legged, with protruding teeth and 'looking like a half-wit'—a description apparently at odds with Im (Hayashi) but consistent with another guard at 131 kilometre camp (evidence of

Sergeant Shimojo). The court showed no interest in clarifying this matter. Furthermore, even if it were agreed that Im (Hayashi) was really the Maggot, the contradiction between the evidence of Krantz that he had nothing to do with the case and the evidence of other witnesses for the prosecution that Krantz had treated Whitfield and given opinion on the consequences of his being attacked should have weakened the prosecution case.

Despite these doubts a guilty verdict was returned. Most extraordinary of all, it transpired that Im (Hayashi) had been convicted once before, on 25 June 1946, on the same charges but that confirmation of the sentence had then been refused by the Judge Advocate-General. Despite all this the Judge Advocate-General on 2 June 1947 dismissed the appeal, a warrant of execution was issued on 27 June, and Im (Hayashi) was hanged at Changi gaol on 18 July. To the end his case was marked by irregularities, since the execution warrant was valid for execution within 24 hours but was not carried out for 3 weeks.

The case of Yi Hak-Nae (Hiromura Kakurai)

The second case is that of the Korean guard–interpreter Yi Hak-Nae, known at the time as Hiromura Kakurai, or the Lizard, then a nineteen-year-old youth.[24] For Australians his case is particularly poignant since the charges arise out of the situation at Hintok Mountain camp, in which all sources agree that Yi (Hiromura) was pitted regularly against Weary (then Colonel, now Sir Edward) Dunlop—the one, despite his lowly status, for a brief period in April 1943 representative of the Japanese camp administration, and required to secure from the other, who was senior officer among the prisoners, co-operation in filling the labour quotas required by the Japanese engineers.

Conditions were very bad at this camp, as many participants have subsequently attested.[25] Men were worked for up to 16 hours per day, at one stage for 3 months without rest.[26] As Utsumi notes, 'The construction of about 50 km of roadbed around Hintok, 155 km from the Railway's point of origin at Kanchanaburi, was fraught with unparalleled difficulty'.[27] And, if one old veteran is to be believed, incompetent Japanese engineers mistakenly put petrol in the jackhammers that had been prepared to cut through Hellfire Pass, with the result that 'We had to carve our way through Hellfire Pass with hammers'.[28]

In a camp of about 800 prisoners, about 100 died, at the worst period at the rate of up to six per day, as cholera, malaria and other ailments took their toll of the weakened men (evidence of Captain Richard Hastings Allen). Here at Hintok, as at other sites of great hardship, the blackest pitch of misery and suffering drew out some of those mythic qualities of comradeship and endurance that helped to form the Australian sense of identity. Tradition was created and renewed.

Formally the camp was under the command of Lieutenant Usuki Kishio (given in Dunlop's account as Lieutenant Osuki and sometimes known as the Boy Shoko), aided by Corporal (later Sergeant) Okada Seiichi (sometimes known as Doctor Death), but Yi (Hiromura) agreed that in April 1943, when the others were all absent or ill, he had had to substitute as commander. At other times, and later, he was a lowly orderly in the camp office, but during this brief and crucial period he stood directly between the Japanese camp authorities and the prisoners, represented by Dunlop. Dunlop recorded in his *Diaries* (17 March) that he came to think of his counterpart as 'a proper little bastard'.[29] While the *Diaries* make it clear that the relationship was tense and bitter, they do not mention any case of Dunlop being beaten by Yi (Hiromura) nor did Dunlop lodge any such complaint against him after the war. Though pressed by the Singapore tribunal to make an affidavit to confirm the allegations that he had been beaten, Dunlop did not oblige. All that the court file contains from Dunlop is a '*Q*' form citing the complaints of two other officers. Of the 700-odd POWs in Hintok at the relevant time, only seven complained in their post-war affidavits of ill-treatment by Hiromura.

The question is, however, whether and to what degree responsibility for the conditions at Hintok should attach to a Korean supernumerary in the Japanese system. In what sense was he responsible for the orders he issued to Dunlop by which prisoners were forced out to work on the line, sometimes regardless of illness and sometimes in the middle of the night? Captain Cecil George Brettingham-Moore expressed in his affidavit what must have been common anger that 'A Korean private [sic] was considered fitter to judge sickness than one of Australia's leading surgeons'. This diffuse evidence of resentment is clear, but such resentment (even hatred) is neither surprising nor evidence of specific war crime.

The closest the tribunal came to consideration of specific allegations concerned the question of whether Yi (Hiromura) had bashed or beaten Dunlop. Only five of the 700-odd prisoners who gave evidence, none of whom attended the courtroom (so that cross-examination was impossible), alleged that Dunlop had been beaten (though they differed on how seriously): Sergeant-Major Austen Adam Fyfe, who swore that he had himself been beaten by Hiromura with a hurricane lamp and a bamboo stick, across the head and body, and that in July 1943 he had personally witnessed Lieutenant-Colonel Dunlop being severely bashed across the head and body by Hiromura; Major Hector George Greiner, who described Yi (Hiromura) as 'one of the most brutal guards I had experiences with'; Major John Chauncy Champion de Crespigny, who noted, however, only that Dunlop suffered abuse, slappings and humiliation at the hands of the Lizard practically daily, but 'I am unable to recall any severe beating' of Colonel

Dunlop by the Lizard; Lieutenant Reginald Gilbert Houston, who referred to Dunlop and Major Corlette as having been 'frequently ill-treated' for their efforts at protecting sick prisoners from work; and Captain Cecil George Brettingham-Moore, who referred to one 'classic occasion' sometime between 25 May and 14 July, when conditions at Hintok had been at their worst, on which Dunlop had been beaten with a bamboo after interceding to try to prevent sick men from being allocated to work brigades. Of the others who testified for the tribunal, Captain Richard Hastings Allen had no recollection of any such beating, and merely described Hiromura as 'no worse than most of the camp staff where beating of PW was a daily occurrence'.

Neither Corlette nor Dunlop, the two specifically alleged to have been beaten, gave evidence. Dunlop's *Diaries*, published much later and meticulous in detail, mention no such beating by Hiromura (though other beatings are recorded). The court did not think it necessary to postpone judgment till this crucial question could be cleared up. Dunlop now says that he was *not* beaten by Hiromura.[30] Furthermore it is clear that the July incident to which Fyfe referred could not have involved Hiromura, because (as Dunlop's *Diaries* also make clear) Hiromura was replaced from the end of April. The incident referred to by Brettingham-Moore must also, because of the date ascribed to it, have involved someone other than Hiromura.

The possibility of mistaken identity is real. There was also a Lieutenant Hirota, a young engineering graduate responsible for work parties on the railway, who enjoyed a reputation for ruthlessness (Brettingham-Moore evidence) and is singled out in the one 'Affidavit' that Dunlop seems to have written after the war (on 27 June 1946) as a man of 'sickening brutality' who was 'directly responsible for the deaths of scores of Australians'.[31] And there was as well a Japanese civilian called Hiromoto (or Hiramoto), who was a clerk in the camp administration (and superior to Hiromura).

Despite the thinness and ambiguity of the evidence, Hiromura was found guilty of having 'inhumanely treated prisoners of war', after a brief hearing on 18 and 20 March 1947. He was held responsible for the general condition of the camp and for the death of 'over 100' Australian prisoners, and duly sentenced to death. Hiromura's time before the court, he later recalled, amounted to about 40 minutes; his character witness, Colonel Ishii Tamie, had about 40 minutes. Since the rest of the 1½ day trial was taken up with the formalities of reading the charges and the sentence, and so on, his actual trial had taken about 80 minutes.[32]

The file was then referred to the Judge Advocate-General (L.B. Simpson) in Canberra for advice. On 2 June Simpson wrote an initial opinion that did not comment at all on the quality of evidence or the degree of Hiromura's responsibility for the camp conditions, but merely concluded: 'I see no reason in the proceedings why the finding and sentence should not be legally confirmed'. A few sentences later in his report, however, Simpson added a completely opposite view: 'In comparison with other cases, this is not a particularly bad one, and I strongly urge the confirming authority to mitigate the sentence to imprisonment for a long period'.

Simpson then turned to consider the most remarkable feature of the whole case: the defence appeal document of 1 April (by Sugimatsu Fumio). This referred, apparently for the first time, to the fact that Hiromura had already once before, in 1946, been arrested, imprisoned, investigated *and then released* on the same charges: ill-treatment of prisoners at Hintok camp between February and October 1943. Lieutenant Colonel Smith, commander of the 1st War Crimes Section, Singapore, had minuted the file on 17 October 1946: 'Case not serious enough to warrant trial. Close file', writing on the same day to headquarters, Singapore district, to say, 'It is now advised that the case against the above-named has been dropped as it is only of a minor nature'. Hiromura, in Changi prison at the time, was told by gaol officers, 'You are not charged'. He was released on 10 December 1946 and set off to return home, only to be rearrested in Hong Kong, retried, and sentenced to death on these same 'minor' charges.

It is true that the case was apparently reopened on 9 January 1947 because of some 'new evidence' (according to a 17 June 1947 memo), but by the time this memo was written the following had to be added: 'There is nothing to show what evidence was available at the time Hiromura . . . was first charged, *nor what fresh evidence was referred to*' (italics added).[33] There is in the file on which the prosecution rested no 'new' material written between May and December 1946. One can only surmise that there might have been *the expectation* of such new evidence, in the form of an affidavit from Dunlop, coming to hand before the trial resumed; none ever did, despite the pleas from Singapore to Melbourne.[34]

However, when Simpson learned of the 1946 proceedings, he wrote his final opinion, on 1 October 1947, reiterating his earlier view that this case was 'not a particularly bad one' and recommending mitigation to a long prison term. On 24 October, Major-General W.M. Anderson, Adjutant-General, ordered the sentence commuted to 20 years' imprisonment.[35] On 7 November, nearly 8 months after his sentence, Yi was told of his reprieve. To this day he has 'not the faintest idea' why he was reprieved, any more than he has of why he was convicted in the first place.[36]

This case alone is enough to raise doubts about the quality of justice dispensed in Australian war crimes trials. It seems that the case against Hiromura, which first was considered not strong enough to warrant prosecution, was then found serious enough to merit death, and finally to deserve 20 years in prison (of which Hiromura in due course served about 10). Though the evidence is clear that Hintok was an awful place, it is much less clear in terms of establishing that Hiromura should be held personally responsible for this awfulness, or establishing that he was brutal in his treatment of POWs (as distinct from resolute and uncompromising in performing his duties to his Japanese superiors). It is unlikely that any court other than a court-martial held soon after a terrible war would have returned a guilty verdict under such circumstances. Hiromura was a very lucky man to have returned from the condemned cells of 'P' block at Changi to the world of the living.

The case of Ch'en Kwang-In (Chiba Korin)

The third case to which I should like to refer is that of Ch'en Kwang-In, the Korean guard known then as Chiba Korin, or simply as Cheebah, a truck driver.[37] Ch'en was charged and tried in a collective action against seven people headed by Captain Suzuki Sohei held at Singapore between 16 and 23 July 1946. The charge against Ch'en was twofold. One concerned the ill-treatment of prisoners in April–July 1945 in a camp in Indochina (which is not considered here). The other concerned his role in the camp administration at Tonchan camp in Thailand, where he was alleged to have stolen prisoners' rations (to resell to Indian labourers), withheld mail, been responsible for 'sadistic treatment of those POW who reported ill'—in effect been in command of the camp and established in it a reign of brutality and terror, bearing particular responsibility for the death of a prisoner named Riddoch, who, having been forced to work while ill, died about 25 days later.

In this case too, large questions went unanswered—more importantly, unasked. The first was the rationale for holding Ch'en, one of the very lowest of the Japanese hierarchy, responsible for the general state of the camp, on the assumption that orders transmitted via him were actually issued by him. The second was the absence of corroborative evidence on any single serious charge of ill-treatment. The third was the absence of any clear causal link between any act of Ch'en's and the death of Riddoch, who had not reported sick and of whose illness it was not established that Ch'en had any knowledge. Yet he was found guilty of ill-treatment contributing to Riddoch's death, and on 23 July 1946 sentenced to death. The Judge Advocate-General recommended that the sentence stand, and he was executed at Changi on 21 January 1947—one of the first prisoners of the Australians to face the gallows.

The statement he made to the court before sentence was passed gives some insight into the thinking of this one lowly Korean guard on the plight in which he found himself:

CHIBA Korin makes the following statement in mitigation of punishment:
'I cannot say that I did anything for the prisoners in sacrifice of my own life, but I think I did my duty as humanely as according to the regulations. I always shared with the PWs about cigarettes, soap and other things, necessary things of everyday life, throughout my three years service in this prisoners camp. I just did my duties as best as I knew how to.

There is one incident which took place in February 1943—my assistant in the truck driving was a man named Mostok—it was at a place called Tarsao. He told me how he came to be captured and about his family life. And he was quite sympathetic about my position. That is to say, the position of a Korean who had to work between the war prisoners and the Japanese Army. That is to say, that he understood quite well my position between the two which is: If I try to be good towards the prisoners, that will reflect rather bad upon the Japanese and if I try to be obedient on the Japanese side, then it will be hard on the prisoners. That position he seemed to understand very well. I had rather more faith in the British Corps. That is how I came to have this tattoo on my arm—this British flag (accused displays forearm to Court). It is designed to show a blade on the British flag. It was this Mostock who put this tattoo on my arm. When this was found out by the Japanese officers I was put in gaol, and as a result I became to embrace a bad feeling towards the Japanese. So the HQ officer was quite cautious about my being with the war prisoners when they were interrogated. I suppose it was from this fear that the Japanese did not like or allow we Koreans to have direct contact with the prisoners. For that I showed on the surface that I treated the prisoners badly, but I never had such heart within me at all. I admit that I had to scold or beat the prisoners in front of the Japanese officers, because if I show any sympathy towards a war prisoner, I shall increase that suspicion, and that would then be quite against me. From such a fact the war prisoner may have thought I was bad towards him but I never had such idea at all. It was not my own intention that I came to be a war prisoner guard. I was forced by the Japanese police that the young men of the age who come in the service—that is why I came. So if there was any case that we Koreans treated war prisoners badly, it was only on the surface—our heart was with them. Until the closing of the war our relationship with the prisoners of war was kept secret. I was referring to the matter of when war prisoners made mistakes, I never informed the Japanese officers. It is due to my spirit as a Korean—the racial feeling, that such of my conduct was brought in. Captain Hiramatsu gave me such work that would be on the surface and he dealt with inner matters. Anything that would appear very bad on the surface they would make the Koreans do and anything that would appear good they would do themselves. That is why we came to be marked as a bad guard.

For three years, I maintained that spirit and at the close of the war, I was quite confident that the war prisoners would appreciate what I had done towards them. On the day of the closing of the war there came an American airplane to Saigon. This American airplane dropped leaflets, stating that the victory is won by the allied side. At that time I learned the fact for the first time by that leaflet. Probably the prisoners did not know until then as much as I. I picket up the leaflet and showed it to the camp head and they were very glad about it. So I went out on the truck and bought several things, wine and fruit and other things and celebrated it with the prisoners—and I gave two shirts and two neck-ties to Bradstreet as a keep sake for the memory of our living together.

On the outside I may have appeared as a monster, but my inner heart throbbed for three years, saying as I have stated. Until I was called to Changi I was quite confident about myself. I never thought that I would be charged on these two matters.

I am twenty-seven years of age and I am single. I have had three years army service. I am a driver by civil occupation.'

The case of Lieutenant-Colonel Nagatomo and others

The fourth case to be considered here is the large collective trial held between 8 August and 16 September 1946 concerning events on the Burma end of the railway, in what was known as Sections 3 and 5, during the period 25 October 1942 to 1 May 1944.[38] The death rate among prisoners in camps in these sections is given in Table 9.3.[39]

Indicted were the overall commander, Lieutenant-Colonel Nagatomo Yoshitada, together with several officers (including a doctor) and four Korean guards: Cho Mun-San (Hirahara Moritsune), Kim Chang-Nork (Kaneko Choroku, also known as Makan or Makin, the Malay word for food), Kim T'aek-Shin (Takemoto Koji, also known as Liverlips) and Pak Yong-Cho (Arai Koei, also known as the Boy Bastard). Ultimately, three Japanese (including Nagatomo) and three Koreans (Hirahara, Kaneko and Takemoto) were hanged, the Koreans on 25 February and Nagatomo on 16 September 1947. In 1991 one of these Koreans, Cho Mun-San (Hirahara), was chosen as the central character in the special Japanese television documentary shown nationally on 15 August—the 46th anniversary of the end of the Pacific and Asian wars.

The case against Hirahara rested on allegations about his behaviour at '80 kilometre camp' and '100 kilometre camp'. While the affidavits compiled in this case are voluminous, and the allegations are in general agreement on the nature of the wrongs complained of, they are the more difficult to reconcile the closer one tries to adjust the focus to particular incidents performed by particular individuals at particular times. The two incidents

Table 9.3   POW death statistics: combined 3 and 5 branch statistics, 15 September 1942 to 20 July 1944

Nationality	Maximum strength	No. of deaths	%
Australian	4851	771	15.8
British	482	133	27.6
American	650	128	19.7
Dutch	5554	697	12.4
Total	11 537	1729	14.8

on which the greatest volume of material was accumulated, and on which the prosecution relied most, were: the beating of American Seaman F.V. Ebaugh, and the beating of an American Army private, Vincent Zummo.

Ebaugh was an epileptic who (according to one affidavit) had had some of the bones removed from his forehead. He died on 14 September 1943, several weeks after a beating by a guard one night in August at 100 kilometre camp, when he had left the line to get his mess kit and been late to return. His death was alleged to have resulted from the effects of this beating. The defence counsel pointed out that, while all accounts agreed on the circumstances under which Ebaugh had been beaten, by a single guard, the fourteen accounts given in affidavits before the court differed very considerably on the question of who had been the assailant. Three people blamed Hirahara (though referring to him as Hitahara, Hitaharia or Hita-Hari); eight gave accounts that seemed to blame the Japanese sergeant, Omi Tadashi (referred to as a Japanese sergeant, a two-star sergeant, Guard Commander Oma, Sergeant Oron, Omi); two more blamed Kaneko Choroku (the Korean guard Kim Chang-Nork, known to them as Makan, or Konico alias Makin) and one blamed simply 'a Korean sergeant'. The defence insisted that neither Hirahara, Omi nor Kaneko (Kim) had been on guard duty at the time of the incident. This point is now impossible to confirm, but it is striking that the court at the time showed no interest in considering the evidence relevant to the question. Though this does not exhaust the discrepancies in the accounts given of the bashing of Ebaugh, it shows well enough the flimsiness of the case against Hirahara.

Vincent Zummo was beaten by a group of guards at 80 kilometre camp late in April 1943. Zummo had apparently been a sort of 'go-between' between the POWs and the Japanese office; and as Hirahara (Cho) put it, 'We helped each other'. Zummo gave his own account of the incident from a hospital in Calcutta in an affidavit dated 13 September 1945.[40] He spoke of a Korean guard (not Hirahara) who had been negotiating an exchange of woollen American socks for sugar. The deal somehow went wrong and led to his being summoned by Sergeant Omi and beaten, for several hours, by Omi and a group of six Koreans. The beatings, he agreed, did not lead to hospitalisation or cause him any permanent injury, and he was unable to name any of the Koreans who had been involved, though one of the interpreters present had been 'Hitahara'. This incident was referred to by many, including a Japanese interpreter, Ishikura, who named Hirahara as one of the guards who had beaten Zummo with bamboo, wood or fists. Other accounts omitted Hirahara's name, however; and while Hirahara himself said that he had interpreted Sergeant Omi's admonitions, he denied any role in the beating. Hirahara (Cho) was renowned for his English ability and, in a striking phrase, told the court, 'About the case of whether I beat Zummo or not, Zummo, God and myself only know, and no other person knows it'.

As a Christian, raised in a Christian family in Korea, and as one of the rare English speakers, Hirahara (Cho) was a prominent figure among the prisoners, and from the court records it seems that he was judged by higher standards than others for being 'false to his principles'.[41] The court was cold to his plea that 'In the Army, the individual private faith and individual conscience is not counted', though it was nothing more than the truth.[42]

Before his case came to trial, he had signed two affidavits while being held at Bankwang gaol in Bangkok. In the first, dated 4 December 1945, he said:

> I admit that I was very strict but not cruel . . . Our instructions were to beat prisoners that didn't obey orders . . .
>
> One of the instructors at the training camp at Fuzan [Pusan] instructed us that we were to treat the POWs like animals; otherwise they would look down on us. We were to be harsh with them and beat them because they were taller than us, and the only way we could show that we were superior was through force, intimidation, and beatings. At the time I was following instructions in beating the prisoners and treating them cruelly. I now realize that I was wrong and I am prepared to take any punishment that may be dealt out to me.[43]

His second affidavit, also signed while in Bangkok, had the following passage:

> It was a standing order in the No 5 POW Camp (Burma), that POWs should be severely punished whenever they gave the slightest reason. The Korean and Japanese soldiers were not only allowed, but encouraged and ordered to beat and kick them.[44]

In court, however, Hirahara challenged the interpretation put on the words of his affidavits, taking exception in particular to the rendering of his word *binta* (which means to slap or box about the ears) as 'beating'. He described *binta* as 'a light form of discipline, seen as an expression of our superior's deep interest for us, so we received it with appreciation that we were not charged with the formal disciplinary punishments'. He insisted in court that only within the limits of such *binta*, 'applied with the open hand and usually applied three or four times', had he punished prisoners.

On this point, the affidavit of Hayashi (Im) in the case referred to above is also worth quoting:

> It was customary for the guards to slap the POWs for offences committed by them. This was an order given to us by the camp commander. It was not necessary for the guard to refer the matter to higher authority.[45]

With the Ebaugh and Zummo cases central to the charge against him, and despite the problems about both incidents, Hirahara (Cho) was convicted of 'having ill-treated PW thereby causing deaths of many of them and bodily injury, damage to health and physical suffering of many others'. He was sentenced to death on 16 September 1946; the sentence was confirmed as 'richly deserved' by the Judge Advocate-General on 28 November, and he was executed at Changi on 25 February 1947.

The case against Takemoto (Kim) and Arai (Pak) was prosecuted in similar vein and to the same outcome. Colonel Nagatomo Yoshitada was found guilty in the same trial and executed at Changi on 16 September 1947.

'F' Force

On 8 April 1943 the Japanese authorities in Changi ordered the despatch of a 7000 man British and Australian 'working party' to an undisclosed location. When told that there were no more than 5000 'fit' men available, they agreed that 2000 sick men might be included, since neither marching nor work would be required, food supply would be easier, and the destination was actually 'health camps' at 'a nice place in the mountains' where the men would have a better chance of recovery.[46] A contingent of 3662 Australian and 3400 British prisoners was organised under the command of Lieutenant-Colonel S.W. Harris, with Lieutenant-Colonel C.H. Kappe commanding the Australian group. The British were inclined to take the Japanese at their word and included sick men; the Australians chose 'the fittest men available', but many of them were suffering from dysentery, beriberi or other diseases.

The contingent set out by train from Singapore, with gear, including a grand piano.[47] The train journey was in steel rice trucks, 27 men to a truck, with only irregular food and water supplies en route. When the thirteen train loads of men detrained at Banpong in Thailand about 100 hours later (around 27 April), 'F' Force found that they faced a long march. Much of their equipment, including the piano but also much of their medical supplies, had to be left in a field.

They marched by night, for 17 nights, over approximately 300 kilometres under steadily deteriorating conditions, often 'in pitch darkness and torrential rain, sometimes knee-deep in water, sometimes staggering off bridges in the dark',[48] camping en route adjacent to groups of South-East Asian *romusha* labourers, then known simply as 'coolies', who were demoralised and in the throes of some dreadful epidemic, till they reached Songkurai around 17 May. When they arrived, exhausted, they found only unroofed huts in a filthy and unprepared camp site. Work on the railway began the next day, but was suspended for '4 or 5 days' when cholera broke out among the prisoners, allowing an opportunity to do essential construction and sanitation works but little chance for the rest that, with proper food, was what was most necessary to allow recuperation. The rain settled in and did not stop for nearly 5 months, and the pace of work, once resumed, grew more and more intense, even frantic.

The British troops suffered worst: of 1600 British troops who marched to Songkurai in May 1943, 1200 were dead by the end of the year.[49] By May 1944, 1060 Australians and 2036 British members of 'F' Force were dead (approximately 60 and 29 per cent respectively).[50] Six weeks after the return of the survivors to Singapore, Japanese doctors could find among them only 125 men fit for light duties only.[51] In terms of disease, cholera was the worst killer, accounting for 750 of the total deaths, with the others falling victim to dysentery, aggravated by malnutrition and generally complicated by malaria or beriberi or both—but the main cause of death was always malnutrition–starvation. In one camp alone there were the following diseases: cholera, typhus, spinal meningitis, smallpox, diphtheria, jaundice, pneumonia, pleurisy, dysentery, scabies, beriberi and tropical ulcers.[52] In June and July 1943 roughly 75 per cent of the camp strength at the Lower Songkurai camp were in hospital, and the numbers that could be sent out to work diminished steadily. The figures for Lower Songkurai camp for the last 3 weeks in June are given in Table 9.4.

The only significant differential in the casualty rate was that of rank. Survival chances increased enormously according to rank: the 44 per cent death rate in 'F' Force as a whole sank to less than 1 per cent for Australian officers and between 2 and 2.5 per cent for British officers.[53] The assumption must be that this was due to the officers' exemption from work, even though some officers were on occasion made to work and some also chose to work, to relieve the burden on sick men by helping fill the quotas.

For those assigned to the work parties, work was hard 'navvying'. The actual hours worked each day varied considerably, starting at first light and continuing usually till about 7:00 in the evening, but at times till midnight or even 2:00 or 3:00 the following morning.[54]

Food and medical supplies were never adequate. A summary of the food position was prepared by Captain Wilson, the British Army's nutrition expert with 'F' Force:

At the fixed camps, the I.J.A. supplied uncooked rations. Theoretically, the

Table 9.4   'F' Force capability, Lower Songkurai camp, June 1943

Date	Strength	Work	Camp maintenance	Sick
14 June	1899	237	237	1390
21 June	1894	399	220	1275
30 June	1889	275	252	1362

ration was the same as at Changi, but in practice the amount handed over each day varied according to the stocks in hand, the state of communications with the outside world and the mood of the Japanese Quartermaster. Another cause of variation was the idea held by some officials and at times openly expressed by them, that sickness even though not feigned in order to avoid work, was a gross breach of discipline and an act of sabotage against the Japanese War Effort. Instructions were actually issued officially from the I.J.A. H.Q. fixing a scale of 600 gms daily for those working directly for the I.J.A. on the road and railway projects, 400 gms daily for those on camp duties, and only 200 gms daily for those classified as unfit or sick. As sick and convalescents always outnumbered the workers, sometimes by three or four to one, the order meant a marked reduction in the amount of food issued to a camp. Although some adjustment and improvement of the sick men's ration was usually possible in our own cook-house, the manual workers dare not be penalized too much for the benefit of the sick . . . Rations for June and July were particularly poor. This was the time when those camps . . . were almost cut off from communication with the outside world. No adequate reserve stocks were laid in before the rains came . . . so rations were cut drastically. In Nieke in the middle of June the whole camp was receiving an issue of white rice 270 gms, dried lima beans 24 gms, dried green leaf 15 gms, fresh meat 50 gms including bone, *less than that required for basic metabolism.*[55] [italics added]

The normal 'ration' for a working man in Japan subsisting mainly on rice is about 1 kilogram, certainly no less; and although rice 'porridge' (*kayu*) is a staple for the sick and convalescent in Japan (in whatever quantity the patient is able or inclined to consume), for weak and ill prisoners, unaccustomed to a rice diet, such rations constituted a form of slow starvation. Desperately, men hunted snakes, rats and monkeys, but reduced rations, nominally meant to affect the sick, affected all prisoners, both sick and well.

The desperation of the Japanese construction units grew as deadlines were shortened by planners in Tokyo and as the labour force of prisoners diminished due to death and illness. It was a grim time. Neither laughter nor the song of birds was heard through that long wet season.[56] This was the section of the railway where the prisoners did not develop nicknames by which to refer to their guards, and even a gallant attempt to cheer the spirits of the sick by holding a singing party in the hospital one night drew rebuke and a beating.[57] Songkurai was probably the worst place on the line.

Criminal responsibility for the fate of the men of 'F' Force was dealt with in a joint British–Australian trial held in Singapore from 23 September to 23 October 1946. Seven men were collectively arraigned on charges of:

1 'inhumane treatment . . . resulting in deaths of many, and in the physical suffering of many others of the "F" Force group';

Table 9.5   The case of Lt. Col Banno and others

Nationality/Rank	Name	Sentence	Outcome (1 January 1947)
J/Lt. Col (o.c. 4th Branch POW Administration	Banno Hirateru	3 years	confirmed
J/Capt. (s.m.o)	Tanio Susumu	5 years	confirmed
J/Capt. (Engineers)	Maruyama Hajime	death	commuted to 15 years
J/Capt. (POW camp commandant	Fukuda Tsuneo	death	commuted to life
J/Lt. (Engineers)	Abe Hiroshi	death	commuted to 15 years
K/Civ Gd	Hong Ki-Song (Toyoyama/Toyama Kisei)	death	commuted to life
K/Civ Gd	Kun Yang-Hyo (Ishimoto Eishun)	18 months	confirmed

Death Rate among 'F' Force Prisoners (to May 1944)

	Maximum Numbers	Deaths	%
Australian	3662	1060	28.94
British	3400	2036	59.88
Total	7062	3096	43.84

Source: The 'F' Force Trial. Singapore Military Tribunal 25 September–23 October 1946.

2 'internment of the said Prisoners of War in conditions which were unhealthy and unhygienic.'

They were: Lieutenant-Colonel Banno Hirateru, commander-in-chief of the 4th Branch, Malaya POW camp; Captain Tanio Susumu, senior medical officer; Captain Maruyama Hajime, 4th Engineers Regiment of the Imperial Guard; Captain Fukuda Tsuneo, commandant of the POW camps at Lower and Upper Songkurai in 1943; civilian Korean guard Hong Ki-Song, then known as Toyoyama Kisei (a member of Fukuda's camp staff); Lieutenant Abe Hiroshi, engineer of the 5th Railroad Regiment, and Korean civilian guard Kun Yang-Hyo, then known as Ishimoto Eishun. All were found guilty of the first charge (although with the words 'resulting in death and suffering' deleted in the case of Ishimoto), and Banno, Tanio, Maruyama and Fukuda were found guilty on the second charge. Death sentences were pronounced on Maruyama, Fukuda, Toyoyama and Abe, while Banno was sentenced to 3 years, Tanio (the doctor) to 5 years, and Ishimoto to 18 months. However, 2½ months later, on 1 January 1947, all four death sentences were commuted: to life for Fukuda and Toyoyama, to 15 years for Maruyama and Abe. The trial dealing with one of the greatest catastrophes experienced by British and Australian troops therefore petered out somewhat indecisively: an outcome that was perhaps inevitable from the moment that the senior Japanese officer, Colonel Banno, was given the light sentence of 3 years.

In no trial was the atrocity so obvious but the attribution of responsibility so difficult. The prosecution attempted to sheet home responsibility to the officer-in-command of the POW camps, but Colonel Banno was described by the court's chief witness, Lieutenant-Colonel Kappe, as 'an incompetent, fatuous old man', 'an old fool' who was 'sympathetic' and would, on occasion, weep over the plight of the prisoners (or spontaneously give them cans of condensed milk), but who 'behaved like a child when very serious events were occurring'.[58] In an affidavit from Captain Benjamin Arthur Barnett, Banno is described as 'a doddering old donkey' (he was about 60 years of age in 1943),[59] although others thought more fondly of him as a 'good old bloke'.[60] Banno had under him Captain Fukuda, a couple of lieutenants and about 50 civilian guards, to cope with the 7000 sick and ailing men dumped on him.[61] He told the court that he 'used to treat the POW's as my children'.[62] But he had little actual power. The decisions that impinged most on the fate of the men were taken at the level of his superiors, and Banno ranked of such little importance that he did not even have his own transport. From its decision it is clear that the court was unable to see him as an evil man.

Likewise, of the medical officer attached to Banno's unit, Captain Tanio, few could be found to speak evil. His Australian opposite number, Major Bruce Hunt, reckoned that Tanio was a man who 'tried' and who 'would not have been indicted . . . for anything I knew', and Colonel Pond (2/29 Battalion) saw him as a man 'who was doing his best under difficult circumstances'.[63] Tanio did not actually arrive at Nieke to take up duties as Banno's medical officer till 24 June, in the depths of the crisis caused by the long march and the cholera outbreak. He claimed that he had regularly pleaded with the Railroad Regiment to reduce the workload required so that the camps could be cleaned up and the sick cared for.[64] Though the medical supplies he received were inadequate and many died, it was not established that that was Tanio's fault. His 5 year sentence indicates that the prosecution attempt to hold him responsible for the health problems of 7000 men scattered across an 80 kilometre stretch of jungle was not very successful.

Captain Maruyama and Lieutenant Abe were officers in the units that drove men to work. As the relentless insistence on sending obviously enfeebled and sick men to work, for long hours, in often appalling conditions was an undoubted cause of suffering and death, the case against them seemed strong. The prosecution argued that 'The officers and men of the Engineers, whose sole responsibility to the prisoners was to make them work, behaved with calculated and extreme brutality from start to finish'.[65] Maruyama's was a semi-autonomous unit under the direct command of the Southern Expeditionary Force Railroad Unit between Banpong and Konkoita, and thereafter acting in co-operation with the 5th Railroad Regiment. He told the court that his unit's responsibility had been to provide food and utensils for the huts, assign POWs to various places and supervise their work, while the POW camp authorities would guard the camps and workplaces and provide daily necessities and wages to the prisoners.[66]

Kappe described Maruyama as 'one of the most brutal and callous Japanese I have ever encountered'.[67] The rations he provided for the men were 'starvation'.[68.] He was also blamed for forcing the sick to work; for the beating administered to the hospital singing party; for keeping exhausted men standing for 6 hours in the sun without food and water after their arrival from Banpong and then allocating them filthy huts; for ordering the 'frightful' march from Timonta to Nieke through knee-deep mud early in June, and later the march southward from Nieke to Tamaran Pat over the period between 18 and 26/27 June—'one of the most brutal marches that POW have ever gone through'[69]—while housing the men en route in huts just vacated by disease-ridden *romusha*. In his defence Maruyama said that he had had a mere 1 day's notice of the arrival of the 700 Australians of Pond's Force at Konkoita (a telegram on 9 May), that the delay that day had been to allow a medical checkup for epidemic prevention, that he had given the men a week's rest before sending them out to work, and that the marches had been on orders passed down to him from his superiors. As for the mid June march, that had actually been undertaken because the 5th Railroad Regiment had cabled that it could no longer supply food either to prisoners or Japanese forces. Instructions had then been sought from the commander of the Southern Expeditionary Forces Railroad Regiment, who ordered the retreat to Takuan. An all-night meeting of battalion and regiment commanders on the night of 16 June had debated whether to follow this order (because of the condition of the men's health) and had decided that, because there were only 3 days' supplies left, there was no alternative. They described it as a 'rescue march'.[70]

The court did not pursue this matter. The case against Maruyama was left to rest largely on his nominal responsibility rather than on particular acts of brutality. In Maruyama's case, as in the case of several other defendants, the ordering of sick men to work was regarded very seriously by the court; clearly such orders had hastened the death of some men. The imperative of building the line, against a deadline that in February was suddenly advanced by 4 months by a decision in Tokyo, placed heavy pressures on all Japanese units along the line. The Australian (and British) politico-military objective of obstructing the construction and the human objective of protecting the men's lives and health were difficult for the Japanese to distinguish. Colonel Pond described well the clashes that ensued:

> When it was apparent that a particular number of workers was going to be insisted on by the Japanese, the policy adopted was to send out as many less than that figure as was thought could be 'got away with', and to reduce that number on subsequent days. This usually worked for two or three days, when the engr offr [sic] would personally conduct a purge of the sick and send many of them out to work.[71]

Pond was the Australian officer closest to Maruyama, and he noted in his diary that Maruyama had done his best, that 'though men were often struck for minor causes, there had been few cases of really heavy beating', and 'towards the end' relations between prisoners and Japanese had been quite good.[72]

The actual death rate of the men in Maruyama's charge was much less than elsewhere among 'F' Force men: 21 per cent, or 150 men, according to Colonel Pond.[73] In the absence of specific evidence of personal viciousness against either, the court decided, nevertheless, to attach greater responsbility to Captain Maruyama than to Colonel Banno. His death sentence was later commuted to 15 years.

The other engineer who was indicted was the twenty-three-year-old 2nd Lieutenant Abe. Abe's main task had been to supervise the construction of the vitally important bridge over the Koi Noi River at Upper Songkurai. Kappe described him as 'brutal and completely insensible to any decency in his attitude to POW's'.[74] Men too sick to walk were carried to the bridge works and often beaten with makeshift whips while on the job—although there was no specific allegation of any beating by Abe. Abe agreed to the court that his unit, the 5th Railroad Regiment (Abe was in command of the 4th Works Section of 6th Company, 3rd Battalion, 5th Regiment), had been responsible for the main work on the Burma side of the railway (actually in Thailand in the area adjacent to the Burmese border at Three Pagodas Pass). He further agreed that, for a period between mid July and 15 August, work had continued as late as midnight (though at other times, he said, the workday was between either 7:30 or 8:00 in the morning until either 4:30 or 5:00 in the evening). However, he was under orders from Colonel Sasaki, his commanding officer, to finish the bridge by 15 August, and the desperation was, at least in part, because 'the forces south of Songkurai were threatened with starvation' when the river rose and the existing small bridge would almost certainly be washed away.[75] Abe told the court that he had felt 'very much dissatisfied' with the lack of planning and preparation on the part of the whole railway project, and added, 'I express my regrets, but we simply had to do our best and we did it'.[76]

In Tokyo in 1992, he recalled with bitterness and anger his time in Burma. He claimed that he too had worked without respite, often to exhaustion, and deeply resented being blamed for decisions over which he had had no control. Ultimately, in his view, the emperor and the top military brass in Tokyo were the ones really responsible.[77] His death sentence was commuted to 15 years.

On the responsibility of Fukuda and Hong (Toyoyama), however, there was wide agreement. Under Banno, Fukuda had exercised general command of the POW camps at Lower and then Upper Songkurai, and his regime was said to have been one of 'continuous floggings, beatings and assaults'.[78] Kappe held him 'directly responsible' for the deaths of 594 British and Australians at the two Songkurai camps: 'He failed to take reasonable action against [sic] reasonable food supplies and drugs . . . He was often drunk. He was lazy, apathetic and callous'.[79] He was also accused of reducing the rations of the sick in order to compel them to work.[80] Perhaps above all he was hated for having apparently handed over authority to the Korean guard Toyoyama, whom he permitted 'to behave like a roaring lunatic'.[81]

Like Maruyama and Abe, Fukuda saw himself as a victim more than an oppressor. He spoke of his indignation when, contrary to previous instructions that the POWs would be transported by 'wheel', that they could carry recreational equipment and that their labour would not be heavy, he found himself having to march 'into this unknown strange land with 7000 men'. He denied responsibility for the accommodation, or for the introduction of (disease-carrying) Asian *romusha* labourers into the camps, which he said had only been done 'against my strong protest'.[82] Once the rains settled in the trucks were virtually immobilised, and the movement of food supplies from Nieke to the camp depended on ox carts or 'on our shoulders'. Even when work hours were longest, the mutual relationship between Fukuda and the prisoners was not necessarily always hostile, and only on certain occasions did supply virtually break down.[83]

Hong (Toyoyama) was the only defendant who was ready to acknowledge in the dock that he had behaved badly, beating prisoners—on one occasion (at Banpong and in front of many witnesses) with a golf club. Evidence was presented of his having forced sick men out to work and berated the prisoners with insults such as 'All English are dogs'.[84] Hong said that he had been beaten more than 1000 times in his own training, and pleaded that he was 'uncultured and unacquainted with the customs of other races'.[85] As well as admitting his own guilt, he defended his superior, saying that Fukuda had done his best for the prisoners and was not a drunkard but accustomed to rise late because he used to 'study and think deeply and plan during the night'.[86]

Captain Robert Howells (2/30 Battalion) thought Toyoyama 'unstable', if not insane. To Colonel C.H.D. Wild he was 'notoriously the worst Korean guard in "F" Force'. Colonel Kappe referred to him as being 'the most cruel, arrogant and consistent in his sadistic attitude'. Had he behaved differently, according to Kappe, 'it would have meant the saving of probably two hundred lives'.[87] Major N. Johnston (commandant of Australian POWs in Lower Songkurai) described him as 'a well-known basher' with an 'ungovernable temper', but noted that his bashings 'had no lasting effect on any PW'.[88] Even Toyoyama's defence counsel represented him as a 'psychopathic case', given to 'tantrums' in which he was irresponsible, and referred to him in the petition for leniency as 'one of those who should be punished most heavily in this case'. In short, virtually everyone, on both sides, seemed to agree that this lowly civilian should bear the heaviest punishment.[89]

Captain Curlewis appears to have been the only Australian to find Toyoyama 'comparatively friendly towards POWs'. Curlewis also noted that he had seen Toyoyama being himself 'badly assaulted by a Japanese officer'.[90] Major Bruce Hunt was quoted as saying that 'the only reasonable explanation of the extraordinary hold which Toyoyama has over Lieut Fukuda is, of course, that Toyoyama is his bugger-boy'.[91] Many Australians came to a similar view.

The matter for which the second Korean guard, Ishimoto (Kun), was tried was obviously considered by the court to be relatively minor, since he was given only an 18 month sentence.

The structure of authority involved in decisions concerning the construction of the railway may be represented in Figure 9.1 The court called as witnesses senior Japanese officers who admitted having given crucial orders—for troops to be moved on foot, for determining scale of rations and issue of medical supplies, and so on—including the officers to whom Colonel Banno and Captain Maruyama had been subject.[92] However, it was unable to pursue responsibility beyond those who were in actual physical contact with the prisoners.

Overall, the problem about the 'F' Force trial was that those tried and punished had not been responsible for the decisions that had the greatest impact on the lives of the men. The senior British medical officer with the force, Colonel Huston, summed up the causes of 'the appalling sickness and death rates' as:

1 initial wrong information about the nature of the operation, which led to the inclusion of many unfit men in the party;
2 inadequate preparation and organisation in getting the men to the Thailand work camps;
3 failure to provide adequate staging camps en route;
4 siting of camps in malarious and insanitary areas adjacent to 'disease infected coolies';
5 not stopping all movement when cholera broke out;

Figure 9.1 Command structure for railway decision-making

Headquarters and General Staff (Tokyo)

Southern Expeditionery Force Railroad Unit (Kanburi)
(Commander: Lieutenant-General Shimada Nobuo, d. January 1943;
succeeded by Major-General Takasaki)

| 2nd Division Imperial Guard (Commander: Major-General Asami Makoto) | 5th Railroad Regiment (Burma side) (Commander: Colonel Sasaki) | 9th Railroad Regiment (Thailand side) |

| 4th Engineers Regiment (Captain Maruyama) | 4th Branch Malaya POW Command (Commander Colonel Banno; staff includes Tanio, Fukuda, Abe, Toyoyama, Ishimoto) | |

6 poor rations and accommodation in the working area;
7 excessive labour demands;
8 reduction of ration scale for the sick 'far below basic metabolic requirements';
9 failure to call a halt to the above conditions even when the results were blatantly apparent; and
10 lack of provision of special transport or accommodation for the sick.[93]

Responsibility for most of these matters was at a level of authority that began only where the indictments and trial stopped. The orders to build the railway (and to advance the completion date by 4 months), to use POW labour, to send the labour force in before food or medical supplies were ready (and on the basis of deliberate deception about their destination and subsequent role), to have the 'F' Force march to their work site, even the orders that determined their rations—all these issued from regimental level or above and did not involve any of the defendants in this case. There is no doubt that these defendants did not abide by the Geneva Convention, but also no doubt that nothing in their training had ever suggested to them that they could or should. The evidence before the court in the 'F' Force case showed a monolithic structure of insensitivity, incompetence and brutality in which enormous pressures operated to deprive soldiers of the moral autonomy to act individually. The authority derived from the supreme command prerogative of the emperor was absolute, and the objective of completing the railway was the end to which all else, as means, was subordinate. Whether the evidence also showed the sort of individual moral culpability commensurate with the common understanding of B- and C-class war crime is more doubtful.

Finally, two particular factors were against 'F' Force. One was geography, for they had to go to the remotest regions, beyond the reach of the more-or-less regular river barge traffic that supplied the lower camps, beyond the trader networks where other units could sometimes supplement their regular rations, and be therefore truly dependent on the Japanese and the weather. Also, they seem to have had weaker and less reliable leadership from their senior officers than elsewhere. Neither the British (and overall) commander, Colonel Harris, nor Colonel Kappe, seems to have been as effective as commanders elsewhere on the line. The hygiene standards of British units seem to have been very low, often arousing disgust and horror among the Australians. The lack of discipline and solidarity between officers and men led to grumbling (unheard in other units such as Dunlop Force), and even among the Australians Colonel Kappe was sometimes known as Kappeama (for Kappe-yama),[94] suggesting that he was so distant from the experience of his men as to have been regarded as virtually 'one of them'. Witness the anguished cry of Stan Arneil in his diary that the officers in his camp were 'all well, have neither ulcers nor itch and are all well shod' (21 September 1943), or (on 3 October 1943) that:

> . . . officers drew more than a quart of gula each and the same of sugar, four tins of fish, tins of milk and as much soap, tobacco and oil as they wanted. We drew 7½ pints of sugar for the Company of 250 men. Our chaps in hospital drew a pint of gula each and we drew a pint of oil each. It was a wicked thing for the officers to do. We drew no milk or peanuts and only three tins of fish for the Company.
>
> Surely these officers do not expect to be respected when they finally discard the uniform.[95]

This strongly suggests that 'F' Force lacked the protection given by the most effective of the British and Australian officers.

Conclusion

Without wishing to draw large general conclusions from such a partial consideration of the Australian Burma Railway trials, several points can nevertheless be tentatively proposed:

1 So far as the question of attribution of responsibility for death and

suffering on such a large scale is concerned, there are two extreme and opposite views: on the one hand, that the human costs were deliberate, in other words that the POWs and Asian labourers were deliberately starved, beaten and worked to death as a matter of policy; and on the other, that the costs were, at least in large measure, due to the inflexibility, carelessness and incompetence of the Japanese, together with unpredictable factors such as the weather. With the passing of the years, the former view has gradually lost ground, and the most recent book devoted to the problem clearly opts for the latter: 'for every prisoner killed or injured [by deliberate brutality] in this way, many hundreds died from malnutrition and tropical disease resulting from neglect and indifference'.[96]

The railway was a military necessity, to which POW labour was committed by decision of Japanese Army High Command in Tokyo (the Daihonei). All major determining decisions came from there, including the initial deadline of November and the orders in February 1943 to bring forward the completion date by 4 months and to complete the project regardless of costs—orders that produced the frenzied maelstrom of activity along the line and led to soaring casualty rates, especially in the most remote, poorly supplied, disease-ridden areas. The further down the chain of Japanese command the imperatives went, the less room there was to manoeuvre or to respond humanely to the plight of the conscripted Asian and European workers, and the greater was the ensuing catastrophe. Ironically, as Colonel Wild, the British Army's Japan expert and Japanese interpreter, told the subsequent tribunal in Tokyo:

> We told the Japanese that the way they were treating their labor, both Asiatic and military, was, from a soldier's point of view, worse than a crime; it was a blunder. We told them, and I consider now, that if they had treated their labor properly and fed it and housed it and given it reasonable working hours, they would have finished that railway by the time they wanted to. We told them then, and I consider now, that as a result of the way they treated their labor they were months later than they intended in finishing that railway, and as a consequence lost a campaign that it was intended to supply in Burma.[97]

2 The lowest levels of Japanese authority were punished with greater severity than their superior officers. The supreme commander of Japanese forces, the emperor, who had taken a close and detailed interest in all aspects of the war, was absolved of all responsibility. Some responsibility for crimes against prisoners was assessed in the Tokyo A-class trial (where Colonel Wild gave evidence of the Burma–Thailand Railway case), but in the end it found guilty (and executed) seven men while *releasing* all the others. Otherwise, the responsibility of the Daihonei (imperial headquarters) in Tokyo, of Southern Expeditionary Force headquarters, and of the Railway Regiment headquarters, was only inadequately pursued.

3 At this low level blame concentrated especially on the Koreans, who were at the very bottom of the Japanese system, beneath the lowest of Japanese soldiers. They were treated judicially *as Japanese*, without any sign of understanding of the cultural and historical specificity of their experience of incorporation within the Japanese empire. Even their names were recorded in Korean in the trial transcript only as a kind of afterthought. The charge of custody of prisoners to a group of people commonly despised and treated with contempt by the Japanese, who were accustomed to being treated brutally by their Japanese superiors, was a recipe for disaster. As Stan Arneil notes, 'There was no love lost between the Koreans and the Japanese. The prisoners were in the middle'.[98] As the war progressed, in fact, suspicion and antagonism deepened, until Koreans came widely to believe that they were targeted for murder—as indeed Koreans in many other parts of the Japanese empire were murdered at the end of the war—and made defensive preparations accordingly.[99] In short, they feared their Japanese masters just as much as did the prisoners. None of them anticipated being treated at war's end *as if they were* Japanese. When a warning was issued from Tokyo to all those within the Japanese forces who might have something to fear from Allied tribunals to make themselves scarce as quickly as possible,[100] nobody thought to pass the message on to the Koreans. From the Japanese point of view, they were a convenient scapegoat, just as, in a different sense, they were for the Australians.

4 In these trials at least, standards of proof were low, the presumption of guilt was strong, and the rules of evidence were applied to make a heavy burden for their defence. Complaints about the quality of the interpreting were common. Review by the Judge Advocate-General was perfunctory (and occasionally quite confused, as is evident in the Hiromura case).

5 The above does not necessarily mean that a spirit of vengeance was at work. There is no reason to doubt the sincerity of statements of ordinary soldiers like Stan Arneil, for example, about 'our complete absence of feelings of revenge or reprisal against the Korean guards and the Japanese. For us they no longer existed'.[101] The non-response by Dunlop to the urgent requests from Singapore for an affidavit to substantiate the charges against Hiromura is an absence in the file that speaks volumes.

However, a judicial reckoning was inevitable. The layer of the Japanese system with which the prisoners had had most contact was that of the guards, and they were therefore blamed for conditions over which they had little or no control—including lack of food or medicine, the compulsion on the sick to work, appalling working conditions and squalid living quarters. A roughness in the quality of justice meted out, especially in the trials conducted soonest after the end of hostilities, is not surprising. It is nevertheless an added tragedy of the war that a group of people who were themselves victims, subtly and profoundly oppressed by Japanese militarism, should have had to bear so much of the blame.

6   The tribunals were confronted with problems that called for the highest levels of understanding in the disciplines of history and politics, but also in sociology, psychology and anthropology, in order to trace the lines of 'responsibility' and attribute 'guilt' within such an unfamiliar cultural context. They failed signally to understand either the structure of military command or the extent to which the moral vortex of Japanese militarism worked to suck up all autonomy and responsibility from the lower levels and concentrate it at the top.

The problem of tracing the locus of responsibility in this society has vexed scholars from Maruyama, writing in the immediate aftermath of the war, to van Wolferen, writing in the late 1980s. Both of these scholars, and many others besides, describe a system in which the source of authority is obfuscated, the heaviest burdens fall on the lowest echelons, and the character of the power to determine goals remains the ultimate mystery.[102] The problem involved in the application of the Western assumption of individual moral autonomy and responsibility even at the lowest levels of the Japanese military hierarchy is such that some commentators have seen the trials as, at root, 'a confrontation between a Western European mentality and Japanese-style morality'.[103]

Some of the prisoners, reflecting on this afterwards, intuited the problem. Thus Albert Coates wrote of his:

> . . . Japanese friend at Tavoy, Corporal Kumada, [who] once said that, if he was ordered to do so by his commanding officer, he would fill me up with rice, then a gallon of water, and jump on my stomach . . . Kumada was quite serious, that though he knew and liked me, he was bound to carry out the orders of his officer.[104]

7   The result of all the above is that the trials lack credibility in Japan itself, even among the most committedly antiwar segments of the people, part of whom are still calling, even today, for a 'people's tribunal', representing the people of Asia against whom most crimes were committed, to determine the issues of guilt and responsibility. The trials as conducted have produced, according to Utsumi, 'hardly any reflection by Japanese on the war'.[105] Equally sobering is the reflection that, *without exception*, those who were sentenced to death by the Allied military B- and C-class tribunals throughout Asia (including the Australian trials at Singapore) went to their deaths believing themselves victims of injustice, even martyrs.[106] Neither the punitive nor the deterrent effects of such trials can be rated very high.

8   A further, profound irony is irresistible. Of all the postwar war crimes trials, the most remarkable, and to some at least 'the closest to what War Crimes trials should be',[107] were those conducted in China (the People's

Republic). Of 1069 prisoners, held mainly in the Fushun prison in northeastern China, only 45 were brought to trial, in 1956, and sentenced to terms of imprisonment up to 20 years. By 1964 all had been returned to Japan. There was no capital punishment. Those held were treated, apparently, with relative generosity, while being made to reflect on their war record—in short, to engage in 'self-criticism'. For many this seems to have stimulated a genuinely penitent spirit, out of which emerged an understanding of the mechanism of the imperial system, a sense of guilt and a commitment to pacifism. In short, the Chinese trials seem to have accomplished a kind of moral regeneration among at least a minority of the men, for which there has been no parallel elsewhere.[108]

This is not to imply a particular moral superiority to the Chinese approach, though humanist idealism did play a role in the early years of the Chinese revolution. Capital punishment was common in dealing with *Chinese* collaborators and war criminals, and the particular policy on Japanese war criminals was influenced by pragmatic and long-term strategic considerations.[109] However, Mao's analysis seems to have been correct: the lenient policy on Japan's war criminals helped to create a strong and ongoing sense of guilt on the part of Japan's political and bureaucratic elite (as well as the prisoners), which has been enormously useful to China, but which harshness might well have quickly dissipated.

Notes

1 *Blood Oath*, directed by Stephen Wallace, Roadhow/Sovereign Pictures, Sydney, 1990. For a critical review of this film, see Hank Nelson's 'Blood oath: a reel history', *Historical Studies* (Melbourne), vol. 24, no. 97, October 1991, pp. 429–41.

2 D.C.S. Sissons, 'War crimes trials', *Australian Encyclopedia*, Sydney, the Grolier Society, 1988, pp. 2980–3; and also by the same author 'The trials: were they justice or vengeance?', *Sydney Morning Herald*, 16 August 1985. Philip R. Piccigallo, *The Japanese on Trial: Allied War Crimes Operations in the East, 1945–1951*, University of Texas Press, Austin and London, 1979, p. 139, gives slightly different figures, but Sissons, more careful to distinguish numbers of those sentenced to death from numbers actually executed, is probably more accurate. The figure given in Japanese sources of '148 confirmed death sentences', while correct, is also therefore misleading.

3 Sissons, *Australian Encyclopedia*.

4 Richard Glenister, 'B and C war crimes trials held by Australia: fair trial and the Geneva Convention', Japanese Studies Association of Australia, 5th National Conference, Griffth University, Brisbane, Queensland, August 1987; also other papers delivered by same author to the History Seminar, La Trobe University, Melbourne, in 1985 and 1986, dealing with both the war crimes trials generally and especially with the Ambon trials.

5 Saburo Ienaga, *The Pacific War 1931–1945*, Pantheon Asia Library, New York, 1978, p. 238.

6 Awaya Kentaro, *Tokyo Saiban-Ron* (On the Tokyo Trials), Otsuki Shoten, Tokyo, 1989, p. 282.

7 The following are the main Utsumi Aiko texts relevant to this question: *Chosenjin BC-Kyu Senpan no Kiroku* (Records of Korean B and C-Class War Criminals), Keiso Shobo, Tokyo, 1982; 'Prisoners of war in the Pacific War: Japan's policy', Proceedings of the 5th National Conference of the Japanese Studies Association of Australia, Griffth University, Brisbane, August 1987, included here as Chapter 8; 'BC-kyu senpan saiban—sabakareta Ajia no shinryaku' (Trials of B and C-class war criminals—Asian aggression on trial), *Asahi Janaru*, 18 Nov. 1988, pp. 27–9; 'BC-kyu saiban' (B and C-class trials), in Shukan Asahi Hyakka, *Nihon no Rekishi* (125), *Gendai* 4, 'Tokyo saiban to jugo nen senso no sekinin' (The Tokyo trials and responsibility for the 15 year war), 18 Sep. 1988, pp. 120–4; 'Chosenjin gakutohei no koto' (The Korean student soldiers), *Wadatsumi no Koe*, no. 88, 21 May 1989, pp. 132–53; 'Nihon no Ajia shihai to senso sekinin' (Japanese control of Asia and war responsibility), *Heiwa Kenkyu*, no. 14, Nov. 1989, pp. 45–56; (with Sumitani Takashi, Akazawa Shiro, Ubukata Naokichi and Otake Yuji), *Tokyo Saiban Handobukku* (Tokyo Trial Handbook), Aoki Shoten, Tokyo, 1989—hereafter *Handobukku*; and 'Kuhaku no sengo—Taimen tetsudo no Chosenjin tachi' (The blank postwar: Koreans of the Burma Railway), *Sekai*, September 1991, pp. 70–4.

8 Sissons, *Australian Encyclopedia*, p. 2980.

9 Utsumi et. al., *Handobukku*, p. 117; note that Utsumi previously (*Chosenjin BC-Kyu*) gives figures of 55 000 POWs and 70 000 to 100 000 *romusha*. Peter N. Davies gives figures of 91 112 *romusha* just on the Thai side of the line, of which 32 996 (36 per cent) died (*The Man Behind the Bridge: Colonel Toosey and the River Kwai*, Athlone Press, London, 1991, p. 196). Hugh Clarke, quoting 2/19 Battalion records, says that 270 000 Asian *romusha* were recruited, of whom only 30 000 were ever subsequently traced and repatriated (*A Life for Every Sleeper*, Allen and Unwin, Sydney, 1986, p. 53). On the 1990 discovery of mass graves in the Kanchanaburi vicinity with the remains of 'up to 500' buried together, see David Lazarus, 'Grave discovery lay ghosts but resurrects the horror', *Sunday Age*, 3 March 1991, or, in Japanese, Takisaka Toshio, whose account refers to 'over 700 persons': *Sekai*, March 1991, pp. 170–1.

10 Figures in Utsumi et. al., *Handobukku*, p. 117; and for Australian figures, Clarke, *A Life for Every Sleeper*, p. xv. Clarke, however, gives the figure of 9500 Australians employed on the railway as too low. The figure given here is suggested by Hank Nelson.

11 Kobayashi Hideo, *'Dai Toa Kyoeken' no Keisei to Hokai* (The Formation and Collapse of the 'Greater East Asian Co-Prosperity Sphere'), Ochanomizu Shobo, Tokyo, 1975, pp. 480–6. For the Australian figures, see Clarke, *A Life for Every Sleeper*, p. xv.

12 Hugh V. Clarke, *Last Stop Nagasaki*, Allen and Unwin, Sydney, 1984, p. 65. Clarke is here speaking of his period at Nagasaki, but the observation is true of Australian attitudes generally.

13 On this question Utsumi's pioneering work is fundamental.

14 Awaya, op. cit., p. 291.

15 Hiroike Toshio, *Taimen Tetsudo—Senjo ni Nokoru Hashi* (The Burma–Thailand Railway: Bridge that Remains on the Battlefield), Yomiuri Shinbunsha, Tokyo, 1971, p. 392. Lieutenant Hirota Eiji, of the 9th Engineers Regiment, was sentenced to death, and hanged at Changi in January 1947.

16 E.E. Dunlop, quoted in Clarke, *A Life for Every Sleeper*, p. 19.

17 *The Burma–Siam Railway: The Secret Diary of Dr Robert Hardie, 1942–45*, London, Imperial War Museum, London, 1983, Quadrant Books, 1984, p. 125.

18 Major Green, 'Q' form, undated, Australian Archives (hereafter AA), ACT, A471/1, 81655, pt 4.

19 Awaya, op. cit., pp. 285–8, and table at pp. 286–7.

20 Utsumi, *Nihon no Rekishi*, pp. 120–4.

21 I am grateful to Hank Nelson for advice on this point.

22 AA, ACT Regional Office, A471/1, 81659, for trial records.

23 Tribunals could take into consideration 'any oral statement' or any 'document appearing on the face of it to be authentic', Piccigallo, op. cit., p. 125.

24 Trial records in AA, ACT, A471, 81640.

25 See E.E. Dunlop, *The War Diaries of Weary Dunlop: Java and the Burma–Thailand Railway, 1942–1945*, Nelson, Sydney, 1986, esp. at pp. 189 ff.

26 Dunlop, in Clarke, *A Life for Every Sleeper*, p. 18.

27 Utsumi, 'Prisoners of war in the Pacific War', p. 11.

28 Jack Flannery, quoted in David McMahon, 'Why the Burma Railway shouldn't be a theme park', *Sunday Age*, 1 April. 1990.

29 Dunlop, *War Diaries*, p. 189.

30 Seminar, ANU, Canberra, August 1991.

31 Affidavit, 27 June 1946, Department of Defence, Army Headquarters, Correspondence files, 1943–1951, AA, Victoria, MP 742/1, 336/1/636A. See also Dunlop's *War Diaries*, p. 195.

32 Yi Hak-Nae, 'Kokuseki no hazama de' (In the loopholes of nationality) (interview), *Sekai*, Sept. 1991, p. 88–91.

33 AA, Victoria, MP 742/1, 336/1/1456.

34 Ibid. Yi himself recalls that there were only four affidavits attached to the original indictment in 1946, whereas there were nine in the 1947 indictment. The content of the allegations did not change, however, and some of the problems of the affidavits are discussed in the text (Yi, op. cit., pp. 88–9).

35 Trial records in AA, ACT, A471, 81640.

36 Yi, op. cit.

37 Trial records in AA, ACT, A471/1, 81242.

38 Trial records in AA, ACT, A471/1, 81655, pts 1–7.

39 Ibid., exibit 2A, pt 4 (attachment to 'Report on conditions, Thailand POW camps' by Lieutenant-Colonel C.G.W. Anderson).

40 Trial records in AA, ACT, A471/1/81655, pt 6, ex. 147.

41 Ibid., p. 841.

42 Ibid.

43 Exhibit 190, AA, ACT, A471/81655, pt 7.

44 Exhibit 191, AA, ACT, A471/81655, pt 7.

45 Exhibit 13, Affidavit of 8 June 1946, AA, ACT, A471/1, 81659.

46 Colonel C.H.D. Wild, quoted in *The Tokyo Judgement*, ed. by Dr B.V.A. Roling and Dr C.F. Ruter, vol. 2, APA–University Press, Amsterdam, 1977, p. 1017.
47 Proceedings of Military Court, Singapore, 25 September 1946 and subsequent, Public Record Office (London), WO 235/1034, 119, p. 332; hereafter cited simply as Transcript.
48 Opening for prosecution, Transcript, p. 7.
49 Ibid.
50 Sir Edward Dunlop, 'Foreword' to James Boyle, *Railroad to Burma*, Allen and Unwin, Sydney, 1990, p. vi.
51 Transcript, p. 13.
52 Opening for prosecution, Transcript, p. 12.
53 Kappe, evidence to court, 9 Oct. 1946, Transcript, p. 205.
54 Kappe's records show the following hours worked on the 4 successive days leading up to 15 August: 08:00 to 02:40, 10:00 to 22:00. 08:00 to 23:00, and 08:00 to 02:45 (exhibit O, Colonel Kappe, affidavit of September 1945, at Brisbane).
55 Appendix G to medical report by Lieutenant-Colonel J. Huston, in exhibit F, Transcript. See also detailed analytical tables of 'F' Force diet in exhibit 12, Transcript.
56 Stan Arneil, *One Man's War*, Alternative Publishing Co-operative, Sydney, 1980, p. 93; and Staff Sergeant Garret George Rickwood (2/30 AIF), first witness to the Singapore court, Transcript.
57 Captain Benjamin Arthur Barrett, affidavit, exhibit A–V, Transcript.
58 Transcript, *passim*, especially at pp. 202, 207, 289, 359.
59 Exhibit A–V, 23 October 1945 (Melbourne), Transcript.
60 *Singapore and Beyond: The Story of the 2/20 Battalion*, 2/20 Battalion Association (Don Wall), East Hills, 1985, p. 174.
61 Defence address, Transcript, p. 334.
62 Ibid., p. 113.
63 Lieutenant-Colonel S.A.F. Pond, 'Report on "F" Force working party to Thailand', 6 January 1944, court exhibit no. 6, p. 5.
64 Transcript, p. 140.
65 Ibid., p. 8.
66 Ibid., p. 180.
67 Ibid., p. 213.
68 According to Colonel Kappe in his evidence to the court, Transcript, p. 210.
69 Transcript, p. 216.
70 Ibid., *passim*, and at pp. 216–9, 294–5, 312–5 for account of this march.
71 Pond, 'Report'.
72 Ibid.
73 Ibid.
74 Transcript, p. 248.
75 Ibid., p. 267.
76 Ibid., p. 269.
77 Interview with Utsumi Aiko, Tokyo, 9 May 1992. My thanks to Professor Utsumi for her account of this interview.
78 Transcript, p. 13.
79 Ibid., p. 226.

80 Ibid., p. 368, and *passim*.
81 Ibid., p. 227.
82 Ibid., p. 282.
83 Ibid., pp. 336–7. (See diary of Captain Adrian Curlewis, exhibit A–R, annexure A, Transcript.)
84 Closing for the prosecution (Captain O. Dixon), Transcript, pp. 372–4.
85 Transcript, p. 293.
86 Ibid.
87 Ibid., pp. 227, 243.
88 29 August 1945 letter to Brigadier Kappe; copy in Transcript.
89 A recent book that describes Toyoyama as 'the curse of "F" Force' adds, wrongly, that it was 'fitting that he was among the first war criminals to be convicted and hanged' (James Boyle, *Railroad to Burma*, Allen and Unwin, Sydney, 1990, pp. 61, 126). Actually Hong (Toyoyama) was released from Sugamo prison on 23 September 1955 and returned to Korea, where he later died.
90 Transcript, p. 338.
91 Quoted in C.H.D. Wild, affidavit, 30 July 1946, Transcript.
92 From Banpong to Konkoita Maruyama said he had been under the Southern Expeditionary Force Railroad Command, thereafter becoming 'a sort of joint force' with 5th Railroad Regiment. Major-General Asami, however, insisted that Maruyama's unit was 'always under my direct command' (Transcript, *passim*).
93 Extract from 'Report of Lt. Col. Huston R.A.M.C.—S.M.O. "F" Force', exhibit 13, Transcript (slightly abbreviated here).
94 *Against All Odds: The History of the 2/18 Battalion A.I.F.*, 2/18 Association (James Burfitt), Sydney, 1991, p. 150.
95 Arneil, *One Man's War*, pp. 130, 133.
96 Davies, *The Man Behind the Bridge*, p. 194.
97 Quoted in Roling and Ruter, *The Tokyo Judgement*, p. 1019.
98 Arneil, *One Man's War*, p. 92.
99 Utsumi, *Wadatsumi no Koe*, p. 141.
100 Ibid., p. 141.
101 Arneil, *One Man's War*, p. 189; and for the same sentiment see Rohan D. Rivett, *Behind Bamboo*, Penguin, Ringwood, 1991, p. 378.
102 See the essays in: Masao Maruyama, *Thought and Behaviour in Modern Japanese Politics*, Oxford University Press, London, 1963; and Karel van Wolferen, *The Enigma of Japanese Power*, MacMillan, London, 1989.
103 Tsukuba Hiraharu, 'BC kyu senpan to sengo shiso' (B and C-class war criminals and postwar thought), Shiso no Kagaku Kenkyukai, ed., *Kyodo Kenkyu—Nihon Senryo* (Joint research—The Occupation of Japan), Tokuma Shoten, Tokyo, 1972, p. 332.
104 Albert Coates and Norman Rosenthal, *The Albert Coates Story*, Hyland House, Melbourne, 1977, p. 108.
105 Utsumi, 'Prisoners of war in the Pacific War'.
106 Over 700 'execution eve' statements, including letters, apologia, last wishes, of B- and C-class war criminals were published in Japan under the title *Seiki no Isho* (Testaments of the Century) in 1953 and reissued by Kodansha in

1984. For this assessment of their content, which seems to me to be fair, see Tsukuba 'BC kyu senpan to sengo shiso', pp. 327–46, at p. 329.
107 Awaya, op. cit., p. 293.
108 Ibid., and works cited there. See also the excellent NHK television documentary film of August 1990, 1064 *Nin Senpan no Jihaku* (Confessions of 1064 War Criminals).
109 Mao Zedong, 'Lun shida guanxi' (On the ten great relationships), speech of 25 April 1956, *Mao Zedon Xuanji* (Selected Works of Mao Zedong), Jen-min Chupanshe (People's Publishing House), Peking, 1977, pp. 280–3, at p. 282. (My thanks to Geremie Barmé for advice on this point.)

10

The man between: a Korean guard looks back

Yi Hak-Nae (Lee Hak-Rae, formerly Hiromura Kakurai)

(translated from the Japanese by Gavan McCormack)

I am Yi Hak-Nae, Korean. Let me say first how grateful I am to have this opportunity to visit this country and to speak to you here about my life. There are several reasons for this visit to Australia. In June of this year I learned from Professor Utsumi and from an NHK television crew about this seminar, and I learned too that Colonel (Edward) Dunlop was alive and well. When I heard the name of Colonel Dunlop, my mind suddenly filled with memories of long ago. Hearing the name Dunlop I could not help but recall vividly the scenes of Hintok camp. From the bottom of my heart I wanted to apologise profoundly, as one of the aggressor side, to Colonel Dunlop and all the former POWs, for the bitterness and pain of the loss of so many of their comrades under those harsh circumstances. Before you all now I apologise from my heart.

Between 9 and 19 of July of this year (1991), I had the opportunity to visit again the Burma–Thailand Railway and Changi prison in Singapore. I left flowers at the graves of the 6000 prisoners at Kanchanaburi and at the cenotaph, and prayed for the repose of the souls of the dead. Surrounded by the old construction sites of the Burma–Thailand Railway and the bridge on the Kwai River, I could not restrain my anger and my tears. And visiting again that dreaded and bitter place, Changi prison, I paid my respects to the graves of those who had been executed, which lay in one corner of the Japanese cemetery. Being able, 50 years on, to express to the former prisoners the apologies that have been so long on my mind, and being able to pray at the graves, has brought me at last a peace of mind and confirmed in me anew my commitment to peace and against war.

The second reason for my visit is to express the hope that you come to understand my position. My country, Korea, became a Japanese colony in 1910. I was born 15 years later, in 1925. From the time I went to primary school and began to think about the world around me, Japanese colonial policy penetrated every aspect of life. Japan was striving to wipe out the Korean race, by educating us to be subjects of the emperor, to see Korea and Japan as one, by making us adopt Japanese names, by thoroughly abolishing nationalist education and popular customs, by having us bow in homage to the imperial palace virtually every day, visit shrines and swear allegiance to the (Japanese) empire.

As is well known, rapacious Japanese imperialism plunged into the Manchurian Incident, the China Incident and the Greater East Asian War, and under its Mobilisation Law almost every day Koreans were forcibly seized and sent to work in the mines, as 'volunteer' soldiers or civilian auxiliaries in the army, or in the fire brigades or youth brigades. One day an elder friend told me that they were recruiting POW guards for service in the south on a 2 year contract at 50 yen per month. I thought that I would learn something from such work, the pay was not bad and I could avoid military service by the 2 year contract; so I signed up. On the surface it was voluntary, but there was a quota for my district, and in effect we were impressed. In June 1942, on the basis of a simple written and oral test, 3000 young men gathered under the Noguchi Unit in western Pusan. We swore an oath, did field training and learned the use of weapons; but though we were to be POW guards, we had no training whatever in the handling of prisoners or in languages. Instead, every day we had beaten into us the military spirit, the glories of the Japanese Army, the necessity for absolute obedience, and the Code of Military Conduct. Every day we were beaten a few times, and after 2 months' training we were sent to South-East Asia.

I was assigned to the Thai POW camps, and from Konyu in No. 3 Section in February 1943 was employed at Hintok subsection (at the 155 kilometre point). This is the place where the problems arose that later led to my being questioned as a war crimes suspect. The camp had been set up with six civilian auxiliaries, including me, and 500 British, Australian and Dutch prisoners to co-operate in the construction of the Burma–Thailand Railway. Later, the main force of No. 3 Section concentrated here.

For the first month virgin jungle had to be cleared and living quarters constructed, and then the railway work began, but the situation at the time was that facilities, food supplies, medical items and clothing were all unprepared and inadequate. The situation was such that, though malaria and cholera were prevalent, adequate medical supplies were not being received. On top of this the conditions of the construction labour got more and more severe. It seemed to me that it was too much to expect to build a railway

*Yi Hak-Nae (extreme left) as
prisoner-of-war guard*

under strict military discipline under such circumstances, but absolute, unconditional and immediate obedience to superior orders was the rule. It seems to me that difference in customs and habits and difficulty in communicating were one cause of trouble.

Though there were many victims, the works were completed on 20 October 1943. Thereafter I was engaged on maintenance works until the war ended with Japan's defeat on 15 August 1945.

I was demobbed, and had waited it seemed an eternity to return to my liberated homeland when in late September I was detained, first in Bankwang gaol in Thailand and later in Changi in Singapore, as a war crimes suspect. I leave the description of the horrors of that living hell that was Changi to another occasion. After a perfunctory interrogation I was charged under an indictment with, from March to August 1943:

1 (having allowed) poor facilities and inadequate food, clothing and medical supplies while I was commander of Hintok camp;
2 causing sick prisoners to work;
3 not having controlled subordinates properly and not having stopped ill-treatment.

A few months later, however, the indictment was dismissed and I was released from Changi prison; but while on my way home on a repatriation ship I was arrested again at Hong Hong, and then sent back again to prison in Changi.

Without any investigation I was charged under an indictment that was the same as the previous time, save that where there had been only four affidavits the first time there were now nine, and that forcing sick prisoners to work was now said to have led to death. Colonel Dunlop's name had also been added to those charging me. The trial was conducted for 2 days on 18 and 20 March 1947. It consisted of simple interrogation as to my identity, recording of plea and questioning of witnesses. None of those charging me appeared in court. After a completely inadequate hearing of less than 2 hours, and on the basis of an examination of documents alone, the hearing ended and judgment was pronounced: death by hanging. At that moment I fell into a state of nervous shock. It is difficult to express what I felt.

I was taken in manacles to the death cells of 'P' block, where there were fifteen prisoners under death sentence. At first I felt a sense of relief as if a burden had been lifted from my shoulders, but as the days passed I reflected that:

1 While on the one hand I was overflowing with joy over the independence of my motherland, on the other here I was under sentence of death for ill-treatment of prisoners; the shame I had brought my country and the loneliness of the abandoned oppressed me.
2 How sad would my parents and brothers and sisters be when they heard such dreadful news!
3 For whom or for what was I going to die? I could find no reason to die.

Day and night I worried over these things. Japanese prisoners, whatever the rights and wrongs of the war, were sustained by the feeling that they were to die for their country, but I could not even share this. This was probably the most bitter thought for those of my friends who were executed. My bitterness and mortification know no bounds when I relive in my mind even now this life on the chopping block, filled with bitterness, and recall my friends who were executed.

Happily, after about 8 months on the chopping block, on 7 November 1947 my sentence was reduced to 20 years in prison. In August 1951 I was transferred from my incarceration in Changi and Outram prisons to Sugamo prison in Japan, and I was released on parole on 6 October 1956. After release I was forced to live in extreme poverty. From that time on until now I have lived in Japan, not just because of circumstances beyond my control, such as the terms of parole, but unable to return to my beloved home country in which I was brought up because of the shame attaching to me as one who had collaborated with Japan to the point of being a war criminal. Japan has become a sort of second homeland.

To sum it up, I have the strong feeling that the postwar trials, which should have been conducted against the enemies of peace, humanity and justice, did not match that objective, especially so far as we B- and C-class war criminals, who were in the very lowest position, were concerned (whatever may have been the case with the A-class trials).

There were in all 148 Korean B- and C-class war criminals, of whom 23 were sentenced to death and 125 to terms of imprisonment. Of 49 families still living in Japan, 32 are families of survivors and 17 families of deceased. I should add that I have one unhappy friend who has been 39 years in psychiatric hospital because of the shock of having been found a war criminal. He will probably end his days there.[1]

As I said at the beginning, I offer my sincere apologies, as one of the aggressor side, over the many victims produced by those harsh circumstances, for all the hardships, bitterness and pain. I can understand and sympathise with the feelings of the former POWs of that time and their situation immediately after the war. However, it is clear that it was not the responsibility of those at the lowest levels, without any authority, that facilities, food, medical supplies and clothing were ill-prepared and inadequate, or that the sick were made to work. Was it not too severe to have exacted death or life imprisonment sentences for ill-treatment such as a few blows delivered in the process of administration and control? Was it not just too severe? As one fortunate enough to have survived after having been branded a war criminal, I was lucky, but I would like to ease the resentments of those who were executed and to help even slightly to clear their names. It may be that it is my destiny to speak on behalf of those friends who were executed and are therefore silent despite all the changes in our times. It breaks my heart when I think of those families. After the years and months have flowed for nearly half a century, I have been given this opportunity for reflection. Though that nightmare period will never be forgotten, from the bottom of my heart I hope that we can mutually understand the position that both sides were in at that time and move forward constructively to the future in a spirit of forgiveness.

Finally, I would like to address briefly the irresponsible attitude of the Japanese governmment. As I said earlier, the Japanese government compulsorily pressed us into service, and we were held, tried and sentenced as war criminals while still in service with the Japanese Army, with our 2 year contracts unfulfilled. On top of the 2 years of service I was held for 10 years as a war criminal. With the issue of the Release Order, the Japanese government threw us out into Japanese society, where the struggle for survival was fierce, where we had neither parents nor brothers and sisters nor acquaintances, without making any provision for our support. Japanese society was a completely unknown society to us. We felt like Urashima Taro[2] on the shores of a deserted island. The difficulties of life and the despair felt after being released caused two suicides. We were filled with bitterness and hated the Japanese government.

From the time when I was still in Sugamo prison I have for 30 years been making the following demands, which I am still making, though without getting anywhere:

1 immediate release and an end to discriminatory treatment;
2 (some address to) the problem of livelihood after release;
3 compensation to the families of those executed and an early return of their remains;
4 state compensation for the survivors.

The Japanese government has taken various legal measures for Japanese war criminals and has provided them with relief, but war criminals of Korean or Taiwanese origin who staked their lives to fight for Japan have been completely excluded from this support on grounds of nationality. When the Japan–Republic of Korea Normalisation Treaty was concluded in 1965, it was emphasised at the bilateral talks that 'everything is settled'. Sincerity was completely lacking. Whatever agreement there may be between Japan and the Republic of Korea as countries, the matter of compensation remains our individual right. We cannot for one moment acquiesce in the utterly insincere words and actions of the Japanese government that treats us as 'used up' or 'disposable'. We are deeply indignant.

As you know, the advanced countries settled their problems of postwar compensation on the basis of the conscience of their government and people. Why is it that the Japanese government, unilaterally and to suit its own convenience, can cause such hardship to others? Does it not see the need to make amends? Its integrity and sincerity must be doubted. In terms of its responsibility as a state, we seek of the Japanese government a legally and morally proper apology and a solution to the problem of state compensation. With the support of Japanese people of understanding, we plan to launch an action in the courts over this in the near future.[3] The 'postwar' will not end for us till the issues of the return of the remains of the executed and the matter of state compensation have been settled. I look forward to your understanding and support.

Notes

1 This man, Pak Chan-Ho, died in hospital in August 1991, almost simultaneously with this reference to him in Yi Hak-Nae's Canberra speech (translator's note).
2 Legendary Japanese figure, equivalent to Robinson Crusoe.
3 Actually launched in the Tokyo court in December 1991.

11

The Korean guards on the Burma–Thailand Railway

Aiko Utsumi

(translated from the Japanese by Gavan McCormack)

Justice and trials

What did those who were convicted of war crimes think of their trials? The representative view among Japanese people, including the war criminals themselves, is that the B- and C-class trials conducted by the Allies who judged Japan's war crimes were 'trials by the victor' or 'revenge trials'.[1]

A survey of the thoughts of the war criminals about the war trials was conducted at Sugamo prison on 22 March 1953. The responses of the 118 people detained at Sugamo, who had been tried at Singapore by British and Australian tribunals, are set out Table 11.1. A glance at the results of this survey is enough to understand that the war criminals harboured strong dissatisfaction with their trials, about both the pretrial and the trial itself.

Firstly, they complained about ill-treatment and torture at the time of investigation and pretrial. Such complaints were voiced without exception by those who had been held in Outram and Changi prisons in Singapore. So far as the ill-treatment was concerned, there were both violence and starvation. Entries such as the following can be seen among those referring to violence:

From about five in the afternoon three soldiers went around bursting into

127

Table 11.1 Opinions of war criminals about their trials

Trial country	USA	UK	Netherlands	China/France	Total
Numbers involved	493	199	260	147	1099
Concerning pretrial investigation					
'Was tortured'	46	14	54	29	143
'Was intimidated or forced'	115	30	71	42	258
Concerning guilt					
'Acted under superior orders'	209	67	115	48	439
'Facts were grossly distorted'	141	43	63	84	331
'Blamed for crimes of others too'	154	31	91	45	321
'Mistaken identity'	58	19	24	37	138
Concerning trial proceedings					
'A mere formality'	259	98	194	99	650
'Testimony not admitted'	171	75	109	87	442
'Felt there was collusion between judge, prosecution and defence'	222	56	68	78	424
'False affidavits were decisive'	163	66	105	47	381
Concerning sentence					
'Inappropriate to acts committed'	356	122	170	95	743
'Penalty too severe'	182	64	137	40	423
'Penalty appropriate'	5	1	0	0	6
'Penalty light'	2	1	0	0	3

Notes:

1. Obvious errors in calculation and typographical errors have been corrected. The figure given for Britain in the original materials, 86, was an obvious error and has been calculated at 199 from the number of respondents. Figures for France and China were small, and have been combined for convenience in this table.

2. Those convicted at Australian trials were returned to Japan in August 1953. At the time of this survey, trials were still being conducted at Manus Island. Furthermore, since sentences were still being carried out on Manus Island, Australian prisoners were excluded from this survey.

Source: Compiled from material in Sugamo Homu Iinkai (Sugamo Legal Affairs Committee), *'Senpan Saiban' no Jisso* (the Truth about the 'War Crimes Trials'), 1952; reissued by Maki Shobo, Tokyo, August 1981.

the cells. It was probably about six o'clock that they came to my cell. Opening the cell door, three Australians came in. Using sign language they asked me had I cut off any heads. When I indicated 'No', suddenly they punched me in the stomach, pinned me down while shouting, and rained blows on my face. This went on for about half an hour, till I was unconscious, when they threw a bucket of water over me and left.[2]

This sort of thing went on almost every evening. There were times when the faces of all the prisoners would show signs of having been beaten when they were let out into the yard in the morning. Two prisoners died at this pretrial stage from such beatings. The ill-treatment of those who were under sentence of death was even more severe, and one prisoner, who feared this violence more than the death penalty, committed suicide.

The other kind of ill-treatment was through starvation. Food at Changi consisted of two meals a day: two biscuits and a bowl of hot water-like soup in the morning, and a bowl of mixed wheat and cornflour porridge in the evening. Under the rational control system in which, after first serving up more of this than one could possibly eat, the quantity was gradually reduced, the war criminal suspects constantly suffered from hunger. They reached the stage where they could not think about preparations for their trials and where they thought, 'I don't care if I die; I just want to eat my fill'. As a result of this postwar ill-treatment, there were many among the war criminals who, rather than thinking about their own war responsibility, came to have a strong sense of themselves as victims of ill-treatment.

Secondly, so far as the trials were concerned, there were problems about interpretation and the inadequacies of legal representation, which was commonly thought to be no more than a formality. Furthermore, they complained about the injustice of the punishment. The Japanese Army was the emperor's army. There was strong resentment over the fact that the special characteristic of the Japanese Army that orders had to be carried out without question was ignored and that the lower ranks were tried.

Such resentments over the trials remain strong among those who were involved, but it is nevertheless a fact that there were crimes committed in war by the Japanese Army. The problem is not resolved by merely pointing to the problems in the trials.[3] Is it not up to us now that nearly half a century has passed since the trials to reconsider the trial records and to leave accurate records of the facts of the war crimes of the Japanese Army?

Construction of the Burma–Thailand Railway

In terms both of numbers and of scale, the largest of the B- and C-class trials were those concerning the Burma–Thailand Railway (120 people indicted). However, in Japan, apart from the members of the Railway Unit and a few 'railway maniacs', since the war hardly any attention has been paid to the Burma–Thailand Railway, and even less to the ill-treatment of prisoners.[4] It was thanks to the film *Bridge on the River Kwai* that people came to have some interest in it. Since the war there has also been hardly any interest in Japan in prisoners. Even without going so far as to bring up the wartime Combatants' Code, interest in the ill-treatment of prisoners has been very slight.

The Burma–Thailand Railway was built by the Japanese Army after it had lost control of the Indian Ocean as a means of transporting by sea the 200 000 men of the Burma Route Army. The Burma–Thailand Railway Construction Order No. 1 was issued on 7 June 1942. According to this order, 50 000 prisoners were to be made to co-operate in the construction. From the start the railway counted on the Allied prisoners as a labour force. On 22 May, just before the issue of this Construction Order No. 1, newspapers announced that Korean youth were to be used as 'civilian auxiliaries' (*gunzoku*) to guard the British and American prisoners who would be held in various places at the request of the army. These civilian auxiliaries were planned from the start to be sent along with the 50 000 prisoners for the construction of the Burma–Thailand Railway. The participating units are listed in Table 11.2.

Table 11.2 Burma–Thailand Railway participating units

Chain of command

Imperial headquarters (Daihonei)
↓
Southern Route Army headquarters
↓
No. 2 Railway Supervision Section
↓
Thai POW camps

Composition of Thai POW camps

Thai POW camps	Section		Section head	No. of POWs
Main camps	Thai side	No. 1	Major Chida	7 200
		No. 2	Colonel Yanagida	9 600
		No. 4	Colonel Ishii	11 200
		No. 6	Major Ebiko	6 000
	Burma side	No. 3	Colonel Nagatomo	9 000
		No. 5	Captain Mizutani	2 000
Backup units		No. 3	Captain Hachizuka	3 000
from Malayan		No. 4	Colonel Banno	7 000
POW camps)				

Note: About 70 000 Asian labourers (Burmese, Malays, etc.) were attached to the No. 2 Railway Supervision Section.

130

However, the construction of the railway began while preparations were still incomplete. Hiroike Toshio, then chief of staff of the Southern Route Army's Field Railway Detachment, wrote: 'The force provided was not just weak, but abysmal. It is incomprehensible that, though it was to be plunged into a nest of epidemics, there was no medical unit'. Until March 1943, while Hiroike was there: 'There was no doctor in the command group; hospitals could not be provided to meet our wishes; the prisoners marched through the jungle on foot: that was the situation. It would have been really astonishing had there *not* been victims.'[5]

Furthermore, he refers to the fact of the composition of the POW camps not matching the actual circumstances, and to the inadequacies of the supply system, as causes of the setbacks. It was impossible for a few hundred Korean guards to watch over 10 000 and more prisoners. They were in no position to either watch over or help the prisoners. For example, at No. 2 Section there were only one Japanese NCO and four or five Korean guards to move 1200 men. It was more or less the same at other sections. For this reason there were no reserves even to be able to gather in those who fell behind from the tail of the detachment. According to Hiroike:

> Had the staff office of the Southern Route Armies been able to glimpse how difficult it was for a few civilian auxiliaries, with only an infantry rifle each to rely on, to conduct through jungle so thick that it was impossible to see fifty metres ahead, or sometimes even 10 metres ahead, a march of up to 1200 prisoners, alternately cursing and cajoling them as they tended to lag behind, they would have realised the drawbacks of this organization.

On top of the difficulties of the actual work, communication was impossible, there were constant pressures to speed the job up, the handling of the prisoners got rougher, and naturally it was impossible to look after the sick. Having seen this reality, Hiroike raised the question of the war crimes of the Korean guards, asking whether these civilian auxiliaries should take all the responsibility.[6]

Furthermore, the condition of the prisoners at the time when the camps took them over was already bad. When No. 2 Section admitted 1800 prisoners, 1000 of them were already sick. There was no proper system for transporting prisoners, no huts for them to move into at their destination, no supply of food and medicines, insufficient food. The basic policy of headquarters in this situation was 'to conform as much as possible to the Geneva Conventions, but it is permissible to use the prisoners unreservedly, without letting this stand too much in the way.'[7]

As early as early January 1943, the order was issued to shorten the period of construction by 4 months, thereby completing the line by the end of August. This was the time when prisoners were beaten and forced to work to shouts of 'Speedo! Speedo!' From late April of this year, the rains began. Work continued through storms and unrelenting rain. Rough bush roads became swamps. Muddy torrents of the Khwae Nooi (Kwai) river swirled and rose. On top of the inadequate food and medical supplies, the starvation and heavy labour, came cholera and malaria. The prisoners weakened and collapsed one after the other. However, the early completion of the railway was an absolute order, necessary for the Imphal strategy, and so the sacrifice of the prisoners was thought to be unavoidable. Lieutenant Abe, who was in command of a unit of the Railway Regiment, said:

> A feeling of fierce hatred for the British and Americans filled the hearts of Japanese at that time. And, since it was the intention of the superior authorities that 'prisoners arriving at the sites should be most efficiently used as a labour force', the real intention of the authorities responsible for the works was that 'to some extent sacrifices will be inevitable'. Naturally, such sentiments were reflected in the thinking of the lower officers and NCOs. It is also a fact that, the worse things got, the more strongly this psychological condition or consciousness was expressed in action. Various misfortunes and appeals were reported from the prisoners, but there was no one among the works unit's commanders to lend an ear to them. Among the highest authorities too they were ignored.[8]

The Works Unit of the Railway Section would demand of the prisoner-of-war (POW) camp the supply of labour it needed for the following day. The camp would retort that it could not meet such demand because of constant outbreaks of sickness. This confrontation was common. One staff officer of the Railway Section said, 'I was constantly arguing with Mr Yanagida [sic for Colonel Yanagida, commander of No. 2 Section] because he was always taking the side of the prisoners'. The head of a section might become a Lieutenant-Colonel but still have to quarrel with staff of the Railway Unit that had the backing of the imperial general headquarters (Daihonei). The Korean guards, however, just obeyed orders, since, however absurd the order, in the army orders were the driving force of military activity and absolute obedience was demanded of subordinates.

The order to speed up the project was ill-prepared and flew in the face of the realities; it led to a spate of POW deaths. At the war crimes trials the actual responsibility for the ill-treatment of prisoners was called in question. The Korean civilian auxiliaries were unanimous that in the Japanese Army non-compliance with an order would have been unthinkable. According to the Army Penal Code: 'Resistance or non-compliance with the orders of a superior officer will be dealt with according to the following distinction: 1. if in the face of the enemy, death, life imprisonment, or a term of more than 10 years'.[9] The slightest sign of incipient insubordination would lead to bashing by a superior.

It was the Korean guards, sharing their lives with them, who were most saddened by the mass deaths of prisoners. This is because it is they who were in contact with the prisoners on a day-to-day basis. But they were

Table 11.3 Burma–Thailand Railway construction-related war crimes trials, by rank

Rank	Indicted	Guilty	Death	Prison
General	2	2	1	1
Field officer	11	11	5	6
Company level officer	37	33	12	21
NCO	23	20	4	16
Ordinary soldiers	12	12	1	11
Civilian auxiliaries	35	33	9	24
Total	120	111	32	79

Note: The civilian authorities (*gunzoku*) listed here were all Korean guards.

Source: Utsumi Aiko, *Chosenjin BC-Kyu Senpan no Kiroku* (Records of Korean B and C-class war criminals), Keiso Shobo, Tokyo, 1982

army employees, at the very lowest level of the army: they had no authority. However, the hatred of the prisoners was directed, not at Emperor Hirohito or (Prime Minister) Tojo Hideki, but at those before their eyes who had to implement orders from them. Living under such conditions, there were times where these guards beat or even tortured prisoners. Within the Japanese Army such behaviour was commonplace. The Korean civilian auxiliaries too had been taught by being beaten. Furthermore, according to Japanese Army custom, in the case of infringement of the rules by a prisoner, beating once or twice without reporting to a superior officer or the Kempeitai was considered a kindness; the act of beating was viewed in a fundamentally different way.[10]

Of 120 people who were indicted at war crimes trials relating to the construction of the Burma–Thailand Railway, 111 were found guilty; 32 were sentenced to death. Those indicted included 35 Korean civilian auxiliaries; 33 were found guilty and nine executed. All nine were *gunzoku* (civilian auxiliaries) from the Thai POW camps. Of the remaining 24 who were found guilty and given sentences of life or terms of imprisonment, some, like Yi Hak-Nae, were originally sentenced to death. Table 11.3 shows the breakup of indictments and trial outcomes by rank.

So far as the unit to which indictees belonged is concerned, 66 people, or more than half the total, came from Thai POW camps; fourteen were from No. 19 Section for transporting the sick, five from No. 9 Railway Regiment, two from No. 5 Railway Regiment, and five from Malayan POW camps. From this the extent to which 'war responsibility' concentrated on the POW camps may be seen.

Why did the Koreans become war criminals?

Of the 984 who were sentenced to death as war criminals, 23 were Koreans and 21 Taiwanese. Of the 3419 who were sentenced to life or various terms of imprisonment, 125 were Korean and 147 Taiwanese. Taking the war criminals as a whole, people from the former colonies made up 7.2 per cent of the total (taking into consideration only those found guilty and given various sentences, not those found not guilty etc.).

Those subjects of Japanese imperialism who had been conscripted into the Japanese Army were made to take responsibility for the system. Why did the victims of aggression have to bear the responsibility for Japan's war of aggression? The existence of the Koreans and Taiwanese shows clearly the problem inherent in the war trials. It may be summed up under the following three heads:

1 Those who came from Japan's former colonies were tried as Japanese.[11] The period taken by the International Military Tribunal for the Far East in Tokyo as that of aggressive war was from 1 January 1928 to 2 September 1945. The control of Korea and Taiwan was not included in the matters on trial. In other words, the Allies took for granted Japanese control of Korea and Taiwan and tried only Japanese aggression against China and South-East Asia. Thus, Minami Jiro and Koiso Kuniaki (Governors-General of Korea) were included among the A-class war criminals, but their behaviour as Korean Governors-General did not constitute material for indictment. This is a problem that concerns the determination of the character of the Asia–Pacific War. The war was, in a sense, a colonial war between the imperialist powers for the colonial division of China and South-East Asia. The sovereign colonial powers fought over these rights. Inevitably, this character of the war also had an impact on the trials. The Netherlands, for example, proceeded with war trials while at the same time suppressing the Indonesian war for independence. France too conducted its trials after announcing the restoration of its sovereignty over Vietnam.

2 In the B- and C-class trials by which the Allies tried Japan's 'conventional war crimes' on the basis of their own law, the greatest emphasis was paid to the ill-treatment of prisoners. Japan's prisoner policy was very strictly questioned, as may be seen from Article 10 of the Potsdam Declaration, which Japan accepted: 'All war criminals, including those who ill-treated our prisoners, should be strictly punished'. Many Korean and Taiwanese young men had been conscripted into the POW administration, which produced so many victims. There were 148 Korean war criminals, of

which 129 were young men who had been conscripted as POW guards. Thus the Korean war criminals who had been conscripted into the army as civilian auxiliaries, rather than those who had collaborated with Japanese imperialism, were made to pay the price for Japan's reckless prisoner policy.

3 The trials conducted by the Allies in accordance with American and British law judged not only the responsibility of the persons who issued orders, but also of those who carried out the orders. In the Japanese Army orders were the driving force of military activity, and absolute obedience was demanded of subordinates. The army Penal Code (Article 4) established the 'crime of opposing orders', where 'anyone who resisted or did not comply with the orders of a superior' was guilty and liable to penalties, which included death. Furthermore, in Article 10 there was a provision concerning 'crimes against prisoners' which prescribed a penalty of more than 3 years and less than 10 years for allowing a prisoner to escape. It could be said that the POW guards, who were army employees on the very bottom stratum of the army, had absolutely no freedom to act on their independent judgment. However, at the trials their responsibility for their actions was questioned whether they had been acting under orders or not.

In this way the Koreans became war criminals. The problem of Japan's colonial control and war responsibility can be seen in concentrated form in this fact. The Korean and Taiwanese war criminals were produced by the gap between the policies of the Japanese Army, which conscripted young men from the colonies as POW guards, and the Allied trials, which ignored the problem of the colonies. Why did the Allies ignore the problem of Japan's colonies? Was it to avoid touching on the colonial problems of the imperialist countries that also possessed colonies? Whatever the reason a large problem remains, not only as to why Japan's colonial problem was not tried either by the International Military Tribunal for the Far East or the B- and C-class trials, but also as to why the Allies tried colonial subjects as Japanese.

Japan's POW policy

The POW policy of the Japanese Army was notorious during the war. The way that the Allies, under the Potsdam Declaration, paid such special attention to the ill-treatment of prisoners out of all Japan's many war crimes shows the difference in thinking about prisoners between the Japanese and the Allies.

The notion of the 'human rights of prisoners' still has an unfamiliar ring to Japanese people today. So how many Japanese can there have been who gave a thought to the human rights of prisoners protected at international law under the Geneva Conventions during wartime, when the idea of 'Never suffer the shame of being taken prisoner alive' from the Combat

Manual held sway? The slogan 'British and American beasts' was much stronger.[12]

The Allied countries protested again and again to the Japanese government about the ill-treatment of prisoners. Protests or inquiries received by the Japanese Ministry of Foreign Affairs via neutral countries alone amounted to 83, and the protests picked up from shortwave radio by the Ministry of Foreign Affairs were countless.[13]

The Army Ministry, which had control over prisoners, promised the Allies 'provisional application' (*junyo*) of the Geneva Convention. However, its use of prisoners for the construction of military facilities, and its supply of food, clothing and medical goods, were not in accordance with the convention. Behind the protests of the Allies lies the fact that 27 per cent of the Allied prisoners who became prisoners of Japan died.[14]

Japan declared war on Britain and America on 8 December 1941, and in the following year set up POW camps in various places within the Greater East Asian Co-prosperity Sphere. Korean civilian auxiliaries were conscripted as guards for the prison camps in Thailand, Malaysia and Java, and Taiwanese guards for those in Borneo. The POW camps, which had only an officer in command, and a few Japanese NCOs under him, were actually run by a few dozen Korean or Taiwanese civilian auxiliaries. The Allies, who saw the POW camps as terror organisations, conducted exposures of suspects by detaining everyone who had worked in them and holding identification parades in front of those who had been imprisoned or detained and local people. Many accusations issued from the prisoners. The railway units and the airfield construction units had moved about depending on the progress of the works, but the POW guards had moved with the prisoners wherever they went. The greater the opportunities for contact with the prisoners, the more they were hated.

These prisoners in due course found themselves pursuing Japanese war crimes as members of the victorious Allied forces. It is not surprising that there should have been former prisoners who would bring accusations. It was no concern of the former prisoners who had been so painfully beaten whether or not the civilian auxiliaries had been acting on the orders of Japanese superiors. The guards who had beaten were prosecuted; those who had made sick prisoners move were prosecuted; shortage of food and shortage of medicines became a matter for prosecution. It was not at all unreasonable that the prisoners should have been all out for revenge over the Japanese Army's treatment of prisoners in that wartime living hell. Their comrades had died one after the other.

However, the problem is not whether this or that Korean civilian auxiliary bore responsibility. An army is a place where everything moves in accord with orders. If an order to beat a prisoner comes from someone in command, the prisoner must be beaten. From eating to sleeping, everything was by order. Any infringement of an order meant imprisonment with hard labour as a 'crime of resisting authority'. These regulations within the Japanese Army may not have been any concern of the prisoners. It was a fact that there were beatings, that there was starvation, that there was heavy labour, and above all that many prisoners died. Naturally responsibility for this had to be pursued. The Korean civilian auxiliaries served that purpose.

According to a Ministry of Health investigation, there were 116 294 Korean soldiers, of whom three became war criminals. Of 126 047 civilian auxiliaries, 129 became war criminals, all of whom had been POW guards. They come from the 3016 conscripted civilian guards. (There were also sixteen who were found war criminals in the Chinese court, but their status is not clear; they were described as interpreters.) A look at these results is enough to show how seriously the Allies viewed ill-treatment of prisoners. Could it not be said, not that the trials scrupulously judged the whole question of war crimes, but rather that they severely judged the ill-treatment of POWs as a special problem?

The death penalties on Korean civilian auxiliaries who were war criminals were carried out at Changi prison in Singapore or Chipinan prison in Jakarta. Prior to the coming into effect of the Peace Treaty with Japan on 28 April 1952, the civilian auxiliaries who had been serving life or various terms of imprisonment were sent one by one to Japan and held in Tokyo's Sugamo prison. Since the Japanese government took over from the Allies the implementation of punishment of the 'Japanese people' under Article 11 of the Peace Treaty, the A, and also the B and C-class, war criminals continued to be held at Sugamo prison. Under the treaty the government it took over the implementation of punishments of 'Japanese people' (*Nihon kokumin*). Detention continued as before.

By the unilateral interpretation of the Japanese government, the Japanese citizenship of Koreans was regarded as terminated as of that date. This meant that, according to the Japanese government's interpretation, the Korean war criminals ceased to be 'Japanese people'. Not only that, but they presumably should have ceased to be proper objects for the implementation of punishments under Article 11 of the Peace Treaty. Naturally they expected to be released; but however much they waited, notification of parole did not come.[15]

On 14 June 1952 proceedings for an order for their release under *habeas corpus* was launched with the assistance of Japanese lawyers. On 9 July of the same year, the supreme court rejected the request of the Korean war criminals. It held that at the time when the crimes were committed they were Japanese, that they had been imprisoned until just prior to the coming into effect of the treaty, and that, since both those conditions were fulfilled, 'even though nationality be subsequently lost or changed, that has no effect on the obligation of Japan to implement the punishment'. In other words, the punishment should continue.

Implementation of the punishment of the Korean war criminals continued. However, because they were not Japanese citizens, they ceased to be eligible for assistance. Though held in the same prison, support systems were set up one after the other for the Japanese war criminals, but nothing for the Koreans. Subsidiary Clause 2 of the Law for the Relief of the Families of Wounded, Sick and Deceased Veterans (passed on 30 April 1952 with retrospective effect from 1 April), which came immediately after the promulgation of the San Francisco Peace Treaty, held that 'for the time being, this law does not apply to those to whom the Household Registration Law does not apply'. In other words, Koreans and Taiwanese were excluded. Starting with this law, those from the former colonies were excluded on grounds of nationality from all laws for relief of war victims. Though impressed and conscripted as Japanese, relief was withheld because they did not have Japanese citizenship.

The Korean war criminals, even when granted provisional parole, had nowhere to go, no work, no friends. Under provisional parole, because of restrictions on residence, they could not return to Korea. In any case the 'travel money' they received on leaving Sugamo prison was only enough to go about as far as the other side of Tokyo. It was hell for them if they stayed in Sugamo, hell if they left. Worse, once out, starvation awaited them: an even more direct suffering than that at Sugamo hit them once they were outside. So they engaged in sit-ins, refusals to leave, petitions to the Diet and demonstrations at the Diet. Through these demonstrations a sum of money equivalent to that paid to Japanese war criminals was paid as 'consolation money'. However, there was no fundamental revision of the Suppport Law, which excluded them on grounds of nationality. All that was done amounted to a series of cheap tricks by the government from time to time. Then with the coming into effect of the Japan–Republic of Korea Normalisation Treaty in 1965, the problem of claims was treated as settled, and no further negotiations were to be entered into.

The Koreans who, as Japanese soldiers and civilians, were made to play a role in the Pacific War were cast off as 'useless creatures'. Still today the Korean civilian auxiliaries continue to press the Japanese government for justice.[16]

Notes

1 Sugamo Homu Iinkai (Sugamo Legal Affairs Committee), '*Senpan Saiban*' no *Jisso* (The Truth about the 'War Crimes Trials'), 1952; reissued by Maki Shobo, Tokyo, August 1981.

2 'Eiryo chiku senso hanzai saiban no jisso' (The truth about war crimes trials in the British areas), '*Senpan Saiban*' no *Jisso*, p. 534.

3 The Japanese Ministry of Justice has not opened to public access the trial records collected by the government.

4 So far no research studies have been published in Japan on the Burma–Thailand Railway, but books dealing with the subject include: Hiroike Toshio, *Taimen Tetsudo* (The Burma–Thailand Railway), Yomiuri Shinbunsha, Tokyo, 1971 (out of print); Nagase Takashi, *Kwai-Gawa Horyo Bochi Sosakuko* (Searching for POW Graves along the Kwai River), Shakai Hyoronsha, Tokyo, 1988; Nagase Takashi, '*Senjo ni Kakeru Hashi' no Uso to Shinjitsu* (Truth and Falsity in 'Battlefield Bridge'), Iwanami Booklet no. 69, Tokyo, 1986; and also several translated volumes.

5 Hiroike, op. cit., p. 114.

6 Ibid., pp. 150–1.

7 Ibid., pp. 154–5. There is also an unpublished note by Colonel Yanagida Shoichi, commander of the No. 2 Section of the Thai POW camps, entitled 'Taimen tetsudo kensetsu no jisso to senso saiban' (The truth about the construction of the Burma–Thailand Railway and the war crimes trials), in which he quotes a high-level staff officer as saying that, so long as the railway was completed, 'it would not matter if all the prisoners collapsed'.

8 Yanagida, op. cit., p. 10.

9 Article 57, chapter 4, of the Army Penal Code (*Rikugun Keiho*, October 1908). Chapter 4 of the code dealt with 'Crimes of disobedience', chapter 5 with 'Crimes of riotous intimidation', and chapter 6 with 'Crimes of insult'. Insubordination or resistance to a superior officer was punished severely.

10 Tojo Hideki at this trial said that *binta* was 'forbidden in the Japanese Army and Navy, but in fact continued to be practised, due to the influence of custom'. He added: 'However, I cannot consider it a crime. It is something which arises from custom.' (Transcript, no. 147)

11 This was agreed at discussions between the chief prosecutor for the Dutch East Indies and the British, held in Singapore on 11 and 13 December 1945.

12 The staff of POW camps in Japan used to conceal their identity when they went to market to buy provisions; otherwise people might have refused to sell them food to feed the prisoners.

13 See Horyo Johokyoku (Prisoner of War Information Bureau), 'Horyo ni kansuru kogi ni kanshi horyo johokyoku oyobi horyo kanribu ga shochi shitaru kotogara o kiroku shiaru shorui no utsushi' (Copies of documents recording the matter of treatment of protests about prisoners by the Prisoner Information Bureau and the Prisoner Administration Branch), mimeograph, n.d. (late 1945), in possession of the author.

14 Judgement of the Tokyo tribunal, section B, chapter 8 on conventional war crimes (atrocities).

15 The Japanese government enacted Law no. 103 in order to give effect to Article 11 of the San Francisco Peace Treaty. In it the term 'people' (*mono*) was substituted for the expression 'Japanese people' (*Nihon kokumin*) used in the treaty.

16 Judicial proceedings for compensation and an apology from the Japanese government were launched in Tokyo on 12 November 1991 by seven former Korean war criminals.

12

Reparations: matters still outstanding

David Barrett

On retiring as Victorian state manager of a Sydney-based publishing house, for the first time since the Second World War, I began to take an interest in the local ex-POW association. By this time I had moved from Victoria to Tamborine Mountain in Queensland. I took the opportunity in October 1986 to attend the national ex-POW reunion being held on the Gold Coast. While there an ex-POW (Japan), George Stevenson, handed me a newspaper clipping relating to the War Amputations of Canada's efforts to obtain reparations from the Japanese government for the brutal treatment meted out to the almost 2000 Canadians taken prisoner in Hong Kong. After absorbing the contents of the clipping and making some low key inquiries from among some of the interstate executives of the association, I discovered to my amazement that no similar claim was being contemplated by any ex-service organisation in Australia.

After being a prisoner of war (POW) for about 3½ years—Changi, Siam–Burma Railway and elsewhere—I had a trip up the railway immediately after the war ended on a search with the War Graves Commission. We actually found more than 12 000 graves in a matter of a few weeks: Australian, British, American, Dutch and other.

I felt strongly enough to start the ball rolling in support of the Canadians' efforts. At an appropriate meeting, on 7 December 1986, of the Gold Coast Branch of the Queensland Ex-POW Association, I proposed the following motion; I am happy to say that it was seconded and carried unanimously. I had also formed a reparations committee by this time, made up of D.W. Barrett, G. Stevenson and P. Collas.

Reparations

Motion of Gold Coast Ex-POW Branch meeting held at Twin Towns, 7 December 1986

1 This Association of ex Prisoners of War is concerned that the heinous, inhuman, brutal and completely unlawful treatment imposed upon Australian prisoners of war by the Japanese military authorities during World War Two has not received the recognition or acknowledgment in terms of reparation or in any other way on the part of the Japanese nation.

2 That this Association is of the opinion that the bashings, the tortures, the starvation and murderous atrocities imposed upon Australian prisoners of war, which brought about the premature death of some 7,700 of them and broke the health of the remaining 13,800 who managed to survive, deserve condemnation of the Japanese by the world community of nations.

3 That with this objective in mind, this Association does, on behalf of all Australian prisoners of war who underwent captivity by the Japanese in World War Two, inclusive of next of kin of those who died in captivity or who have died since, embark on the necessary action to claim reparations from Japan for the unlawful acts so wilfully perpetrated.

4 Furthermore, in pursuance of this objective: this Association investigate the feasibility of enforcing such reparation claims in the international arena, including utilising, if thought fit, the instrumentalities of the United Nations Organisation, the Sub Committee of Human Rights at Geneva; and implement the necessary action as may be feasible and lawful to enforce such reparation claims accordingly.

David W. Barrett, AFAIA
Chairman of Claim Committee

After some disagreement from the Federal President, Sir Edward (Weary) Dunlop and a few others, the motion was eventually agreed to at both state and federal levels.

We proceeded to publicise the committee's work on behalf of all ex-POW (Japan), their widows or immediate next of kin, at the same time requesting all those desirous of doing so to write or phone for a claim form. Advertisements were taken out in the major Australian newspapers. The response was immediate: the flood of claim forms with their $10 processing fee and donations became a torrent. The media supported our actions with wide-ranging publicity from the major to the regional and weekly newspapers. Eventually radio and television joined in with interviews. The claims kept coming, resulting in more than 10 000 in the final count, and some $180 000 were raised with the processing fee, donations and an art union—conducted and promoted by myself and with a block of land donated by a friend as first prize. As treasurer I invested this money carefully, resulting in a sizeable income that was sufficient to pay our day-to-day accounts.

An office was opened in Southport, a photocopier and furniture were procured, and later a fax machine was purchased to further facilitate communications with overseas and particularly Japan. During this period I had commissioned a retired A-grade journalist to research and prepare a submission of claims giving evidence of the brutality and atrocities committed by the Imperial Japanese Army in all the countries it occupied during the Second World War. An international lawyer from the University of Queensland did a feasibility study on the legal aspects of our claim. His conclusion was, I am happy to say, very positive indeed.

In March 1990, accompanied by Peter Collas, I visited Canada, Britain, Switzerland, Singapore and Japan. The question of reparations was discussed with the relevant heads of ex-POW associations, and agreement was reached on the appropriate United Nations procedures. While in London a meeting was arranged with Sir Bernard Braine MP at the House of Commons. Sir Bernard had previously addressed the House on the need for the Japanese government to compensate all victims of the Imperial Japanese Army. A meeting was also arranged with the British ex-POW association barrister, Mr Lloyd-Jones, who is helping the British Survivors formulate their United Nations claim. I also presented him with a copy of our submission for reference.[1]

At Geneva we had two meetings with Mrs Franciska Ize-Charrin, Principal Administrator of the Human Rights Division UNO. She was most impressed with our two-volume submission, copies of which were presented for distribution to the member nations, including Japan. I also had rewarding discussions with representatives of the International Red Cross, The International Health Professionals, Amnesty International and the International Commission of Jurists. All were advised that our submission had been filed.

At Singapore we visited the Kranji War Cemetery and paid our respects to our fallen comrades who now lie in peace.

Our visit to Japan was filmed by NHK television and shown on prime time after our departure. However, I believe that it was well received by a viewing audience of some 33 million. I met Nagase Takashi after 46 years on his home town railway station at Kurishiki City. He had been our interpreter on our search for graves on the Siam–Burma Railway in August 1945. Nagase supports our reparation claim. I also met Father Tony Glynn of Nara City, who is another keen supporter and an expert in Japanese language and customs. Mr Toshikazu Kokubu, a Japanese Navy veteran of the Second World War whose father was executed as a war criminal, was most helpful in arranging a meeting with Mr Shiro, who I understood was the Chief Secretary to the Minister for Foreign Affairs. He commented as follows:

Mr Shiro was aware of our committee and our submission before the conference. He believed the reparations claim was fair and that the Japanese people would regard it as a debt which should be paid. He also considered it essential that the Japanese government address this serious problem at its earliest opportunity.

The six nations involved in the claim for reparations from the Japanese Government have all signed a letter of intent authorising the War Amputations of Canada, with Cliff Chadderton as chairman, to head the thrust for reparations. A meeting was held in Ottawa on 17 September 1991. All national groups were represented, and all agreed that the War Amputations should continue to pursue claims for compensation through the Human Rights Commission in Geneva. Delegates representing thirteen organisations have claimed on behalf of approximately 200 000 survivors, which would involve a payment by Japan of 4 billion US dollars.

After a particularly heavy workload for almost 5 years and failing health, my wife and I decided to realise an ambition of many years and retire to Tasmania. As the thrust for reparations was now in the hands of the War Amputations of Canada, I felt that I had achieved 99 per cent of my objectives. Accordingly, I resigned my positions as chairman and treasurer of the Queensland Ex-POW Reparations Committee and secretary and treasurer of the Gold Coast Branch of the Queensland Ex-POW Association.

Notes

1 I was fortunate in meeting a publisher in Brisbane, Lester Padman of Boolarong Publications, who agreed to publish an expanded edition of our United Nations submission. *Nippon Very Sorry—Many Men Must Die*, Brisbane, was published in 1990, with all royalties to be used for the welfare of needy ex-POWs and their families. The book was prefaced by the Hon. Justice Marcus Einfeld, Justice of the Federal Court of Australia. Mr Einfeld was also President of the Australian Human Rights and Equal Opportunity Commission in 1987–90.

13

Reflections, 1946 and 1991

Sir Edward Dunlop

Sir Edward (Weary) Dunlop is perhaps the most famous Australian survivor of the railway. Here we reproduce first his 1946 sworn statement, followed by his 1991 statement at Canberra. In neither does he refer to his own personal privations or even to the occasions when he was beaten. The sanity and humanity that sustained him (and the men in his care) at Hintok in 1943 was still evident in 1991.

August 1946

I, Ernest Edward Dunlop, of 66 Walsh Street, South Yarra, in the State of Victoria, make oath and say:

Prior to discharge, I was VX259 Lt. Col. E.E. DUNLOP.

I was taken PW at Bandoeng, Java in March 1942. At that time, the Japanese Commander in that area was Col. Minnamoto, and his Adjutant was First Lt. Sumiya. Lt. Col. Odakua was in charge of medical services, and his staff officer was Capt. Nakazawa.

In Jan. 1943, I embarked with a party of 878 PW's for Singapore, and from there we were sent to the Konyu Area, where we were employed on the construction of the Burma/Siam Rly. At this period we came under what was known as No. 4 group, the Japanese commander of which was, for most of the time, Lt. Col. Ishii. The group consisted of about 13000 men and in July 1943, I was senior Australian Medical Officer in this group. Of the Japanese, my immediate Commander was Lt. Osuki [sic for Usuki], and my immediate medical superior was Cpl. Okada. Also in that area, and subsequently in charge of Australian troops was a Japanese, Lt. Tanaka.

Between Jan. and Aug. 1943 in the Konyu–Hintok Area, Lt. Osuki was directly responsible for causing the deaths of many PW under his care, by callous neglect to provide food, adequate shelter, hygiene arrangements or medicines and repeatedly stated that the sick should not receive as much food as the fit. He also stated that if the sick died, the working percentage was correspondingly increased. At a time, when there were hundreds of sick men, he forced medical orderlies to work on the railway, thus depriving the sick of essential attention. Under Lt. Osuki's command, it was permitted, and at times, personally ordered by him, that the sick be forced out to work. This was a daily occurrence for months, and cost scores of lives of PW. Lt. Osuki was personally responsible for defrauding PW, in that he demanded 'Commission' from Thai bargemen; this extra cost causing increased prices to PW. On June 8, 1943, Lt. Osuki compelled PW at Hintok to purchase for him 5794 packets of cigarettes, which they had not ordered and could not afford. Those Osuki had bought as a private trading venture.

Cpl. Okada (Doctor Death) was responsible for the medical arrangements of thousands of men, though he appeared to have no medical training. For many months, and particularly in June–July 43, he daily over-ruled experienced medical officers, forcing them to send sick men to work under the most exhausting conditions and brutality and thereby directly causing many deaths. On 10 May 1943, a Japanese General paid a visit to Hintok Camp. Okada promised me that if 43 sick men were removed from the hospital into the jungle, they would not have to work, and the sick figures would thus be improved. The men were to return to hospital after the general's inspection. Instead of this, Cpl. Okada handed these men over to the engineers, and though these 43 were suffering from huge tropical ulcers and were bloated with beri-beri, they were compelled to roll heavy drums of oil some miles over rough mountain tracks. In June–July 1943, Okada had men who were too sick to walk carried on to engineers works parade for allotment of duties. Cpl. Okada was well known for trading in the belongings of PW and was responsible for delaying the evacuation of the sick unless they sold watches etc. at a fraction of their value.

Lt. Col. Ishii (The Laughing Colonel) as commander of all Group 4 PW, was responsible for the deaths of hundreds of men by his neglect to ensure provision of sufficient food, clothing, shelter and medicines, to the working camps during 1943. At Hintok and Konyu PW under Lt. Col. Ishii's administration were treated with the utmost brutality and violence, the sick being daily driven to work in large numbers, thus directly causing many deaths. Lt. Col. Ishii visited those Camps and was completely aware of the conditions. In point of fact, his visits were accompanied by an especially increased severity in the ill-treatment of sick men. On May 8 1943, following his visit to Hintok Camp, extra workers were required from the hospital and were driven to work in spite of the protests of the doctors in charge, including my own repeated strenuous protests. Also on the occasion of this visit by Lt. Col. Ishii, when shown by me emaciated dysentery cases massed in tents, I told him that no drugs had been made available by the Japanese, not even magnesium sulphate. This, in spite of repeated requests by the medical staff. I told Ishi that the only possible alternative treatment was by starvation and fluids. He asked, 'How long no food', and I told him 2–3 days. He then replies 'In future remember—no food one week.'

On June 12, 1943, at Hintok Camp, a Japanese whom I do not know, but who, though wearing no badges of rank, called himself a doctor, had the sick paraded, and without any examination, caused 45 unfit men to be sent to work.

During the period I was at Hintok, Lt. Hirota was in charge of the engineer section. This officer is directly responsible for the death of scores of Australians who worked under him in inhuman conditions on railway construction in the Hintok Area. In 1943 he daily forced extremely sick men to work and treated all workmen with sickening brutality, and sadistic punishment. In May–June and July 1943, it was a daily spectacle to see scores of emaciated sick men forced out to gruelling labour tottering along with the aid of sticks. Others too sick to even walk, were, by his orders carried to the engineers lines to labour in the lying or seated position. These sufferers were flogged and ill-treated for their inefficiency as workmen and some died in direct consequences. As one example of sadistic measures, this man caused workmen with horrible inflamed and festering feet, to work barefoot in sharp rocks or haul logs in thorny jungle, and forced men with dysentery to soil themselves while working. He personally struck men with sticks and threw stones at them, and his tours of the works area were accompanied by waves of brutality.

Murder of TX 2361 Sgt. S.R. Hallom, 2/3 M.G. Bn. A.I.F.

This soldier was extremely ill with malaria and high fever and collapsed on the way to work, 12 Jan. 43; with difficulty he made his way back to the camp and his illness was formally reported to the Japanese and he was admitted to hospital. Nevertheless, by order of Lt. Hirota, he was removed from hospital and, along with several other soldiers who had fallen out of work parties with exhaustion, was mercilessly flogged, kicked and tortured for some hours. This was carried out in Hirota's presence by a Japanese engineer Sgt. known to Australians as 'Billy the Pig', and another 'Molly the Monk'. He was carried back to hospital deadly pale, with his face, neck and chest contused and swollen, and abrasions to his body and legs, and a sprained right ankle. He never recovered from this savagery and died on 26 June 43, due to internal injuries.

On 22 June 43, Cpl. Cully of 'P' Bn. AIF was admitted to Hintok Camp Hospital with an injured neck and cerebral irritation sick and vomiting. The following account was given by him to me and was substantiated by witnesses.

'Hirota' came to inspect a gang of light duty men of which Cpl. Cully was in charge. He ordered that instead of the gang having felled trees up a slope in teams, each man must carry one. When Cpl. Cully demurred and said that the condition of the men rendered this impossible, he seized a felled sapling about 6 feet long 4 inch butt and 3 inches at the top and

Sir Edward Dunlop (with the ball on his back) representing Victoria against NSW, Sydney 1935.

felled the corporal with a blow on the back of the neck, then rubbed the lesson in by a few more blows and a sawing motion. His order was then cruelly enforced.

Though men were dying of malnutrition Hirota repeatedly refused to allow his empty lorries to be loaded with canteen stores for them. Instead, after their days work, they were obliged to volunteer for gruelling night marches to carry these stores to camp.

In August, I went to another working camp called Kinsayok. It was there that, on the 3rd Oct. 43 I was attacked and struck about the head with heavy sticks by a Korean guard. The reason for this was he resented the fact that I had not seen and saluted him while he was bathing in a bath house. This Guard was known to Lt. Hatori (Camp Commandant) and Cpl. Okada, to whom I made protest.

Between Jan. and Dec. 1943, a Japanese named Lt. Moroka, as medical staff officer to No. 4 Group, was also responsible for lack of medical supplies, adequate hygiene, anti-malarial arrangements, a shocking lack of hospital facilities. To my knowledge he did not personally drive sick men to work, but this was done repeatedly by medically untrained junior NCO's and privates in areas under his control.

I left the Railway camps in late Oct. 43 and went to Tarsau and other hospitals. At Nakom Paton hospital, I was summoned to the guard house on 10 July 44 at 0930 hrs. and accused of reporting in late the previous night. In consequence of this, I was repeatedly struck on the face by a Korean guard and then compelled to kneel on the sand in the sun for a prolonged period. The POW Japanese interpreter at Nakom Paton Camp (Mr Cohen NEI army) stated that he knew the guard commander responsible.

SWORN at Melbourne in the State of Victoria this 27th day of June '46.

Sgd: E.E. Dunlop (o.w.s.)

Before me: R.S. Hitch

A Commissioner of the Supreme Court of Victoria for taking affidavits.

August 1991

I must confess that I have not had any great heart in war trials. It just seemed to me that, although I cannot entirely forget Japanese behaviour in prison camps, there are a whole lot of things that we had better take into account. I suppose the most significant of all is that German people, with all that civilisation behind them, Beethoven and so forth, could have behaved so badly as to eliminate about 6 million people. This extraordinary crime against humanity was by a country with so much fine culture behind them. Similarly the Russian–German conflict is a story of appalling loss of human life in which people did not seem to obey any of the conventions of war. I have recently been involved in the special Red Cross Year to alleviate the sufferings of victims of war, and what appears to emerge is that about 12 per cent of those who died in the First World War were civilians, and in the Second World War II civilian casualties rose. In some 100-odd wars and revolutions since then, the civilian casualties have been 10 to 1. That is the background to our experience.

I personally felt that the Japanese had an excuse for getting involved in the last war. I think that the Americans put them down as a tinpot economy and really screwed them down as a minor power. There was a lot of provocation. They had been locked up for 250 years, trying to do things their own way, only to be pushed into the world by Commodore Perry (in 1853). They only got involved in war as late boys. However, as one who was a 'toad beneath the harrow', there was an awful lot to excuse—so many people died so wretchedly from ill-treatment. The prisoners were in countries in which there was plenty of food, but they were just put on a starvation ration and expected to work and die cheerfully.

There is a good deal to be forgiven. I think that war trials are very difficult things to feel happy about, particularly when there is a considerable delay after the war. As one who was quite prepared to forgive the Japanese and get on and do business with them in the world, one thing has just irritated me a little: they do not seem to me to really teach history. The last thing that Japan has really got down to, I think, is the self-analysis that comes with the teaching of history. So I am rather pleased that we have had this meeting and discussion in which at least we can put our points of view. For example, to me it is totally horrifying that Japanese prisoners awaiting trial should be on a starvation ration and hardly able to crawl. That seems to be inconceivable behaviour by major powers that are trying people for similar so-called crimes. These are facts that we should know about—if they did occur.

My own experience was of over 2 years in the European and Middle East war. Then in Java I became a prisoner after the fall of Singapore. We had a not unreasonable experience there for a good many months. We lost a good deal of weight, and we got no pay, and none of the conventions of war were observed, but there was not too much death or anything like that. The Burma–Thailand Railway was the real cutting edge of my experience as a prisoner. I felt that there were some terrible indictments against Japanese behaviour in their treatment of prisoners of war, even allowing for all the excuses. I remember one particular camp where I had an interpreter that I got on well with. He proposed to me that Japan was the case of a desperate vagabond fighting a rich man with a top hat; you had to understand that in such a contest the rules of the game were not clean and gentlemanly. I suppose we have got to accept the fact that Japan was a fairly late entrant into the modern world. In the First World War the Japanese escorted our troops overseas and behaved extremely well. Their performance was based on that of the British Navy. After World War I William Morris Hughes was totally averse to giving Japan a few islands around the Pacific as a reward. So perhaps we should have expected a bit of payback.

Although I could develop a friendship with a few Japanese in prison camps, and I even had my life saved once or twice by Japanese who seemed to have a more kindly approach, at most their behaviour really was terribly bad, and I think that the Japanese should address themselves to some aspects of their behaviour during that phase. Admittedly there is a good deal to be said on both sides. I think that they were really forced into the war by the Americans' not giving them some place in the Pacific and in trade relationships, but I do not think that it is going to do any good in the future to try to completely whitewash them for what went on in the Second World War. I do hope that Japan will have the courage to teach history in the future.

However, as a country that is now a major trading partner, we can hardly be screaming for vengeance and at the same time putting out a hand for trade. I hope that in the future there will be a meaningful relationship between Japan and Australia. Recently I was put down strongly by Gareth Evans. I said that we had plenty of problems around us in Asia—for example, conflicting interests and other things, and territorial problems. Might it not happen that we would need the Japanese to lay a restraining hand on the neck of an Indonesia, saying 'Our pitch, son'? I think that there are all such possibilities of future relations with Japan—things we have got to work on. I do not think that we are helped by the Japanese denying the fact that their behaviour was quite bad in the Second World War and that they should give up teaching history.

Notes

1 In a letter of 15 July 1992 to Hank Nelson, Dunlop added that Usuki had been 'a whisky sodden no-hoper', of the kind 'reduplicated in any society.' Lieutenant Usuki was executed at Changi on 22 November 1946. Of the others referred to by Dunlop, Lieutenant Hirota was executed at Changi on 21 January 1947, and Lieutenant-Colonel Ishii Tamie was executed at Changi on 26 March 1947. Corporal (later Sergeant) Okada Seiichi was sentenced to 10 years in prison.

14

Conclusion

Gavan McCormack and Hank Nelson

Fifty years is a long time, whether in the life of a man or a woman or a state. The young Australians who went off to war in high spirits in 1941, confident in the superiority of their British way of life—now watch bemusedly as their government struggles to find policies that will win favour in Tokyo and their grandchildren pore over their Japanese lessons. The young Japanese, mobilised into the gigantic war machine and imbued with equally unshakeable belief in the superiority of the imperial way, who in a matter of months humbled and razed the proud European empires of Asia, only to be themselves defeated by the forces they had unleashed—they now return as tourists to the scattered graveyards of their old comrades, and watch their grandchildren mature into a culture that ridicules the values for which they once fought and died. The young Koreans, who thought to find adventure (while avoiding direct military service) in a world beyond the rural backwaters of the then Japanese empire, who were bashed and humiliated and struggled to adapt to identities as super-loyal (as is often the case with those whose loyalties were always suspect) subjects of the Japanese emperor—they now grow old as exiles from their homeland, wondering what identity their grandchildren will pass on to future generations and in what soil their bones will eventually find rest. To the grandchildren of all three groups of young men who found themselves parties to the conflict of the 1940s, the passions and the struggles of 50 years ago seem almost as remote as palaeolithic time. All now are likely to enjoy a very similar culture of work, consumption and leisure, mediated to them through identical computer, VCR, auto and karaoke.

Imperial and racial ideologies held sway almost universally in the 1940s

151

world. Young Australians believed in the superiority of the 'white' race and were the unthinking and (mostly) uncritical heirs to a long history of Western imperialism and aggression in East and South-East Asia. Young Japanese believed in the superiority of the 'yellow' race (especially those descended from the sun goddess), and Japanese of whatever political persuasion rejoiced at the collapse of Western empires. Both sides believed that the dominance they offered other peoples was just, beneficial and benevolent, while the other side was illegitimate, exploitative and evil. These world views were sharply antipathetic. The Japanese who, literally and figuratively, came to hold the 'whip hand' over the British and Australians in Thailand and Burma, spontaneously strove to destroy the moral authority of British imperialism by humiliating officers and driving a wedge between British and Australians. The much resented Japanese practice of *binta* (face slapping), which inevitably degenerated at times into general bashing, conveyed a clear message of racial assertion—a symbolic turning of the tables on Asia's Western masters—in which the Japanese took some understandable pleasure. For their part the prisoners treated their captors with contempt, in some cases showing their feelings by display of 'stiff upper lip', which in turn fed the Japanese rage even more.

The desire to match and worst the Western soldiers, especially the officers, occasionally took some bizarre forms at an individual level. Thus Captain Maruyama (in private life chief physical training instructor to the Tokyo police and director of its anti-Communist squad) once challenged Captain Roy Mills to fight to the death 'in order to show his superiority to the British'.[1] There was also Lieutenant Hirota, who arranged a series of athletic contests between himself and Colonel Dunlop—standing jump, long jump, spring, shot put—which ended only when Dunlop—an outstanding athlete—had the good sense to 'allow' his opponent to win the high jump. At this he was rewarded by being taken to a filmshow in the Japanese quarters (where he learned for the first time, by seeing it on film, of the sinking of the *Prince of Wales* and the *Repulse*).[2] The violence with which some of the Korean guards occasionally exploded also reflected the enormous psychological strain on them: a despised and discriminated group at the bottom of the Japanese military system, regularly bashed and beaten themselves, who could be expected, when given power over the prisoners, to take out some of their frustration and alienation on them.

In mid 1940 Australia most men of the 8th Division responded to the call for volunteers for overseas service with a high sense of duty, and they were held in high esteem by the Australian public. They had every right to believe that they were good and valuable citizens. They were endangering themselves, bringing honour to their nation, fighting evil, responding to the call of empire in desperate times, and helping Allies in need. But later many felt that they had gone into battles with little support—battles where defeat was conceded before the first shot was fired. Little was done to protect them in the prison camps, and they have been given little recognition in peace. Whether true or not, they *believe* that they have been neglected, both in practical terms and in the eyes of the public. There is a contrast between their expectations, the 'send-offs' and farewell parades before they sailed to war, and the contempt with which they were treated as prisoners and what they think has been public indifference since the war. They believe that young Australians know almost nothing about the experiences of prisoners of war (POWs). In fact young Australians probably know as much about prisoners (probably more) than they know about comparable events: Greece, Crete, Tobruk, El Alamein, or Australians in the air battles over Europe—and over 5000 Australians in the Royal Australian Air Force (RAAF) died in the war against Germany.

The Australian POWs fear that their experiences, so intense and terrible at the time, so dominant in the lives of most of the survivors for the next 50 years, will be given no place in Australian history. The impact will have been on 22 000 lives, and not on the 7 million Australians they left in 1941, nor on the 17 million Australians who hear fragments of prisoner biographies 50 years later.

But they were the first Australians who went en masse into South-East Asia. They went when the old empires of the British, the Dutch, the French and the Portuguese were at their height. They saw the old Raffles Hotel (reserved for officers); Kader Bux & Sons, 'official contractor to the army', offered them dhoby, tailoring and bootmaking services; they went through the 'modern mosaic entrance' of Robinson & Co., 'the finest departmental store in Malaya', and tested the guarantee of courteous and obliging service; and they bargained in Change Alley and thought that it would take 1000 cakes of Lifebuoy soap to 'prevent the nose working overtime'.[3]

They were attracted and repelled by the empire about which they had so often read, heard and sung. Captain Adrian Curlewis wrote soon after his arrival in Singapore: 'Talk about the Outposts of Empiah and all that, by Gad, it's simplay too shattering'. But in the same letter he said, 'My Chinese boy Foo Che Hang neglected me this morning so I abused him all around the room and scared hell out of him'.[4] Later, when Curlewis was staying in a bungalow at the highland resort of Fraser's Hill, he observed people who were 'so very English' and decided 'We are really a different race in Australia'.[5] The reality of the empire the Australians had volunteered to defend was much as they had imagined it; but in that empire most of them were outsiders, and even the patrician Australians became more conscious of their differences from other peoples.

As prisoners the Australians met Asians as few white people then encountered other races: they were without prestige, power or wealth, and they claimed to bring no superior message about the sacred or profane world—except faith in an ultimate Allied victory. The Australian public has impressions of prisoners being killed, bashed and starved—of lines of young skin-and-bone diggers, ankle deep in mud, struggling with teak railway sleepers while a screaming guard swings at a passing prisoner with a pick handle—and the public believes that the prisoners are still angry about their treatment, and make broad statements of condemnation about Asians.

Of course ex-prisoners denounce brutal guards. One said recently:

> The bloody Korean guards . . . well they would knock you arse over head with the butt of a rifle, kick you in the shins, kick you in the balls, kick you anywhere, do anything with you. Bastards all the way through.[6]

Of course some ex-prisoners generalise from their experiences. John McGregor, who suffered more than most prisoners, wrote at the start of his reminiscences:

> . . . victory over the white man turned the Japanese into monsters. They fed themselves on sweet-tasting morsels of racial hate, swelled up with pride, and disclosed in full a trait of sadism, the like of which no civilised race would have believed possible. It has since been claimed that this monster is now dead . . . But the people who were present when this Japanese child of infamy was born assert that this is not so.[7]

John Lane, captured in Singapore and shipped to Japan, has turned his memories into a novel. The back cover proclaims:

> Today, money-hungry Australian parasites are selling to the Japanese the very land for which Joe Barry [the central character] and his mates fought and died. No wonder they are bitter! In another fifty years, the Japanese flag will be flying all over this once proud nation. The betrayal will be complete.[8]

The anger is there, and news reporters wanting their one-line response to the death of Hirohito or to the announcement of a major Japanese investment in Australia go to the ex-prisoners, and those who presume to speak for them, for words of outrage.

What is generally unknown to the Australian public is that the ex-POWs had a variety of encounters with Asians, and since the war have praised and acknowledged debts to some Asians when many other Australians have been ignorant of, or indifferent to, distinctions. McGregor praised the Chinese he met when he tried to escape and those who were with him in Outram Road gaol:

> No British or Australian soldier who served as a prisoner of the Japanese in the Malayan campaign will ever forget the debt owing to the Chinese who flaunted Japanese authority consistently in order to bring aid to the men in captivity . . . The full story of the heroism and loyalty of the Chinese in Singapore and Malaya will, I regret, never be fully assessed.[9]

Often in their reminiscences the prisoners refer to acts of generosity from unknown Chinese. Soon after the surrender on Singapore, Bill Young was with a group scavenging for whatever could be eaten or traded when a young Chinese boy signalled them to follow him. He took them to a house where a meal was ready, and disappeared. The Chinese, knowing that they would be killed if caught helping prisoners, just left them to their feast, and the only sign of appreciation the prisoners could leave was 'the empty bowls and a brief wave towards the figures toiling up on the hillside'.[10] Since the war the ex-prisoners have funded scholarships for nurses from Malaya and Singapore to study in Australia, given gifts of books to schools and sometimes, when they met to remember their own, drunk a toast to the Chinese.

On Sumatra the prisoners praised the Atjeh, and the Old Sandakians, the survivors from Borneo, often mention the '13 gallant men of all races' who were executed or died in prison after being arrested by the Japanese for helping the prisoners plan an escape. After the war the Australian government sent a mission to Borneo to find and reward over 280 people who had helped the prisoners. John Funk, brother of one of the executed men and himself imprisoned by the Japanese, was granted Australian citizenship in 1951, and was made a life member of the ex-POW of war association. On Ambon Arthur Young wrote in his diary of the people who were protecting and feeding them: 'Surely we will never forget these friends of ours'.[11] They did not. Ambon has become central to the way the survivors of Gull Force remember their imprisonment. In 1992 one ex-prisoner celebrated his fifteenth consecutive Anzac Day on Ambon, and much of the welfare work of the Gull Force Association is directed to hospitals, schools and village improvement schemes on Ambon.

The intensity of the experiences that Australians and Asians shared under the Japanese, the acts of compassion by Asians for Australians who could not command or repay, and the postwar response of Australian ex-POWs to those who helped them are unknown to most Australians. It is not that the work of the Gull Force Association has been unreported. The Ambon pilgrims (their term) have often taken a writer with them, but annual newspaper articles on inside pages do not influence public perceptions.[12] The ex-prisoners are widely believed to be those most likely to hate 'Asians'; they are thought to be 'racist' (but their prejudice is patronised as understandable), when in fact they could be seen as pioneering closer Australian relations with Asians. To the detriment of the ex-prisoners and Australia, the negative and conservative reaction of the ex-prisoners is known, and their positive response has been ignored. Australians, it seems, have preferred and cultivated a stereotype of the ex-servicemen as reactionary and ethnocentric. As a result another generation can praise itself for educating Australians about the lands and peoples to their north and defining a role for Australia in that region.

The Australian ex-prisoners have not been given sufficient recognition for the way that they survived. Australians were in situations as bad as any suffered by Allied prisoners, but there does not seem to have been one case where an Australian camp deteriorated into absolute despair or anarchy. The strong did not attack and exploit the weak, and even in the most desperate camps on the railway, on Ambon and in Borneo, men struggled to do the most basic tasks to sustain life for the group: they burnt or buried the dead, they dug latrines, they carried water and cooked food. Among escaped convicts or in cases of shipwreck, fighting and cannibalism occur. On 'hell ships' transporting prisoners to Japan some American prisoners screamed, murdered and attempted to drink the blood of the dead.[13] Australians saw camps where they thought that the British had 'chucked it in'—where the men could not 'bury their dead or shit'.[14] The comparisons may be unfair: the groups of prisoners who became violent or despondent might have suffered peculiar and terrible forces, or they might have had less training, lacked their own military unit organisation, or been less fit at the start of the ordeal.

The Australian prisoners seem to have been beneficiaries of those characteristics of nationalism that they most hoped would transfer from the diggers of the First World War to themselves. They were more likely to work in groups, share hardships and windfalls, be less dependent on officers for direction, and take the initiative to adapt and improvise. So in one of the camps of the despondent the 'Australians set about cleaning it up . . . the surface was scraped clean and burnt, water laid on to the camp by a bamboo pipeline from a spring on the hill, showers were provided, ample firewood provided for heating water'.[15]

The ex-prisoners have carried their cohesion into the postwar period. The magazines that circulate (sometimes with names enforcing the association with Asia (*Makan* and *Tidapa*)[16] are dense with details of the comings and goings of members, reunions, trips back to the railway, reminiscences of war, notes of relevant books, requests for information from the compilers of family histories, and results of research—such as a list of the ships constructed at Kawasaki shipyards while the men of 'C' Force were there.[17] The group strength extends to the non-front-line units with few and dispersed members, such as field ambulances, for the intensity of the experience of being a POW, unlike that of battle, was shared by all those who were captured.

The Australian ex-prisoners may hope then that their experiences, understood by so few, and which incite pity when they do not look for pity, may be placed in a context where they are seen as embodying and exploiting the ideals of an older Australia and as pioneering Australia's mass engagement with the region. Sir Edward Dunlop and Tom Uren both drew on their POW experiences in their later lives, and that has been obvious, for they have been public figures who have often spoken about the bases of their attitudes and actions. Their ideals came from an Anzac Australia, with a breadth and compassion that came from camps on the railway. That is also

Yi Hak-Nae, Sir Edward Dunlop and Tom Uren, 1991.

true of some who acted but did not express philosophies, men such as Curly Heckendorf. For many ex-prisoners there was in their lives a new breadth, compassion and anger, and it has been the anger that has become most known.

The locomotive that chugged the Burma–Thailand route in the last years of the war now rests in the confines of Tokyo's Yasukuni, Japan's central shrine to its war dead. Each year veterans, mostly of the 5th and 9th Railway Regiments, gather there to celebrate the achievement of building the line. Uppermost in their minds is pride at the engineering feat accomplished. The cost—in lives—and the crimes committed to build it are treated as 'unfortunate' accompaniments to a great venture, more or less as official Japan continues to treat the war as a whole, responding with begrudging and carefully calibrated expressions of regret as the diplomatic occasion calls for them, but exerting constant pressure to prevent the simple truth from being known in school texts.

Associations of ex-servicemen play a more limited role in Japanese than in Australian society, their influence on broader political or social life being slight. The voice of those who look back on the war as aggressive and unjust in origin, brutal and disgraceful in conduct, is very muted indeed. It took courage for the Korean guard Yi Hak-Nae to come to Canberra in 1991 to apologise to Colonel Dunlop and the former Australian POWs; it also required a moral clarity and sense of responsibility for which Japanese society as a whole is not noted. As terror gradually emerges again as an instrument of political influence—with attacks in recent years on the life of the governor of Nagasaki, the deputy prime minister and a prominent film maker for opposing in one way or another the prescribed consensus—voices calling for honest recognition of the past, repentance and reconciliation, will not find it easy to be heard.

In 1943 young men from Japan, Australia and Korea entered into closer contact along the railway line than ever before in their history. Despite the structured hostility and the terrible human suffering exacted, there were also expressions of common humanity, which stand out in the record as moments of light. Thus Captain Adrian Curlewis mentions in his diary a Christian Korean guard 'who sings Onward Christian Soldiers with me on working parties' and who visited him in his hut at midnight bringing 'his mess tin of rice with sweet potato in it' to help him recuperate. On other nights he describes the same thing and refers to 'Korean sentry Uminaga' (possibly the same man) with whom he had had a long talk.[18] Some days, even when hours of work were long, passed without violence amid 'jokes and pleasantries'; relations with sentries sometimes warmed to be 'on a most friendly basis'; and occasionally special issues of sweet coffee, cigarettes or condensed milk were made. On such occasions Curlewis could be moved to wonder at the sight of 'Japanese, Chinese, Dutch POW, English, Australians, Tamils, Burmese and Malays, Thais, all talking in their own tongue' and visible from where he lay.[19]

As the last spikes were struck and through trains began to run, tension eased. Curlewis reflected: 'Without doubt it has been a marvellous achievement . . . Its value to Britain some day will be immense'. A few days later he made the following entry in his diary:

> November 1. Strangest of days. 10 swimmers were asked for. We went to the river where gelignite was thrown in for us to collect the stunned fish. Canoes were pinched from the Thais and it finished up with Nips and selves swimming, canoeing, smoking, eating peanut toffee, like the best of friends. In the evening a ball was produced and international catching took place. General goodwill and chats.[20]

The construction work that had begun (as Hugh Clarke recalls) with a fishing and barbecue party that degenerated into a brawl, this time proceeded more harmoniously. This did not mean that what had been endured for the preceding months was forgotten. The horror of it was burned indelibly into the minds of those who survived. However, the strength of the human capacity to survive and to overcome adversity, and the desire to reach beyond the conflict to find the ground of common humanity where ordinary young Australians, Japanese and Koreans could relate to each other, is

Conclusion

movingly attested. The achievement of such a world, and of such a relationship, the men of the railway left to their grandchildren.

Notes

1 Colonel S.A.F. Pond, 'Report on "F" Force working party to Thailand', 6 January 1944, court exhibit no. 6, Transcript of 'Banno Trial', Public Record Office (London), WO 235/1034, 4119.
2 The contest occurred on 20 March 1943. Thanks to Sir Edward Dunlop for this story, told during the 1991 Canberra meeting and recounted in a letter to Hank Nelson dated 15 July 1992. Dunlop went on in his letter to describe Hirota as 'a rather nasty zealot', but added 'think of those good priests who ran the inquisition'.
3 *Through*, official journal of the Signals 8th Australian Division, vol. 1, no. 1, December 1941, has paragraphs on what men did on leave.
4 Philippa Poole, *Of Love and War: The Letters and Diaries of Captain Adrian Curlewis and His Family, 1939–1945*, Lansdowne Press, Sydney, 1982, p. 30.
5 Ibid., p. 53.
6 Quoted in James Burfitt, *Against All Odds: The History of the 2/18 Battalion A.I.F.*, 2/18th Battalion (AIF) Association, Sydney, 1991, p. 234.
7 John McGregor, *Blood on the Rising Sun*, Bencoolen, no date or place, p. 6. McGregor was sent to Outram Road gaol for attempting to escape from Singapore.
8 John Lane, *Sayonara Australia*, John Lane, Yunderup, WA, 1991. John Lane's reminiscences were published in *Summer Will Come Again*, Fremantle Arts Centre Press, Fremantle, 1987.
9 McGregor, op. cit., p. 54.
10 Bill Young, *Return to a Dark Age*, privately published, Sydney, 1991, p. 46.
11 *Barbed Wire and Bamboo*, official organ of the ex-POWs, June 1992, p. 12.
12 In 1992 the *Age* published articles by Kate Cole-Adams, 'Piped water flows to repay an Anzac debt to Ambon' on 24 April, and further reports on 25 April.
13 Donald Knox, *Death March: The Survivors of Bataan*, Harcourt Brace Jovanovich, New York, 1981, ch. 11.
14 Burfitt, op. cit., p. 152; and Don Wall, *Singapore and Beyond: The Story of the 2/20 Battalion*, 2/20 Battalion Association, Sydney, 1985, p. 180.
15 Wall, op. cit., p. 180.
16 *Makan* is the magazine of the 2/30th Battalion, and *Tidapa* belongs to the 2/4th Anti-tank.
17 Magazine of the 2/19th Battalion AIF Association, June 1944, p. 32.
18 'Private diary of Adrian Curlewis, 18 April 1943 to 2 January 1944', 27 pp., exhibit A–R, annexure A, entries for 22, 29, 30 September (see Poole, op. cit., for published text). Curlewis in his affidavit of 15 November 1945, signed in Sydney, referred to 'three Koreans who definitely tried to help us—Miamoito [Miyamoto?], Yastah [Yasuda?] and Kagawa', Exhibit A–Q, Transcript, 'Banno Trial', WO235/1034, 4119.
19 Curlewis, diary, entry for 22 August.
20 Ibid., entries for 24 October and 1 November.

Appendix A
Australian forces on the railway

Hank Nelson

Burma

'A' Force (3000 men) left Singapore in May 1942.
Shifted to Thanbyuzayat in Burma, it began work on the railway in September 1942.
Williams Force (total 884) and Black Force (593 Australians) arrived in Burma from Java in October 1942.
Group 5 (385 Australians commanded by Major L.J. Robertson) arrived from Java in January 1943.
Total strength of Australians in Burma: 4851.
Total deaths from September 1942 to July 1944: 771. Death rate: 15.8 per cent (Wigmore, p. 561).

Thailand

Dunlop Force went from Java to Singapore to Thailand, January 1943: 873 men at Konyu 25 January 1943 (E.E. Dunlop, *The War Diaries of Weary Dunlop*, Nelson, Melbourne, 1986, p. 154).
Additional men shipped from Timor and others from Java (became Q Battalion): 375.
Another 538 were shipped from Java in two groups.
Total: 1788.
Approximate deaths: 200. Death rate: 12 per cent (Long, p. 571).

'D' Force left Singapore in March 1943: 2220 Australians.
Approximate deaths: 400. Death rate: 18 per cent.

'F' Force left Singapore in April 1943: 3660 Australians.
Deaths to May 1944: 1060. Death rate: 29 per cent.

'H' Force left Singapore in May 1943: 670 Australians from Singapore and 35 from Timor and Java.
Deaths: 179. Death rate: 25 per cent.

'K' Force left Singapore in June 1943: 55 Australians.

'L' Force left Singapore in August 1943: 73 Australians.
Total deaths uncertain, but probably less than 10.

Totals

About 13 000 Australians went to Burma or Thailand.
The deaths listed above total just over 2600. That was also the estimate of the Allied War Graves Registration units in 1946. Later the estimate of deaths was increased to 2815 (Wigmore, p. 588).

(Major sources of published statistics: A.J. Sweeting in Lionel Wigmore, *The Japanese Thrust*, Australian War Memorial, Canberra, 1957; and David Nelson, *The Story of Changi Singapore*, privately published, Perth, 1974.)

Appendix B
Prisoner-of-war death rates: some comparisons

Hank Nelson

First World War

4044 Australians became prisoners of war (POWs).
288 died of wounds while prisoners.
109 died of illness.
Death rate was 10 per cent, but most deaths were a result of the severe wounds suffered by many of those captured.

The Australians were fortunate that only about 150 were captured by the Turks. Had many been imprisoned (and it could easily have happened), then the Australian attitude to 'Johnny Turk' might have been different. Perhaps two-thirds of POWs of the Turks died. Of some 13 000 men captured at Kut, marched to Anatolia and employed in harsh labour camps, including building railways, only some 2000 survived. (T.W. White, *Guests of the Unspeakable*, 1928 and 1932, republished by Little Hill Press, Sydney, 1990, is an account of an Australian prisoner of, and escaper from, the Turks.)

Second World War

8184 Australians became prisoners of the Germans.
265 Australians died while prisoners of the Germans. Death rate: 3 per cent.
22 376 Australians became prisoners of the Japanese.
8031 Australians died as prisoners of the Japanese. Death rate: 36 per cent.
Half of the Australians who died in the war against the Japanese died as prisoners.
Out of 142 319 British prisoners of the Germans, 7310 died. Death rate: 5 per cent.
From 93 154 American prisoners, 2038 died. Death rate: 2 per cent.

The extraordinary contrast is not between the behaviour of Germans and Japanese, but between the treatment of prisoners on the west and the east of the European theatre.

About 1.5 million or 45 per cent of the Germans captured by the Russians died, and 60 per cent of the Russians imprisoned by the Germans died.

The number of Japanese and Chinese who died after capture between 1937 and 1945 is unknown. Nor do we know how many Japanese died as prisoners of the Russians after 1945.

(Sources: Lionel Wigmore, *The Japanese Thrust*, Australian War Memorial, Canberra, 1957; and R.J. Pritchard and S. Zaide, eds, *The Tokyo War Crimes Trial*, Garland Publishing, New York and London, 1981, vol. 16, p. 40, 537.

Why did millions become prisoners in the Second World War? The basic reason is that from the first modern war, the American Civil War, entrenched well-armed men with adequate rations and ammunition could hold out almost indefinitely. With the weapons then available defence was superior to offence. That was obvious on the western front in the First World War. But by the Second World War, offence was superior. Attacking forces moved through, over and around defences. The Second World War was therefore mobile, attack and counterattack covering vast distances backward and forward across North Africa, east and west across Europe, and through South-East Asia and the Pacific. Vast numbers of troops were constantly being cut off, and within weeks might be 1000 kilometres or more behind their own front lines. Prisoners were the victims of world war occurring at that time when technology gave the advantage to the offence, and when defence planners and public sentiment, influenced by previous wars, exaggerated the benefits of holding particular pieces of land.

Table 13.1, calculated soon after the end of the war and submitted to the Tokyo war crimes trials, varies from later figures, but the percentages and the relative numbers from one nation to another are reasonably accurate.

The interesting comparison rarely made is between the Canadians and the Australians. The Canadians were training for war against the Germans and spending their time on garrison duties before being sent to Hong Kong with a false idea of the British strength there. The Winnipeg Grenadiers left the West Indies, went by train across Canada and then by ship to Hong Kong. There is a parallel with those Australians who went to Darwin and then to the Dutch East Indies. Like the Australians in Ambon and some units that sailed for Singapore, the Canadians had just 3 weeks in Hong Kong before they went into battle. The Canadians lost 290 in battle, including those killed by the Japanese immediately after the fighting. One of the worst incidents was the killing of patients and staff and the raping of nurses at St Stephen's College Hospital. In January 1943, 1184 Canadians were shipped to Japan. Among the Canadians, twenty-three officers died in

Table B.1   Prisoner deaths in the war against Japan

Country	Total deaths	Prisoners	Death rate (%)
Australia	7 412	21 726	34
Canada	273	1 691	16
United Kingdom	12 433	50 016	25
New Zealand	31	121	26
United States	7 107	21 580	33
Dutch (white)	8 500	37 000	23
Totals	35 756	132 134	27

Source: R.J. Pritchard and S. Zaide, eds, *The Tokyo War Crimes Trial*, Garland Publishing, New York and London, 1981, vol. 16, pp. 40, 537.

battle and four as prisoners. In the ranks 267 died in battle and 260 as prisoners. (There is a summary in C.P. Stacey, *The Canadian Army 1939–1945*, King's Printer, Ottawa, 1948, ch. 26; and see the evidence of James Barnett in *Tokyo War Crimes Trial*, vol. 6, pp. 13, 222 ff.)

Korean War

Australians: 29 captured, 1 died in captivity. Death rate: over 3 per cent. Americans: 7140 captured, 2701 died in captivity. Death rate: 38 per cent. (See below for those missing in action, MIA.)

Vietnam War

No Australian serviceman became a POW.
500 Australians were killed in action or died of wounds.
43 605 Americans killed in action or died of wounds.
605 American ex-POWs had returned by 1980.
115 Americans are known to have died as prisoners.
About 2500 Americans MIA.

It is not known how many MIAs were killed in air crashes, died in battles, deserted, were killed immediately they were captured, or died of wounds, torture, disease or malnutrition while prisoners. The minimum percentage of American prisoners who died in captivity is 15 per cent. If it is assumed that a quarter of the MIAs became prisoners the figure is 50 per cent. Some prisoners in Vietnam were incarcerated for twice as long as any prisoners in the First or Second World Wars with correspondingly greater chances of suffering from malnutrition, disease and despair. (Basic statistics are given

Prisoner-of-war death rates

by: Harry G. Summers, *Vietnam War Almanac*, Facts in File Publication, New York, 1985; and James S. Olson, ed., *Dictionary of the Vietnam War*, Greenwood Press, New York, 1988.)

The question of MIAs also distorts the Korean War figures. Over 5000 Americans in Korea were posted as missing, and presumably some of these were prisoners, at least briefly. The 38 per cent mortality among the American prisoners in Korea is a minimum figure.

Index

Numbers in italics refer to photograph captions